DATE DUE

A TEAM TO BELIEVE IN

A TEAM TO BELIEVE IN

······································

Our Journey to the Super Bowl Championship

Tom Coughlin

with Brian Curtis

BALLANTINE BOOKS · NEW YORK

Published in the United States by ESPN Books, an imprint of ESPN, Inc.,
New York, and Ballantine Books, an imprint of The Random House Publishing Group,
a division of Random House, Inc., New York.

BALLANTINE and colophon are registered trademarks of Random House, Inc.
The ESPN Books name and logo are registered trademarks of ESPN, Inc.

Library of Congress Cataloging-in-Publication data

Coughlin, Tom (Thomas Richard).
A team to believe in : our journey to the Super Bowl championship / Tom Coughlin
with Brian Curtis.
p.   cm.
ISBN 978-0-345-51173-7 (hardcover : alk. paper)
1. Coughlin, Tom (Thomas Richard), 1946–   2. Football coaches—
United States—Biography.   3. New York Giants (Football team)
4. Super Bowl.   I. Curtis, Brian, 1971–   II. Title.
GV939.C668A3 2008
796.332092—dc22
[B]   2008026266

Printed in the United States of America on acid-free paper

www.ballantinebooks.com
www.espnbooks.com

1 2 3 4 5 6 7 8 9

First Edition

Book design by Susan Turner

To Judy,

You are the love of my life and the one most responsible for making our coaching journey possible. Throughout our more than forty years together, you have allowed me to focus on my profession, while you took care of *everything* else. We barely had enough money in the early years to make ends meet, but it didn't matter. We had fun.

You raised our four children. You were there as they embarked on life's new adventures from the first days of kindergarten to the freshmen days of college. You were the friend, the disciplinarian, the chief financial officer, the chef, the chauffeur, and the fan, but most important, you were Mom.

You were the one who found us a new house to make a new home on so many occasions, and you instantly became a hit in the neighborhoods with your warm sense of humor and nurturing personality. When we moved away—as we inevitably did—the neighbors wept for you while they barely even noticed you had a husband.

I often kid you, "If you knew what you were getting into would you do it again?" . . . I know the answer.

You are a source of strength for me and for our family, and simply, the best.

Tom

FOREWORD

• • • • • • • • • • • • •

by Bill Parcells

I sat down on my couch in my living room in Jupiter, Florida, in early February to watch Super Bowl XLII: the undefeated New England Patriots and the resilient New York Giants. There was no one else in the living room with me, just the way I like to watch football games. Just me and the TV. To be honest, my loyalties were torn. On one sideline stood Bill Belichick, who had worked with me for fifteen years in stops in New England and New York (twice). In the front office of the Patriots worked my good friend Scott Pioli, the vice president of player personnel, who also happens to be married to my daughter, Dallas. On the other sideline, the New York Giants were a piece of me, from my eight seasons as a head coach and three more as an assistant. Tom Coughlin had been our wide receivers' coach in New York for three of those years, and he had earned his way to this Super Bowl. Many of the Giant coaches and employees were still friends of mine. My loyalties may have been torn, but my faith in football was not. It was a historic march toward an undefeated season against the unexpected journey of the underdogs.

In what has to be one of the greatest football games ever played, forgetting the fact that it was a Super Bowl, the teams battled back and forth until the final seconds when the New York Giants completed a stunning comeback. Like most football fans, I marveled at Eli Manning's escape from the grasp of New England defenders to launch a ball that somehow, some way, was caught by David Tyree. I sat on the edge of my seat when Eli hit Plaxico Burress with thirty-five seconds left to take the lead. And I held my breath when future Hall of Famer Tom Brady had four last gasps to pull off a miracle. The Giants' win ranks up there with the greatest upsets in NFL history.

In order for a champion to really have a worthwhile accomplishment, he must have overcome quality opposition, and boy, did the Giants ever. First of all, playing in the NFC East, the most daunting of divisions, is a weekly challenge of storied rivalries—Dallas, Washington, Philadelphia, New York. Then it was onto the play-offs, where the Giants passed the test at Tampa Bay. Surely, they couldn't do it again the following week in Dallas? But they did it. And then they overcame ferocious cold in Green Bay to beat a very good football team led by a Hall of Fame quarterback. Finally, to cap it all off, they beat arguably one of the best teams in the history of the National Football League. *That* is quality opposition.

Winning a Super Bowl championship is not easy. We coach and work in a highly competitive industry without much gray area. With free agency, injuries, talented coaches and players, and intense scrutiny from the media and fans, getting to the Big Game doesn't come easy for anyone. That's why the New York Giants' accomplishment in 2007 was so special.

The Giants, and their coach, were resilient. When critics shouted that Tom Coughlin should go and Eli would never develop into a winner, they didn't listen. They didn't fold after a 0–2 start in 2007. They didn't lose faith when they were demolished by the Minnesota Vikings at home. They didn't give up when they lost their best chance at clinching a play-off spot in a home loss to Washington in December. They didn't waver when they missed a game-winning field-goal kick in Green Bay in January. They never stopped believing.

One of the amazing aspects to their success in 2007 was their ability to win on the road. The Giants won ten games (seven in the regular season, three in the play-offs) on the road in 2007, including road wins over Washington, Chicago, Philadelphia, Buffalo, Dallas, and Green Bay. Do you have any idea just how hard it is to win *one* game on the road in the NFL let alone ten? That is toughness.

Tom is credited with changing his approach, and it became clear as the season wore on that something was different about this coach and these Giants. I have known Tom a long time, and I knew that, like me, he was set in his ways. We were born, raised, and coached in an era when toughness, discipline, and a firm hand was the only way to coach. I am certainly not very flexible, and I give Tom all the credit in the world for taking a hard look at himself in the off-season and making the subtle changes that made a difference in 2007. I am reminded of the words of Anton Myrer, a combat marine corporal and World War II veteran, who penned the popular military novel *Once an Eagle* in 1968.

> *Inflexibility is the worst human failing. You can learn to check impetuosity, overcome fear with confidence and laziness with discipline. But for rigidity of mind, there is no antidote. It carries the seeds of its own destruction.*

Yet even though Tom made self-improvements, he never lost a grip on his core beliefs, on those values that he has always stood for. He adhered to what Abraham Lincoln once said: "Important principles may, and must, be inflexible."

Perhaps the Giants and Tom needed a slightly different approach as the game of professional football has changed in so many ways. The money certainly has had an impact. Too often insignificant by-products of success get in the way of what the game and competition is all about.

The real athletes, those true to competition, seek the ultimate achievement, and the game of football will forever be about that. The ultimate achievement is the Super Bowl. And the Giants can lay claim to it.

Repeating that victory in 2008 will not be easy, but at least for a year, the Giants' coaches and players are at the top of their profession. And they will always remember their 2007 journey. The lessons taken from what the Giants accomplished—never giving up, believing in the team, never listening to critics—will reverberate throughout the NFL and, frankly, throughout sports.

Sitting on that couch in Jupiter in early February was emotional for me. I couldn't have been more proud of the men coaching in the game, of the way the game was played, and of what the Giants' victory means for every team in every sport.

ACKNOWLEDGMENTS

· ·

Tom Coughlin

There is so much gratitude to give to so many in my life—past and present—so I thank you all. My parents, Lou and Betty; Judy's parents, Paul and Eleanor Whitaker; my wife, Judy; my children and their spouses, Keli and Chris Joyce, Tim and Andrea Coughlin, Brian and Susie Coughlin, and Katie and Chris Snee; and our beautiful grandchildren, Emma, Dylan, Cooper, Shea, and Caroline, who bring an automatic smile to our faces and bring joy into our hearts. One day I hope that my grandchildren and my grandchildren's grandchildren will read these pages and be inspired by how a group of men came together, believed in themselves, and persevered against all odds to achieve victory.

The 2007 journey was not about me but rather about a group of players and coaches, and a proud organization, who never stopped believing, and for that I give my thanks. My gratitude to Pat Hanlon, who has been invaluable in his time and guidance.

Finally, to those who have been a part of the Jay Fund, my sincerest gratitude for helping to make the world a little bit better by contributing time and resources to the Tom Coughlin Jay Fund Foundation.

> The mission of the Tom Coughlin Jay Fund Foundation is to assist children with leukemia and other cancers and their families by providing emotional and financial support to help reduce the stress associated with treatment and improve their quality of life.
>
> www.tcjayfund.org

BRIAN CURTIS

My heartfelt thanks to Tom, Judy, the entire Coughlin family, the New York Giants' players and coaches, Pat Hanlon, Peter John-Baptiste, Chris Pridy, Kim Kolbe, and Ed Triggs; thanks to Mike Anderson, Steve Brauntuch, Mark Taglieri, Scott Waxman, Sandy Montag, and our editor, Mark Tavani, and the great professionals at Random House.

My gratitude to Tamara, my rock and my love, and to the lights of my life, Emily and Daryn, who bring so much happiness into my life.

INTRODUCTION

. . . .

THE MERCURY SITS BELOW ZERO AND the wind chill makes it feel like −24 degrees. My ears are frozen, my cheeks are red, even my mind is cold. But the temperature is only a distraction, just another bump in the road for our team. It is overtime in the NFC Championship Game on famed Lambeau Field in Green Bay on January 20, 2008. Cornerback Corey Webster has just intercepted Brett Favre on the second play of OT, redeeming himself after he slipped and was burned by Favre and receiver Donald Driver earlier in the game on a 90-yard touchdown play.

Eli Manning jogs onto the field with the change of possession. With great field position at Green Bay's 34, we need to gain a few more yards to set up Lawrence Tynes for the game-winning kick. Then again, that kick is not as simple as it seems. Tonight, Lawrence has made field goals from 29 and 37, but he also missed from 43 and 36 in the fourth quarter—one done in by poor mechanics on the snapper-holder exchange, the other simply a poor kick.

We attempt two running plays with Ahmad Bradshaw, then Eli's 3rd-down pass to Steve Smith goes incomplete. Suddenly, it is 4th and 5 from Green Bay's 29 and it is going to take a 47-yard field goal to send us to the Super Bowl. No postseason opponent has ever made a field goal at Lambeau Field from over 40 yards. That said, prior to kickoff, we determined that any field goal attempt with the ball inside the 30-yard line would be makeable. The ball is now on the 29. In the moment I have to give the go-ahead for the field goal, I see Lawrence running onto the field. He couldn't possibly miss a third straight kick, could he?

I KNOW WHAT YOU'RE THINKING: our team had a memorable season, so now I think I can write a book, right? There are thousands of talented coaches at all levels of sport who never win a title. Does that mean they don't have something to say? Of course not. But as the days and weeks passed after our 2007 journey ended, and as I had time to reflect on just how far we had come from the depths, I began to understand what an amazing journey we had just experienced. It is a story that deserves to be told; in many ways, it's the all-American success story. It is a story about a group of underdogs who were told, "You can't win," but went out and proved everybody wrong.

I've been a football coach for more than forty years at the collegiate and professional levels, and I had never experienced such despair as I did in January 2007. At the end of a disappointing season, the New York media were calling for my head in a personal and vindictive way. My bosses, the owners of the New York Giants, had yet to tell me if I was going to be their coach in 2007. My family, unbeknownst to me at the time, was under an enormous amount of stress thanks to their concern for my welfare. As for me, I kept my head down and tried to work through it, but it was difficult. From those dark days forward, I didn't look back, only ahead. And what transpired over the next thirteen months is an experience like no other, so profound that it has changed my life and the lives of our coaches and players.

When I think back to how it all came together, it certainly wasn't magic. The coaching staff didn't pick up some manual last off-season that contained the ten steps on how to win a championship. There is no guidebook that tells you how to rise up. There were no franchise-defining changes to the roster from one season to the next, no major free agent acquisitions, no new ownership, no new playmakers. What did change, however, was the depth of our self-confidence and the seriousness of our commitment to putting team above self.

As for my role in our success, let's just say that this sixty-one-year-old man was willing to change, and that may have played a small part in the story. I took a hard look at myself and demanded that *I* improve. I learned to be more patient, to be more understanding. In 2007, I was the same coach I had always been, but with a new approach.

In the pages that follow, I will share our memorable journey with you, how we were able to come together as one to achieve the unbelievable.

When you think about our season, you may think of David Tyree's amazing catch in the Super Bowl or Eli Manning's scramble on the same play or maybe Plaxico Burress' game-winning touchdown catch. Maybe your thoughts turn toward the goal line stand against the Washington Redskins in week three, which earned us our first victory, or perhaps you think of the storm that brought snow, rain, and hail to Buffalo on the season's second-to-last weekend, when we clinched a play-off berth. Or maybe it's the season-ending clash with the undefeated New England Patriots, which attracted millions of viewers to their television sets. Those are just some of the moments that you know, but there are thousands of others that transformed our team into champions.

There was the remarkable overseas trip to London, the first-ever regular-season game played outside North America. There was our unforgettable meeting with Greg Gadson, an Iraq War veteran who lost both legs on the battlefield and who became a true Giant in 2007. There was the sudden death of a player's mother, and there were painful decisions concerning injuries. Who made these moments happen? The players, coaches, video staff, trainers, personnel department, player development staff, office assistants, and everyone else who is a part of this organization—they made these moments happen.

Moments such as the one in Green Bay.

ON THE FIELD LAWRENCE TYNES goes through his usual prekick routine, though this kick is anything but routine. His missed kicks in the fourth quarter are on everybody's mind. Now, how can he possibly block out those misses and kick one *farther* than those attempts?

Our holder, Jeff Feagles, indicates a spot on the frozen field approximately 8 yards from the line of scrimmage. Lawrence marks off the spot with his foot, as the kicker is responsible for making sure the spot is at the right distance. He puts his plant foot into position and takes three steps back and two to the left. He and Jeff make eye contact, signaling they are ready, and Jeff makes contact with snapper Jay Alford.

The ball is hard as a rock and Lawrence's foot is already black and blue.

But the snap is good, the hold is perfect, and Lawrence strikes the ball with a thump.

So how did we get here? How did we go from nowhere to 47 yards from the Super Bowl?

A TEAM TO BELIEVE IN

ONE

· · · · ·

The difficulty lies, not in the
new ideas, but in escaping from old ones.
—JOHN MAYNARD KEYNES

I T IS JANUARY 7, 2007. WE HAVE A 1ST AND 10 ON PHILADELPHIA'S
44-yard line with just over six minutes to play in the first half of the
NFC Wild Card Play-off Game. Eli takes the snap, turns to his right, and
hands the ball off to Tiki Barber, who explodes around the left end and
scampers down to the Eagles' 3, where he is forced out of bounds by
Lito Sheppard, giving us a 1st and Goal from the 3. I immediately call
time out to give our big linemen a chance to run to the new line of scrimmage, but also to give our coaches a chance to figure out exactly what
we want to call. It may seem like seven points is a given, but all one has
to do is look at the first twenty minutes of the game to realize nothing is
a given with this New York Giants team.

After starting off the game with a penalty on the first snap from
scrimmage, Eli drove our offense from our own 33 to the Philadelphia
17, when he connected with Plaxico Burress on a well-executed touch-

down pass and catch to give us the early lead. During the regular season, we scored first in thirteen of our games, so playing with a lead is nothing new for us. But neither are frustrations. On our next four possessions, we manage zero points, and that is with starting field positions that included our own 48 and the Eagles' 49 and 46 yard lines. How bad was our offense? After the opening touchdown, we moved the ball 12 yards on four possessions. Putting points on the board when we had the ball in plus territory has been an issue all year. And just because this is a play-off game does not mean our tendencies—both the good and the bad—fade away.

So though we are confident we can score with a 1st and Goal from the 3, nothing is guaranteed. On first down, Eli's short pass to Tiki falls incomplete. On second down, Tiki gains just 1 yard on a carry, stuffed by Mike Patterson and Darren Howard. On third down, Eli's attempt to loft the ball to our big tight end Jeremy Shockey is not a good one. With 4th and 2, trailing by three, I elect to kick a field goal, which Jay Feely converts to tie the game. We give up a late touchdown pass, and at halftime we trail 17–10.

During the regular season, we split road wins with the Eagles, and the loss to Philadelphia at home in December was especially devastating, another low moment in a difficult season. Just getting to the play-offs was a relief to some in our organization, and probably to Giants fans as well. But there is no relief for me. Just getting there isn't part of my philosophy, and after a year of injuries and team turmoil, I want to finally prove what we're capable of. Trailing by just seven on the road in the play-offs, considering how poorly our offense played for most of the first half, is certainly not a death sentence. We can do this. The 2006 season has gone south for a lot of reasons, but I'm hopeful that today is our chance to erase the bad memories.

On the opening series of the second half, we force the Eagles to go 3 and out, despite a face mask penalty on the first snap, but again we cannot find our rhythm on offense and actually move *backward*. The teams trade punts, and the only scoring in the third quarter comes when our defense holds Philly to a field goal with under three minutes to play in the quarter.

Eli Manning has showed brilliance at times in his career, but whether he is having a great game or a not-so-great game he always maintains his poise. Starting from our own 29, after Tiki runs on first and second downs, Eli scrambles for 2 yards and picks up a first down. We take a shot downfield. Eli's pass, intended for Plaxico, is short, but Eagle corner Sheldon Brown is called for interference and the ball is moved from our 39 to Philadelphia's 14. A pass to Jim Finn picks up 8 yards; a run by Tiki gains nothing. As the game moves into the fourth quarter, we face a 3rd and 2 from the 6. After Eli's pass to Sinorice Moss is incomplete, we settle for another field goal to cut the lead to 20–13.

There's 12:13 remaining in the game, and our season rests on the outcome of our drive. The foolish penalties, the inopportune turnovers, the failures in the green zone—these mean nothing as Eli and the offense jog onto the field. Starting from our own 20, we quickly run the ball into Eagles territory, aided by a holding call on Mike Patterson. After we pick up 6 yards on a reception, I call our first time-out with 7:48 to play in the game. The very next play, Tiki is ruled to have gained no yardage on 3rd and 1 at the Eagles' 25, but our coaches who are watching replays in the box insist he picked up the first down, so I challenge the ruling on the field. The call is overruled, and we do indeed get a fresh set of downs. First down from the 23: false start. The next snap: false start. The next snap: offensive holding. That quick, we go from 1st and 10 from the 23 to 1st and 30 from the 43. Penalties have hampered us all season long, which is especially frustrating since I make it a point every week to remind our players that penalties lose games.

Eli's pass attempt on 1st and 30 is incomplete, but then he and Plaxico hook up again, this time for 18 yards, and I quickly use our second time-out. It is 3rd and 12 from the 25 and the pair connect again, this time for 14 yards. On the very next snap, they do it yet again, and now it counts for six. Jay Feely converts the extra point, and our comeback has tied the game at 20–20.

All we need to do is get a stop and send this game into overtime. All we need is to keep the Eagles in their territory. Eagles back Brian Westbrook has already done damage to us, gaining 108 yards rushing up to this point, including an electrifying 49-yard touchdown run early in the second quarter. On that run, he burst through the line, bounced outside, regained his balance after being tripped, cut back at the 20, and reversed directions at the 15 before running into the end zone. Now, we figure Eagles coach Andy Reid will rely on his back on this final drive.

We are right.

Westbrook gets the call on three of the first five plays, helping take the Eagles from their own 34 to our 32 with two minutes remaining. He runs right at the spot left vacant by All-Pro Michael Strahan, who went down in early November with a season-ending injury. After the two-minute warning, Westbrook picks up 13 more yards and Philadelphia is in field goal position. We use our last time-out with 1:48 to play. Over the next three snaps, the Eagles simply chew clock and use their time-outs wisely to set up a 38-yard field goal attempt by David Akers.

Last night, Dallas had a chance to convert a seemingly easy go-ahead field goal late in the fourth quarter in their play-off game against Seattle, but quarterback Tony Romo, the holder on the kick, mishandled the snap, costing the Cowboys a play-off win. Nothing is automatic.

Jon Dorenbos is the snapper, Koy Detmer is the holder. The snap is good, the hold is clean, the kick is up. It is good.

Our season has come to an end.

In the postgame locker room I am positive, pointing out that despite our struggles and injuries in the second half of the season, we stayed together as a team.

"I am proud of you," I tell them, whether they are listening or not. I talk as if we will be together again.

The media want to talk about my future. I don't. The strained relationship I maintain with reporters is put to the test once again in the bowels of Lincoln Financial Field. I speak briefly with Giants owner John Mara, general manager Ernie Accorsi, and director of player personnel Jerry Reese, and we agree to sit down later in the week.

It's a talk that can't come fast enough for many inside and outside the Giant organization.

THOUGH THE DISAPPOINTING END TO the 2006 season ushers in a difficult time in my life, professionally and personally, I honestly do not believe that I *won't* be the head coach of the New York Giants in 2007. I am not panicked. As frustrated and disappointed as I am on Sunday night after the loss, I drive into the office in Giants Stadium early on Monday morning. I think about the Philadelphia loss and how things went wrong in 2006. And I think about my years in New York.

When I arrived in 2004, we knew what the Giants needed—discipline, mainly. We started off 5–2 before the bottom dropped out. We lost back-to-back games behind veteran quarterback Kurt Warner, and I made the decision to replace Kurt with the top draft pick, Eli Manning. It's safe to say that decision created the first big media frenzy of my head coaching tenure in New York. The media crushed me for supposedly giving up on a potentially play-off-bound team simply to give the rookie experience. Obviously, that's not the way I saw it, nor the way Wellington Mara did, who smiled and told me, "We think the same way."

Why did I go with Eli? A young quarterback cannot learn the game of football by merely watching from the sidelines and holding a clipboard. He needs to be on the field, in the huddle, facing the ferociousness and speed of a blitz, to understand the challenge. We knew Eli would be under fire, defensive coordinators around the league salivating at the thought of blitzing the rookie, and they did just that. Washington and Baltimore blitzed play after play that we, not just Eli, couldn't handle. The rookie came into my office the morning after the Baltimore loss and told me, "I know I can do better, Coach." He knew he could be an effective starting quarterback of the New York Giants, and he was willing to do whatever it took to get there.

Critics continued to bash me as Eli struggled in 2004, but I kept reminding myself that playing quarterback in the NFL is difficult. The multitude of decisions that must be made in a matter of seconds on any given play is mind-boggling, and despite the losses, Eli was learning.

The on-the-job training would benefit us in seasons to come. Still, with Eli in as the starter, we lost six of seven games to finish 6–10. I've never regretted the decision to play him.

The criticism from the media wasn't merely about the losses or my decision to play Eli. No, they also played up that I instructed our players on how to put on their socks properly. Most fans didn't know at the time that our players had been experiencing a rash of blisters and I wanted to stem the tide of sore feet. Then, too, one of the men I most respect, legendary basketball coach John Wooden, used a whole practice every year teaching his players to put on their socks properly, so I felt I was in good company. That, of course, saved me no grief from the press.

In 2005, things couldn't have been more different. We cut down on silly mistakes, Eli improved in every game, and we won the NFC East title, going 11–5. In our play-off game against the Carolina Panthers, we were without players but we practiced and prepared the whole week, coming off a season-ending win over Oakland, just as we had done the week before and the week before that. With our three starting linebackers out and the offense unable to move the ball, we were shut out 23–0. The loss to Carolina was tough to take, and I deserved blame. We did not play with the same intensity as Carolina—it was clear they were more physical—and it is my job to make sure the team is ready to play its best.

After the game, Tiki Barber was critical of me and the coaches in his postgame interviews. I had never been on a team where grievances were aired for all to hear, and it was something I wouldn't stand for. I spoke to Tiki privately about being a part of the solution, reminding him that a football team is a family.

Despite the play-off loss, the stage was set for a tremendous run in 2006 led by our now veteran QB.

We knew going into the 2006 draft and into the free agency period that we needed difference makers, especially on defense. In the draft, we selected Boston College defensive end Mathias Kiwanuka with the last pick of the first round, and we took Miami wide receiver Sinorice Moss in the second. We were busy in free agency, hoping to sign the handful of players who could take us a step further in 2006. We brought in veterans

LaVar Arrington, Sam Madison, Will Demps, R. W. McQuarters, and Brandon Short. As for returning players, Eli would be playing in his third season, with Tiki running behind him. The defense looked solid, anchored by All-Pro Michael Strahan and rising star Osi Umenyiora.

We started off on the right note, winning all four of our preseason games. I know those games are meaningless to some, but to me, a win is a win is a win. Winning makes it easier to improve, because the players get so much positive reinforcement. The 4–0 preseason also gave us confidence heading into the opener and gave the media something positive to say and write.

We opened the season in a nationally televised night game against the Indianapolis Colts on September 10. The Colts, of course, were led by Peyton Manning and were a favorite to win the Super Bowl. The media hype for the game was intense, particularly because the Manning brothers would be competing against each other for the first time. After we dug a 13–0 hole, our offense awoke with just over two minutes to play in the first half, and Eli led the team on an 86-yard drive that culminated in a 34-yard touchdown pass to Plaxico Burress. The Colts added a field goal in the second quarter and led 16–7 at halftime. In the second half, the offense continued to play well and we closed the gap to 16–14. Even so, despite Eli's efforts in the fourth quarter, the Colts and Peyton were too much, and we fell short, 26–21. Still, we'd proved we could play with one of the NFL's best teams.

The following week on the road in Philadelphia, we pulled off our best win in my three seasons with the Giants. It was perhaps the greatest comeback in New York Giants history, and it was certainly the greatest quarterback comeback in a single game. Trailing 24–7 in the fourth quarter on a hot day on which the Eagles relentlessly blitzed, Eli engineered a remarkable comeback and Jay Feely kicked a game-tying field goal, sending the game into overtime. In OT, Eli found Plaxico for a touchdown and we won, 30–24. Eli finished 31 of 43 for 371 yards, completing 20 of his last 26 passes. All seemed well in Giants land, and after Eli's performance against the Eagles, the media began to believe that this could be his breakout season. A loss the following week at Seattle tempered those expectations, but we then reeled off five straight wins to climb to 6–2. We looked play-off-bound.

Then came an eighteen-point loss to Chicago, a game in which Eli gave his worst performance of the season. It was also a game in which the Bears' Devin Hester ran back a field goal attempt for a touchdown. I knew that I had to do something to jump-start our team, as we trailed by four at the time, so I called for a 52-yard field goal attempt. I thought the kick might go wide, but not short. The blame belongs to me.

The Chicago loss was followed by one at Jacksonville and—that quick—the media smelled blood. They panicked, our team panicked. Players chirped their frustrations in the press and pointed fingers in the locker room. On November 26, we played Tennessee in Nashville, hoping to stop the bleeding. Both sides of the ball played well for fifty-one minutes, and we held a commanding 21–0 lead with under ten minutes to play. It appeared that we were finally back on track. And then turnovers, dumb penalties, and a missed sack opportunity allowed Tennessee and Vince Young to come back in a big way.

In the last ten minutes, not only did they tie the football game, they won it on a field goal as time expired. It was a crushing defeat. Postgame, I took a lot of heat for my obvious chewing out of Mathias Kiwanuka after he allowed Young to escape his grasp and make a huge run. I admit it: I lost my cool as the frustration got to me. But from my vantage point, I saw Young get wrapped up, and the coaches up in the booth were telling me through the headset that it was over, as we would have the ball back on downs. Next thing I knew, Young was run out of bounds right in front of me. The following day, I tracked down Mathias and asked him if it was a big deal; he said it wasn't, and we moved on.

After a loss to Dallas the following week, we were suddenly 6–6, and the play-offs seemed out of reach. The topic du jour in the New York media was when—not if—I would be fired. Every day, that's what was written about. The collapse at Tennessee. The collapse in the second half of the season. The collapse of my prospects as head coach. It was all about me. Never mind that injuries had killed us the second half of the season. Never mind that we had lost Justin Tuck, Amani Toomer, LaVar

Arrington, Michael Strahan, Luke Petitgout, and Osi Umenyiora to injuries over the year. Never mind that Tiki Barber had announced early on that this would be his last season in the NFL. But it is the media's job to cover the team, and it is my job to shoulder responsibility for the team. We split our remaining four games, winning the season-ender at Washington to clinch the wild-card berth and a trip to Philadelphia. The 2006 season had not gone as planned, and many believed my job was the consequence.

WHEN I ARRIVE AT THE office on Monday morning, just hours after the loss to Philly, I begin the process of evaluating our players and coaches, just as I always do immediately at the conclusion of a season.

If you know anything about football coaches, you know that we suffer from a peculiar form of tunnel vision. We spend almost every waking hour in meeting rooms or on football practice fields. There is little time to do anything else, let alone read the papers and listen to sports talk radio. In the days before the Philadelphia loss, the noise from the all-sports stations didn't hit my ears; the words written in columns in newspapers didn't pass before my eyes; the screams from our loyal fans didn't reach inside our walls. And I wanted it that way.

But sometimes you can't block it all out. In the seventy-two hours after the game, the hysteria to fire me and get rid of Eli Manning (and, really, all of the players) is at a fever pitch. The newspapers are looking for blood. What are the headlines? "Coughlin Must Go. Ax Can't Fall Fast Enough." "Coughlin Should Be Through with Little Blue." "Keeping Coughlin Would Be a Big Blue Boo-Boo." In the days following the loss, the organization remains silent.

On Monday evening, I leave the Meadowlands complex and head toward our home in northern New Jersey, thinking about the meeting I have scheduled the following day with Giants owners Jonathan Tisch and John Mara. As I pull into our driveway, I notice two cars parked in front—one belonging to our son Tim, the other to our daughter Katie. Now, it isn't unusual for the kids or their kids to be at our house, but something just feels different at 9:00 P.M. on a Monday. I get out of the car, pick up my bag, and walk into the house. Tim, Katie, and Judy are sitting at the kitchen table, and I can tell from their faces that something is wrong.

"Dad," says Katie right away, "why are you putting up with this?"

"Is it worth it?" Tim asks. "They are dragging your name through the mud. You're getting hammered out there."

Clearly, Tim and Katie have been listening and reading. In fact, as it turns out, all four of my children and Judy have been e-mailing back and forth for weeks about what is being written and said. I am a bit taken back at what they are telling me, especially what's being written by certain sportswriters who I believed had always been fair to me. Judy wants to know why I *don't* know what is being said and written. She thinks I *should* know.

I look over at Tim and see the concern of a father—not of a son—on his face.

I sit and listen. Tim points out that I have been in tough situations before, but it has never gotten as personal as the attacks of the past few days, not even at the ugly end of things in Jacksonville. Judy echoes the sentiment.

My kids live in the real world, where every day they have been hearing the vicious rants and the nasty names and the calls for my head. Most of the time I don't live in that world. But on this night, in this room, I understand more than ever what family means and what being a football coach can do to a family. Even so, this late-night gathering is not an intervention to convince me to quit. Rather, my family wants me to stand up for myself and be prepared to voice the important issues with the team's ownership the following day. Most important, Tim and Katie know how painful the past weeks have been, and they don't want me to suffer. And they are right: 2006 and early 2007 have been tough. They make it clear that if I want to stop coaching, they are behind me.

We talk for an hour or two. Then Tim and Katie drive away, and for a moment I feel the strain that they must be feeling at work and in their neighborhoods as Tom Coughlin's children. This is a difficult part of the profession.

I am not exactly sure what to expect in the meeting with the team's owners, but I do know that I will stand my ground on what I believe is right, and I am confident I will be the head coach. In John Mara's office in Giants Stadium on Tuesday, John, Jon, and I talk about the direction of the organization in a professional and productive meeting, lasting about forty-five minutes. We talk about the attitude of the team and the coaches and the play at some of the key positions. As we talk, I get a sense that they are gauging my attitude and my belief about winning in 2007. Do I think I can make this work in New York? As I walk out, I am satisfied that they believe I can. Though it is unspoken, it is clear: it is time to win.

The Giants announce a one-year contract extension within twenty-four hours of that meeting. I will be back, but 2007 will be a mandate to turn things around, and the price of failure will be my job. I sit in my office over the next few days making notes, taking an inventory of the positives and negatives of the 2006 season, for the team and for myself. We simply cannot go through another season like 2006.

THE PLAYERS TRIED HARD IN 2006, yet we were insufficient in several aspects of the game, and I take the blame for that. But what can I do to ensure that 2007 is not a repeat? It starts with the coaching staff.

Kevin Gilbride, who as the quarterback coach had taken over play calling the last two weeks of the season from John Hufnagel, is officially promoted to offensive coordinator in January. Kevin has been coaching since 1974, with stints at five different colleges, six NFL teams, and one year in the Canadian Football League. He has called plays for the Houston Oilers, the Jacksonville Jaguars (with me in 1995 and 1996), the Pittsburgh Steelers, and the Buffalo Bills, and I have no doubt that his experience will benefit a rather young offense.

On defense, we also need a change, a new approach. I inform Tim Lewis, our defensive coordinator, that he will not be back in 2007. It is always difficult to let a staff member go, knowing full well the impact that his family will feel, but making difficult decisions is a big part of a head coach's job description.

My search for a new defensive coordinator centers on Philadelphia, since I have been keeping an eye on their impressive linebacker coach, Steve Spagnuolo. As a head coach, I am always keeping track of assistant coaches around the NFL who I believe could make great coordinators. Steve has done a tremendous job in Philadelphia, coaching the linebackers, corners, and safeties over eight years under well-known defensive coordinator Jim Johnson. In addition, Steve served as an assistant coach under my former boss Jack Bicknell with the Barcelona Dragons in NFL Europe, and I knew that if Jack had hired him, he must be a quality coach. I contact the Eagles and head coach Andy Reid drives into the office on an off day Saturday to sign the permission form, allowing Steve to interview with us.

By six o'clock the next morning, Steve and I are sitting in my office in Giants Stadium. We talk about his family and his previous coaching experiences, and we reminisce a bit about Jack Bicknell. Then we dive into football and spend the next six hours talking defense. His defense will be disciplined and will get more pressure on the quarterback, stopping the run and forcing the pass. It doesn't take me too long to realize that Steve is a leader our defense can rally around. I decide he is our guy. Sure, it is a risk offering the job to someone who hasn't been an NFL coordinator, but I believe he is the right man for the job. After some back-and-forth between Steve's agent and Jerry Reese, we have our new defensive coordinator.

But there are more staff changes to come. My longtime friend Mike Sweatman, the well-respected special teams coordinator, decides to retire, and Tom Quinn moves up to take his place. Chris Palmer, my offensive coordinator in Jacksonville for two seasons, joins the Giants as our quarterbacks coach. Chris has the task of continuing to develop Eli Manning into an All-Pro quarterback. Thomas McGaughey joins us as the assistant special teams coach, and Sean Ryan comes on board as the offensive quality control coach. With that, the new staff is in place.

But even now, the changes are only beginning.

Longtime Giants general manager Ernie Accorsi announced his retirement in 2006, and the director of player personnel, Jerry Reese, was elevated to GM just days after the Giants announced my contract extension in January. Jerry brings passion and enthusiasm to the post, and he can often be seen sitting in coaches' offices talking football. He has emphasized the idea that we are all in this together, and he will play a huge role in shaping our roster.

Making changes to a roster is a never-ending process in the National Football League. Moves are made nearly every week of the year in an attempt to find the best possible fifty-three-man roster and eight-man practice squad. But it is not always as simple as determining who is the best player. In today's NFL, there are salary concerns, free agency issues, position depth battles and draft prospects, and a long list of other factors that contribute to player personnel decisions, and we take all of them into account now.

It's never easy to release a player, especially a veteran, but in collaboration with the personnel department and Jerry, we make the tough decision in mid-February to release linebacker LaVar Arrington, left tackle Luke Petitgout, veteran linebacker Carlos Emmons, and return specialist Chad Morton. We also do not re-sign kicker Jay Feely. The free agency period starts March 1, and by that date we are $20 million under the $108 million salary cap. Over the next two months, after careful evaluations, meetings, and negotiations, we sign Chiefs linebacker Kawika Mitchell, quarterback Anthony Wright, and defensive tackle Marcus Bell, among others. With the retirement of Tiki Barber, we look for some depth in the backfield and trade for Cleveland running back Reuben Droughns.

The coaching staff and the roster have taken shape, but there is more work to be done.

THE TESTY POSTGAME EXCHANGE BETWEEN me and the media after the Philadelphia loss was the culmination of a season-long tug-of-war. The personal attacks in the columns and articles in the days after the loss, most of which called for my firing, did not help soften my attitude toward the media in any way. I understand that being a head coach in New York isn't supposed to be easy, and I also know full well that dealing with reporters is part of my job. More than that, I understand I am not a "sound bite" coach, and I get it that reporters hate my short answers, especially to repetitive questions. But I have not tried to win over the media, and I certainly will not play favorites, as some coaches do. Nevertheless, the strained relationship between me and them has made life difficult for me and for my players. Last season, it was all about me, and it shouldn't be that way. So just as I evaluated and made changes to the coaching staff and to the roster, I think about how to adjust my give-and-take with the press.

Pat Hanlon has been working in communications for the New York Giants since 1993, and before that he was with New England and Pittsburgh. Pat knows football and, more important to me, he knows the media business. He is always a great sounding board and one of the few people around me who tells it the way it is. When I *need* to know, he tells me. When I *need* to improve in an area outside of football, Pat makes no bones about it. The noise of the media criticism reached eardrum-shattering levels in January, so something needs to change, and Pat has some ideas.

One of his ideas is one-on-one, off-the-record meetings for me with beat reporters and columnists from around the New York area. I am initially reluctant. *You mean meet with the guys who have been calling for my head the last four months?* Pat believes that sitting down in a calm setting will allow both sides to air frustrations and will crystallize ways to improve the relationship going forward. With some input from Judy, I come to recognize that there might be some benefit to this, so I agree to the meetings.

Pat decides that there are eight beat writers and three or four columnists with whom I should meet in the ensuing weeks. First up is Neil Best from *Newsday,* who got to know me when he was a beat reporter covering the Giants but who now is a media columnist for the paper and not involved in the day-to-day coverage. Given his perspective and experience as a Giants beat reporter for ten years, Pat believes Neil can present the overriding concerns on behalf of all of the writers.

Before Neil comes into my office, Pat and I spend a few minutes reviewing his reporting history and his coverage and opinions of me. As with the meetings that will follow, my time with Neil goes way past the scheduled thirty to forty-five minutes. I take notes as we talk. He is candid with me, which I respect, and even a bit humorous. Neil explains the issues as he sees them, including the fact that the media wants more access to coaches and the fact that I am disliked because of how impatient I am with reporters. From my perspective, the meeting with Neil is helpful, so Pat and I decide to continue on with other local writers, who come from the *Bergen Record*, the *Star-Ledger*, the *New York Post*, the *Daily News, The New York Times,* and most of the other major newspapers in the area. In each case, Pat preps the reporters before the sit-downs so that they know what to expect. And these sit-downs do not become shouting matches; I simply ask my counterparts what they need from me and how they believe our relationship could be more harmonious. One reporter comments that I act like I don't have time for the press, and that sticks with me. In some of the meetings, I sense a genuine interest on the part of the reporter in improving the relationship; in others, not so much.

The conversations allow me to gain a better understanding of the media, their concerns, and how they perceive me. Afterward, I review my notes. Just what do reporters seem to want?

- They want more access to me and the assistant coaches.
- They want more patience and understanding from me.
- They want fewer statistics and more insight when I answer questions.
- They want shorter opening statements so they can get in more questions.
- The beat writers want more time with me on Fridays.
- They want me to call reporters by their names.
- They want me to watch my body language and tone.

After talking it over with Pat, I do agree that the media can have increased access to assistant coaches as compared to previous years, something the NFL has been pounding on all teams to grant. Also, reporters can visit with assistants a few times in the off-season, on the first day of training camp, and during our bye week in the regular season. In addition to those times, coordinators will also be available during minicamp and every other week during the season. As for increased access to me, in addition to the Monday, Wednesday, Thursday, and Friday media opportunities, I agree to allow for more one-on-one time.

As for my attitude toward the press, it is clear that patience is a virtue I need to develop. But with this input from reporters, I intend to show more respect toward the men and women of the media and to be slower to fly off the handle at redundant or provocative questions. The truth is that I never want anyone to believe that I do not respect his or her job. I value hard work and always have, so why haven't I been valuing the hard work of reporters? I also vow to think things through more before meeting with reporters during the year, anticipating their questions and constructing answers. I may be sixty-one, but I'm not too old to make some adjustments. Whatever I can do in 2007 to make it not about me, I will.

OVER THE COURSE OF FOUR DECADES, I have coached at three colleges and with five NFL teams, and at three of those stops I was the head coach. Never once did I question my approach or my process. I knew one way to coach football and deal with my players, and it had worked on both levels. It didn't mean I never took a hard look at myself to improve, but I never sought out a new way to interact with players. I simply have never believed that a head coach must be friends with his players or tell them how great they are every day to be successful. Rather, my job is to help them be the best they can be, and by doing so win football games.

So it would be accurate to state that in my first three years in New York I wasn't the most beloved figure in the Giants organization. In fact, most players seem to avoid me at all costs, often looking down as we pass in a hallway or the locker room. Apparently, the players believe they have to walk on eggshells around me, for fear of my wrath. Maybe I have created that atmosphere on purpose, never wanting players or coaches to relax. I do have an open-door policy, but rare is the occasion when players *voluntarily* enter my office. After all, when they do step inside, it is usually never a good thing. Maybe it is because I never really reached out to players; maybe I never let them see the real me, afraid that if I let my guard down, it would make me vulnerable. Maybe my tendency to wear my emotions on my face during games and practices—as the television cameras often notice—sends a bad message. A bad pass, a dropped ball, or a silly penalty can elicit all sorts of facial contortions, and I have been criticized by some for my demonstrations and outbursts. As a coach, it's who I am. It's all I have ever known. But why does it seem to push away players now when it didn't twenty years ago?

There is no denying that the age gap between me and the men I coach plays a role. There have been many successful coaches in a lot of sports who seemed not to have had an issue with age difference—Phil Jackson, John Wooden, Tom Landry, and Tom Lasorda, to name a few—but for me it's an issue. Most of our players were born in the 1980s, and my own children are older than many of the men I coach. When I talk about Vince Lombardi, they wonder who that was. When they play Jay-Z, I say, "What is that?" When I bring up FDR, they think I'm talking about a highway in New York City. But as obvious as the differences in generations are, the solutions to the problem are not readily apparent.

Change is the theme of the 2007 off-season, so why not a change in how I relate to our players and staff? The truth is, if 2007 is going to be my last season with the New York Giants, I just want—and need—to be me. The *real* me, not the football coach with the facade.

Our director of player development, Charles Way, puts it to me this way: "Be the guy that you are when you are with your children or grandchildren."

He has a point. I *am* different around my loved ones, particularly the grandchildren. Funny, crazy, down-to-earth, involved. Obviously, I won't be building sandcastles with Eli Manning or playing tag with Michael Strahan, but perhaps I do need to open up to more fully connect with the players. I need to make it obvious that I do care and that the caring is sincere.

With prodding by Judy, I decide on one more change for 2007: to make things more fun. I am going to enjoy the 2007 journey, and I want the players and coaches to enjoy it as well, regardless of where it takes us.

With that, the tough self-analysis is over, but the tests still lie ahead. Will Steve Spagnuolo make our defense into one that is feared? Will I smile and graciously answer a reporter's question about the poor play of one of our starters? Is there any chance that I can be the real me, the "new" me, even when adversity comes upon us? We will know soon enough.

Every year shortly after the season ends, Judy and I take four or five days and travel somewhere together: Puerto Rico, Costa Rica, Turks and Caicos Islands. It is a tradition we started in Jacksonville, and we usually go during Super Bowl week. We attended the Super Bowl in Miami in 1995, but I have no interest in ever attending again as a spectator. I only want to go when I'm coaching in the game. This year we go to Sonoma Valley in California with good friends, but I still watch the Super Bowl, sitting in a chair in the Silverado Country Club with a pen and pencil in hand, taking notes as the Indianapolis Colts defeat the Chicago Bears.

I find myself wondering if next year I'll be taking notes once again.

TWO

• • • • • •

Optimism is the faith that leads to achievement.
Nothing can be done without hope and confidence.

— HELEN KELLER

PLAYERS WIN CHAMPIONSHIPS; COACHES HELP THEM GET THERE. An organization can assemble the most experienced, most highly regarded coaching staff in the National Football League, but without the talent on the field, it is impossible to win big in professional football. Chuck Noll had a tremendous staff in Pittsburgh in the 1970s and early 1980s when they won four Super Bowls, but they never would have gotten that far without drafting the likes of Terry Bradshaw, Lynn Swann, Franco Harris, Joe Greene, John Stallworth, Jack Lambert, and Mike Webster. Drafting players who help you win games has always been complicated, however, what with the advent of free agency, teams must commit to a philosophical position when it comes to drafting and signing players. Making mistakes, especially in the early rounds of the draft, can haunt an organization for years. That is just one of the reasons why the New York Giants, like all of the other thirty-one NFL teams, put so much time and money into the draft process. We simply can't afford to make mistakes.

Coming off the 2006 season, it is clear that we must field a transformative draft class in 2007. We need to select players who can contribute immediately, particularly at cornerback and at wide receiver, to constantly add playmakers to our roster. The money available to sign free agents to fill the gaps can take us only so far, so we look to the draft for answers.

The NFL draft itself has become a spectacle. Analysts on television and "experts" on the Internet break down hundreds of players and spout off on which ones teams need to take. Type the words "2007 NFL draft" in Google and 489,000 hits come up. The noise reaches a crescendo in mid-April, days before the draft. Then, over forty-eight hours in New York City, press from all over the world descend on the Big Apple to cover the event as if it were the Super Bowl itself. Two television networks broadcast the draft live, and hundreds of Internet sites track the picks in real time. But while those two days in April are the most visible to the public, for an organization such as the New York Giants the draft begins almost a year earlier, and the 2007 draft is no different.

The Giants personnel department includes approximately twenty people, tasked with identifying those players who can help us win. There are the pro personnel directors and scouts who continually evaluate players currently in the NFL, and there is a director of college scouting and a large college scouting department that evaluates all of the best college players in the country.

The evaluation and draft process starts long before prospects are even on the draft board. Like many teams, the Giants are part of a large scouting service, BLESTO, comprising scouts from around the country who provide thousands of bits of information on all of the college prospects a year before those players are even predicted to be in the draft. It allows teams to identify and evaluate prospects who are still only in the spring of their junior year. After spring meetings by the scouting service, our scouting department has a good idea of whom they need to take a look at over the ensuing year.

They start in the summer and watch college practices, talk to coaches, and study tape on campuses around the nation, then retreat to their hotel rooms and their laptops to fill out evaluation forms to send back to New Jersey. They grab a few hours of sleep, then wake up and move on to the next school. All told, our scouts will evaluate in person approximately five hundred of the top prospects during the college season and report back to our scouting director. The pro and college scouts also attend our training camp in August and evaluate our Giants players.

When the college and pro football seasons are over, things really pick up. Seniors play in all-star games such as the Senior Bowl in Mobile, Alabama, all of which are generously attended by NFL scouts, coaches, and general managers. Prospects begin to participate in individual workouts for interested teams, and top schools now hold Pro Day events, not only to benefit the players and scouts but also to show off their programs to recruits and fans.

Roughly 330 players flock to Indianapolis for the National Invitational Camp, otherwise known as the NFL Combine, for a week of mental and physical tests as well as interviews. Before we even go to Indianapolis, we give all of the prospects preliminary grades. In Indy, you can usually find me perched at the 10-yard line, stopwatch in hand. I also am involved in all of our player interviews at night.

Immediately following the Combine, I sit down with our director of college scouting, Marc Ross, and we discuss the prospects. By the time of our final organization-wide draft meetings in April, we are focused on those players who grade above a certain cutoff at their position. Prior to those meetings, the director of college scouting pulls together information from the scouts, the position coach, Giants vice president Chris Mara, general manager Jerry Reese, and me, and puts together a packet on each prospect.

Usually it is in the second week in April that we start our draft meetings in New Jersey. They last all day long, every day for ten days. Before heading into each session, I personally have already studied tape on the top players and have all kinds of information and statistics in my notebooks. Each day of the April meetings we focus on a different position. The coaches, scouts, Jerry, Marc, and I talk about the pluses and minuses of potential players and whether or not we think their grade and ranking are too high or too low. We move quickly, not spending a lot of time on any one player.

Like most other teams, in April 2007 we invite prospects to Giants Stadium to meet with us, get a feel for our organization, and participate in formal in-person evaluation. Among the twenty-three who visit in April are USC wide receiver Dwayne Jarrett, Ohio State running back Antonio Pittman, Western Oregon tight end Kevin Boss, and Miami safety Brandon Meriweather. Brandon is perhaps the top safety prospect. He has speed and great instincts, but there were some incidents involving Brandon at Miami that need more explanation. We spend time with Brandon and come away impressed. But is he our guy?

When draft weekend finally arrives on April 28, we are still hard at it, working the phones, talking to agents, analyzing possible trade scenarios. During the draft, coaches work in their offices until our picks draw near, and then we rejoin the others in the conference room, surrounded by televisions and draft boards. With experience comes skill in evaluating players and therefore more accurate grades.

Our big need in 2007 is a top-flight corner who can start right away, and we have our sights set on Aaron Ross, the All-American corner from the University of Texas. We like his toughness, his hands, and his tackling ability, and Aaron can also return punts. But in the first round, we pick twentieth, and there are teams ahead of us also in need of a corner. We breathe a sigh of relief when, with the eighteenth pick, the Cincinnati Bengals take another corner, Michigan's Leon Hall. We take Aaron two picks later.

In the second round, Carolina takes Dwayne Jarrett, and we take his teammate, wide receiver Steve Smith, six picks later. Our other picks include Jay Alford, Zak DeOssie, Kevin Boss, Adam Koets, Michael Johnson, and Ahmad Bradshaw, Ahmad in the seventh round out of Marshall University. Typically, you hope your top three picks contribute in their first season. There is no way for us to know just how important a role *all* of these rookies will play in the upcoming season.

The draft process itself has become something of a game. Organizations try to camouflage their intentions so as not to attract other suitors to a prospect. I never try to give away a real need or pigeonhole myself when talking to the media about the draft. Some teams use the prospect meetings in the days prior to the draft to throw other teams off the scent by inviting prospects they have no intention of taking or by not inviting those they do want.

Once a player leaves college and gives up his eligibility, the agents, parents, and inner circle control him. Agents don't want their clients to do anything in the months leading up to the draft that could hurt their draft position and cost them money, so some top players do not even participate in all-star games or all Combine events or even their own school's Pro Days and will be clocked just once in the 40-yard dash. Of course, on the flip side, the all-star games and workouts give unrecognized players all of the exposure they need. You have to take it all with a grain of salt, and experience is your best asset. You have to have faith and belief in your evaluation process and abide by the final grade. When all is said and done, when the games and charades of the draft are over, what are you left with? We are confident that our 2007 draft class can contribute. We just aren't sure who, how, and when.

EVERY COLLEGE PLAYER HAS HIS "welcome to the NFL" moment. It might be a jarring hit in a training camp; it might be a two-hour tape study with a position coach; it might be the drain of two-a-day practices in the heat of July in an NFL camp. Whenever it happens, and however it happens, the game changes for them. They are no longer coddled college superstars but men fighting to earn a living. For some, the adjustment is quick; for others, it can take more than a year. In 2007, we need them all to adjust in the blink of an eye. We have no choice.

On May 11 we welcome the draft class, a few rookie free agents, and some tryout players to minicamp in New Jersey, where over the course of three days they are introduced to NFL football. There are offense, defense, special team, and position meetings; jog-throughs; practices; an introduction to strength training and player development; and everything else that exposes them to the New York Giants. The rookies are usually wide-eyed, and 2007 is no exception. They are looking to make an impression on the coaches and trying to feel their way in the NFL and in the Giants organization in an attempt to find out just what is expected of them.

From what we can tell in just the few days we are together, the draft class is as advertised. Yes, they make simple rookie mistakes, fumbling the ball and getting beat on pass attempts, but we are impressed with their willingness to learn. Aaron makes a few mistakes but is otherwise impressive with his physical skills. Steve opens some eyes with a few tremendous catches. Zak DeOssie and Jay Alford prove that they belong, impressive both in position drills and in their long and short snapping. And our last pick, running back Ahmad Bradshaw, earns perhaps the most praise in those three days, with a few memorable runs. But these are just rookies in noncontact drills going against other rookies, many of whom won't even be on an NFL opening-day roster. How will they perform against our veterans?

The league allows teams to hold up to fourteen voluntary organized team activities (OTAs) in late spring, lasting no more than four hours. Though they are voluntary, most of our players tend to show up. In 2007, we decide to hold nine official OTAs starting in late May. Now, keep in mind that the majority of players have been hard at work since March or earlier, working on strength and conditioning with our strength coaches. Some of them have even worked out in the practice bubble, running routes, throwing passes, and honing technique. In early May, right before the official start of the OTAs, Eli starts throwing to receivers, including Plaxico Burress, who has showed up, but not to Jeremy Shockey, who has not. Since I have been back in New York, Plaxico and Jeremy have often worked out on their own in the off-season and don't often attend the voluntary sessions, so it's a good sign for us that Plaxico is here.

Out of the eighty-eight players on our roster, eighty-four of them are on hand at the start of the OTAs on May 22. Burress has gone back to Florida; there is no Shockey, no Michael Strahan, and no Jim Finn, who is injured. By the sixth OTA on June 5, Shockey is with us. Also now in the fold is kicker Lawrence Tynes, for whom we traded a conditional pick to Kansas City.

For the first time since I was named head coach in New York, the NFL mandates some access for the media during our OTAs. Our first two OTAs are focused on the individual position drills; the other seven begin with individual drills, progress through seven-on-seven, and end with team drills. Mixed in with the meetings and practices are team barbecues and the Giants' golf tournament on Tuesday, May 29.

We can see the building of a team in the May and June workouts. And if you are wondering, then yes, I am a bit more relaxed with the players, a bit more "inviting." I am not sure what I—or they—make of it, but the days keep moving swiftly, and before we know it, the mandatory team minicamp is upon us in June and all players are in attendance.

On June 13, the first day of minicamp, I ask former Giant Jessie Armstead, who returned to the Meadowlands to officially retire as a Giant after so many great seasons on Giants teams in the 1990s, including the 2000 NFC Championship team, to speak to the team. Jessie knows all about Giants pride, and in heartfelt fashion he explains to our players what being a Giant means to him and what it should mean to them, a new generation of players. Whether or not the words stick, time will tell.

The theme for the off-season and the minicamp is "Less Talk, More Work" or "Talk Is Cheap—Play the Game." In 2006, we did too much talking. Players spoke out in the media about the coaches and their teammates, and they played the blame game in the locker room. It was the most poisonous team atmosphere I have ever been around. In 2007, at least so far, we've been working more than talking. It is evident early in minicamp that Steve Spagnuolo has mixed things up a bit on defense. Every time the ball hits the ground, all eleven defenders run to scoop it up. Perhaps the aggressiveness that we were seeking is starting to emerge. On offense, Eli looks sharp, and it becomes clear that replacing Tiki Barber will fall on the shoulders of a committee of backs, including Reuben Droughns, Brandon Jacobs, and perhaps Derrick Ward.

Whether or not Ahmad Bradshaw will be in the rotation is yet to be determined.

Work must be balanced by play, of course. All spring, I put an enormous amount of thought into how I was going to change and how my relationship with the players could change, and I kept coming back to the same conclusion: just be myself. But how could I show them my fun-loving side? And then an idea is born: poker! Charles Way makes the suggestion of a casino night to break up minicamp and to work on team building. We hire a company to set up a full casino right in Giants Stadium so the coaches and players can enjoy a night out.

So on Thursday night, June 14, we give it a go. Beforehand, I can tell the players are skeptical, offering looks that say, *Okay, Coach is just trying to do this for show, to prove how he's changed.* But they're wrong. Nobody enjoys it more than I do. I lose all of my play money very quickly at the poker table, sharing laughs and commiserating with Osi Umenyiora and a few of his teammates. We share stories about our lives, eat wings and drink soda, and just hang out like men. And I start to realize that giving an inch doesn't mean giving a mile.

As minicamp comes to an end, we are content with the progress. The rookies are fitting in, the veterans are in great shape and focused, and the new coordinators are starting to make an impact. On the last day, I gather the players to talk about the concept of team. What does it truly mean to be a team? It means putting aside ego. It means no finger-pointing. It means we go through the good times and the bad times together. It means placing team above self.

"The San Antonio Spurs won last night," I tell them. "They won another NBA championship. In my mind, they embody the team concept. I mean, they have stars like Tim Duncan and Tony Parker, but every player sacrifices for everyone else. That is a team."

I hope the message is sinking in.

THREE

● ● ● ● ● ● ● ●

Tomorrow is in large part determined by what you do today.
So make today a masterpiece.

—JOHN WOODEN

OUTSIDE OF THE DOOR OF MY OFFICE IN GIANTS STADIUM HANGS A picture of an eagle with a stern look on his face and the words "I *am* smiling" plastered above, a gift from Judy many years ago. Though it may accurately depict my disposition many times, it is also an inviting wisecrack for those who walk through the door.

You can learn a lot about someone by what he surrounds himself with. On the walls of my office are dozens of family snapshots: single ones of Judy, large colorful ones of the extended family at a beach, and plenty of our grandchildren. There's a picture of my son Tim and I, Rudy Giuliani, a picture of the scoreboard from when our Boston College team upset top-ranked Notre Dame in 1993, a picture of me hugging some New York City firefighters, and even a few pictures of Mother Teresa.

A Vince Lombardi poster explains what it takes to be number one. A sign reads, "The destination is marvelous but the real joy is in the journey." There is a framed list of John Wooden's words on preparation, like "Preparation is where success is truly found" and "Early on I came to believe that you should learn as if you were going to live forever and live as if you were going to die tomorrow."

My bookshelves at the office don't even compare to my vast collection of books at home, but here rest books on football, of course, including *Tom Landry: An Autobiography, Run to Daylight, Oklahoma Split T Football,* and *Vince.* There are books on success and leadership, including *Time-Out Leadership, Joe Torre's Ground Rules for Winners,* and *The 17 Essential Qualities of a Team Player* by John Maxwell. There are military books, such as Patton's *War as I Knew It* and the *First American Army*; history books, including *Jefferson's Great Gamble*; and books on faith, including various copies of the Holy Bible.

It is often during the months of June and July that I have the most time to devour books. The off-season work is done, the players are enjoying what's left of their summer, and the coaches can stop worrying— at least for a few weeks. July 2007 is particularly special for us because our oldest daughter, Keli, is going to be married. She wisely plans the wedding for our vacation time, and the weekend on Amelia Island is a wonderful time with family and friends. Walking my eldest child down the aisle is emotional, and I am so proud. And when the music starts playing at the reception, old Tom Coughlin is encouraged by his sisters and hits the dance floor. Even as the weekend unfolds, I find myself thinking about just how much fun I am having, perhaps because so much of my family is together. Just as I made the conscious decision to try to enjoy the 2007 football season, I also remind myself to soak up every minute with my loved ones. Soon enough, the hot days and nights of training camp will beckon, and the time with loved ones will have passed.

TO THE CASUAL FOOTBALL FAN, what happens on Sundays in December is what matters. A game-winning kick, a tough goal line stand, an athletic interception—those are the moments that propel teams forward. But to the trained eye, to the real football aficionado, victories are made in the hot summer days of July/August when the groundwork is laid for the upcoming season. It is here that work ethic and personality are born. On these fields, often in 100-degree temperatures, offenses develop their tempo and defenses develop cohesiveness. Teams are made in August, not December. Every training camp is a new beginning, and we need one.

I am a football coach, so I can't wait for July 27. I absolutely love training camp—the practices, the two-a-days, the team unity, the hard work, the sweat, the optimism—all of it. So I am thrilled to get to the University at Albany. I'm more anxious than normal to get here because it means we are officially on to 2007, the memories of 2006 now distant. And if the spring practices are any indication, I believe things will be a bit different this year with this team. I'm not sure how just yet, but I have a good feeling.

Do we have players on the roster who are capable of success and will they fit together as a team? The answer to those questions is yes. But there are also plenty of unanswered questions as well: Who will emerge as our go-to back and how will David Diehl perform at left tackle? How fast will Mathias Kiwanuka pick up the linebacker position after we have moved him from defensive end? How healthy will guys such as Amani Toomer and Michael Strahan be? And, of course, will Michael even be a New York Giant this year? He is absent from camp, mulling over retirement. How fast can rookie Aaron Ross contribute at corner? How will our kicking game look?

Then, too, there is the unspoken cloud hanging over everything that we do: that I am a one-year coach whose job rests on the wins and losses in 2007.

There is one thing we do know: we have veteran leaders at every position. The quarterbacks have Eli Manning, the wide receivers have Amani and Plaxico, the offensive line has Shaun O'Hara, Chris Snee, and David Diehl, the tight ends have Jeremy Shockey, the defensive line has Michael (I hope) and Osi, the linebackers have Antonio Pierce, the defensive backs have Sam Madison, and on special teams Jeff Feagles and David Tyree lead the way. If they are on board with the team concept, if they maintain a positive attitude, then I am confident it will trickle down to the rest of the team. If not, we'll be dealing with a disaster.

THE PLAYERS HAVE THEIR OFFICIAL weigh-ins and medical checks on July 27, and after lunch they participate in the mandatory and dreaded conditioning test. The test consists of ten "half-gassers," sprints from one sideline to the other and back, with thirty-second rests in between. The receivers, running backs, and defensive backs must complete each half-gasser in sixteen seconds or less, the linemen in twenty or less, and everyone else in eighteen or less. After running five of the half-gassers, the players are allowed a three-minute rest before completing the final five. It is a great way to start camp: right away intensity, pressure, and competition against the clock. I am pleased that so many Giants pass on their first attempt. Those who fail will continue to run the ten half-gassers daily until they, too, pass the test.

As a man in love with statistics, I tend to be long-winded at times when speaking to the team. I have always believed that numbers don't lie and that they often are the best illustrators of points of emphasis. But the use of so many numbers can make my presentations a bit lengthy. So, too, does the idea that I have to cover everything, leaving nothing unspoken. Before training camp starts, I make the decision to try to keep my talks short and to be less intense during them. It starts with our first team meeting in the old gymnasium meeting room on campus.

"Our objectives in 2007," I begin, "do not have to do with wins and losses, but rather our hearts and minds." They appear on the video screen:

1. The key to our success will be unselfish play.
2. We need to trust and support one another in the good times and the bad.
3. We must develop a feeling of one, to experience a team that plays for each other.
4. We must learn that if our hearts are in the right place, we can accomplish anything and overcome all obstacles.

5. We must establish a state of mind that demands a higher level of achievement and a greater sense of ownership and accountability.

6. No toughness, no championship!

"If we meet these objectives, if we stick together as a team, if every one of us puts team above self, then I really believe we can be something this year," I say. "Remember, talk is cheap—Play the Game."

During last year's training camp, there was a lot of talk about the Super Bowl and expectations, and we all know how 2006 turned out. So this year in camp, there won't be much talk of the holy grail, even if some of us privately believe we have the talent to get there.

As for training camp itself, there are also objectives, team bonding simply one of them. We want to come out of camp healthy, avoiding serious injuries; we want to have full evaluations of all of our players in order to select a final fifty-three-man roster and a practice squad that gives us the best chance to win; we want our offense, defense, and special teams to learn and embrace our systems; we want young players to develop the knowledge and experience that can elevate their play; and we want to come out of training a better football team.

The University at Albany is a perfect location for camp. There are five practice fields plus the stadium field, as well as a workout facility and training room in the basketball arena, which also doubles as our locker room during the stay. Meetings are held in the Physical Education Building, which also houses the coaches' offices. The players' dorms are more than half a mile away, so most players drive their cars to the facilities for our meetings and workouts.

The first few days of camp in 2007, we are full with energy and enthusiasm. With new coaches running their units, there are new voices bellowing around the five practice fields at the University at Albany. I keep a close eye on the rookies and a few of the free agents, but I also intently watch as the defense attempts to adjust to Steve Spagnuolo's defense. There are numerous mistakes early on in camp, as expected: missed assignments, blown coverages, incorrect personnel. Those things will be ironed out in the coming weeks . . . I hope.

From the first whistle of camp, we begin evaluating everyone. We work a variety of guys in the backfield, including Reuben Droughns, Derrick Ward, Brandon Jacobs, Ryan Grant, and Ahmad Bradshaw, and after just a few days of work it is clear both that we will be fine with our depth in the backfield and that Ahmad is going to play some sort of role. Our main off-season pickup on defense, Kawika Mitchell, proves that we made the right choice. He is fast and athletic and adjusts well moving from middle linebacker to the outside.

As training camp progresses, a handful of players, Plaxico and Amani among them, sit out at least one if not both of the sessions. Plaxico is recovering from off-season ankle surgery, and Amani has his own issues after surgery on his anterior cruciate ligament.

The initial enthusiasm is difficult to maintain as the days wear on. Training camp, as you might expect, is a tough hill to climb, especially on days when we practice twice. But it's more than the physical exertion, it's the mental energy required to stay focused in hours of meetings. Take a look at a typical two-a-day schedule, this one for Saturday, July 28:

6:00 A.M.	Early wake-up
5:45–8:00 A.M.	Breakfast (mandatory)
6:30 A.M.	Treatment for players listed as "out" (mandatory)
6:45 A.M.	Wake-up
7:00 A.M.	Treatment (mandatory)
7:00–8:30 A.M.	Tape and dress (rookies and vets)
8:40–8:50 A.M.	Special teams/C-QB run and stretch
8:45–8:55 A.M.	Team run and stretch
8:50–9:00 A.M.	Special teams period/C-QB exchange
9:00–10:40 A.M.	Practice
10:40–10:45 A.M.	Head coach with media
10:45–11:10 A.M.	Treatment (mandatory)/strength development
11:15–12:45 P.M.	Lunch (mandatory)
11:30 A.M.–12:15 P.M.	Players with media
12:15 P.M.	Lunch open to staff, media, and guests

12:25 P.M.	Coaches A.M. tape review (sp. tms./off./def.)
1:00 P.M.	Staff A.M. tape review (sp. tms./9 on 7/team)
1:15 P.M.	Training room open for tape and dress
1:30 P.M.	Coaches prepare for afternoon meetings
2:30–3:10 P.M.	Offense/defense meetings
3:20–3:30 P.M.	Special teams/C-QB run and stretch
3:25–3:35 P.M.	Team run and stretch
3:30–3:40 P.M.	Special teams period/C-QB exchange
3:40–5:10 P.M.	Practice
5:10–5:20 P.M.	Conditioning
5:25–5:50 P.M.	Treatment (mandatory)/strength development
5:30–7:00 P.M.	Dinner (mandatory)
6:30 P.M.	Dinner open to staff and guests
6:30 P.M.	Coaches P.M. tape review (sp. tms./off./def.)
7:00 P.M.	Coaches prepare for evening meetings
7:00–7:30 P.M.	Special teams meeting: KO/KOR/FG/FG BLK
7:00–7:30 P.M.	Quarterbacks meeting
7:30–7:50 P.M.	Team meeting: lecture, nutrition
7:50–9:30 P.M.	Offense/defense meetings
9:30 P.M.	Training room ice and snack distribution
9:40 P.M.	Staff P.M. tape review (sp. tms./blitz/team), review next-day schedule and practice
11:00 P.M.	Bed check

That's a long day for the players and for the coaches.

DURING THE FIRST WEEK OF training camp, I receive a mailed envelope, addressed to me at the University at Albany. The return address, typed in the upper left hand corner:

Headquarters
Office of the Commanding General
Multi-National Corps—Iraq
APO AE 09342
Official Business

What in the world is this? Am I being drafted?

I carefully open up the envelope and begin to read the handwritten note on stationery labeled "Office of the Commanding General."

Coach Coughlin,

> *I was in one of my daily commander's updates last evening and out of the corner of my eye, I caught you being interviewed, so I thought I would drop you a line.*

> *We have been very busy here in Iraq since I took over command last November. It is quite a responsibility to be in charge of 165,000 soldiers and Marines. It is a tremendous honor to serve alongside these wonderful men and women. Every day they face extremely difficult conditions (today it was 125 degrees). But they never hesitate to conduct operations.*

> *They truly believe in what they are doing. They believe in their leaders but most importantly, they believe in each other!*

> *I wish you the best of luck this year. I know it has probably been a long wait for you to get back out onto the field. You will have a fan here in Iraq and I will be watching whenever I can. You're a great leader on and off the field and you have my utmost respect. Push them hard and remind them of Team First!*

Ray Odierno
LTG, Commander MNC (I)

Wow. This short handwritten note carried a powerful punch. It wasn't just the message; it was the messenger. General Odierno and his family have suffered like many other families. His son, Tony, lost his left arm to an improvised explosive device while fighting on the ground in Iraq. That General Odierno took the time to sit down and send encouragement my way made me proud to be a coach—and an American.

His words further cement my belief that I, and this team, will be okay. We believe in what we are doing and who we are. I share parts of the letter with our team during training camp, hoping his message of Team First is not lost in the details.

But as we work on the team concept, the media is focused on a big part of our team who, so far, is not with us.

AS THERE ALWAYS SEEMS TO be, there is a large media presence in Albany, and the early headlines involve the absence of Michael Strahan. After fourteen seasons, Michael cannot decide if he wants to play another year of football. It isn't a holdout, as some suspect, and it isn't about money. It is about a man's desire. Every day the questions from reporters come my way, and every day I tell them there is nothing new to report. It is the first real test of my new relationship with the media. I do get frustrated, but I think I do a good job maintaining my cool.

I speak to Michael over the phone near the start of training camp as well as a few weeks in, and we are both open and honest. He is unsure if he has the heart to come back, and although we all want him back, and I tell him so, I also indicate that I want him back only if his heart is truly in the right place. Michael has a great deal of pride, and even though he's coming off an injury, I am confident he can return to All-Pro status. We miss his smile, his presence, his competitive fire in camp. But life goes on without him.

The days of training camp move forward, and as the players work on skill development, assignments, and upgrading our execution, I continue to work on being more open. It is difficult during practices to open up, especially when there are so many things to correct. But in those moments when we are not in the heat of improving ourselves, I try to open up. For example, in previous years at camp, I sat and ate dinner with the coaches, albeit quickly. In 2007, I often sit with players and occasionally talk about families, vacation trips, or the New York Yankees, albeit quickly.

I also add some new wrinkles, a few of which have been suggested by others. We are about a week into camp when our veteran punter, Jeff Feagles, comes to me with an idea. What if, he says, at the end of practice our field goal kickers take kicks in front of the team, with each kicker representing either the offense or the defense? The winner of the kicking contest earns the side he is kicking for an extra hour before curfew that night. At first I am skeptical—not only about breaking our routine but also about giving the guys an extended curfew. After giving it some thought, and considering from whom the idea originated, I give it my blessing.

I have so much respect for Jeff Feagles. Jeff has been in the league for twenty years, playing for five teams, and yet could probably play for another five years. His work ethic and understanding of what it means to be a professional have allowed him to stay in the league long past his contemporaries. A knee injury almost ended his career, and after the 2005 season, Jeff was in so much pain that he simply couldn't keep going and unofficially retired. He packed up and moved his wife and four boys to Phoenix to begin the next stage of his life. But the weeks went by, and as Jeff underwent additional medical tests and corrective procedures, the knee began to improve. Soon he started to reconsider his decision to step away from football.

During those months away from the game, Jeff and I grew close. We talked a lot over the phone, often sharing stories and concerns about football and family. He said that if he did decide he wanted to return to football, he was hesitant to move his family back to New York again. I understood the gravity and consequences of the decision, as I have moved our family ten times, often at inopportune times in their lives. I wanted Jeff to come back if his fire was still burning. In the end, he did choose to return for the 2006 season, which I am not sure he would have done had our discussions not dug deep in his heart.

From that point forward, my respect for Jeff grew immensely. I relied on him. When we were on the train headed to play Washington in the last game of the regular season in 2006—a game we had to win to make the play-offs—I was contemplating what to tell the guys that night in our meeting. It had been a long season and the players had probably heard it all from me, so I thought a different messenger might bring a fresh approach. I asked Jeff on the train ride down if he would talk to the team that night. He agreed and spoke eloquently about the opportunity before us and just how rare it was. Those moments furthered my trust in Jeff, which is why when he brings up the idea of a kicking contest, I consent.

Lawrence Tynes kicks for the offense, Josh Huston kicks for the defense. They are in a battle, by the way, to be our kicker in 2007. As the contest commences, the players are into it, knowing that an extra hour of free time is riding on the foot of their teammates. They cheer on their guy and distract the other. I have to admit that even I get into it, yelling, grimacing, feeling as if a game is on the line. In the end, Lawrence hits his second try from 50 yards and the offense gets an extra hour that night.

PRESEASON GAMES ARE JUST THAT—preseason. They don't count in the standings, they usually don't cost coaches their jobs, and they often do not showcase teams' best efforts. But they do provide excellent opportunities for young players to get game experience, for coaches to evaluate players in game situations, for offenses and defenses to test what they have learned, and, frankly, for teams to break out of the mundane stretch of training camp. Great teams make the best use of preseason games. They may not win them all, but they get the most out of them. For us, we set specific objectives for each preseason game. We want to win the game, of course, but won't stray from our objectives. Those objectives could include evaluating specifics on offense, defense, or special teams, such as how player A would do returning kicks or putting the number three QB in with the second unit. Our second objective is to get players a predetermined number of snaps, especially in the first game, in order to allow the coaches and personnel staff to evaluate the long list of players who have been in camp with us. Our third goal is to create specific situations, such as a two-minute offense or short yardage packages, if the game itself does not create them.

Every coach has a different way of managing preseason games. Prior to heading down to New Jersey for our first preseason game, I have already decided that the starters will play the first quarter, the second unit will play the second quarter into the third, and the third unit will finish the game. We split our special teams units by half, with the first unit playing the first half. The individual position coaches then fill in a grid with player jersey numbers so we all can keep track of who is in the game, who needs to be in, and when.

So fifteen days into camp, we finally leave Albany and head home to play the Carolina Panthers at Giants Stadium on Saturday, August 11. On Friday night, we stay at the Marriott in nearby Teaneck, our hotel for all of our home games. Even though it is a preseason game, I want our players to dress and conduct themselves as if we were in the thick of the regular season. That implies a dress code, a curfew, and the regular-season routine of meetings, videos, voluntary Mass and chapel, and lights-out at 11:00 P.M.

On Saturday night, we lose the game to the Panthers with a final score of 24–21, but the loss is not what concerns me. Even though it is the first preseason game, our defense plays nowhere near the level at which they are capable of playing. Carolina's offensive starters maul our defense in the first quarter, picking up five first downs on one thirteen-play, 81-yard drive. They do it through the air, with Carolina quarterback Jake Delhomme passing for the touchdown, and they do it on the ground, rushing six times for 55 yards. Our interior run defense has way too many holes and missed tackles, and Mathias Kiwanuka struggles at times with his assignments in his adjustment to linebacker. I remind myself that this is what training camp is for, to correct those problems. There are some positives, including Eli's scrambling sidearm touchdown pass to Jeremy Shockey and a 67-yard kick return by Derrick Ward. David Tyree makes a nice catch. I try to stay positive as we head back to Albany.

Even more impressive than the progress on the field is the support the players exhibit for one another on and off the field. The veterans are leading the rookies, and the rookies are listening. Jeff Feagles has taken our rookie snappers, Zak DeOssie and Jay Alford, under his wing; Sam Madison has developed a strong relationship with Aaron Ross; Reuben Droughns provides insight to Ahmad Bradshaw; Jeremy Shockey introduces wide-eyed Kevin Boss to the NFL.

On Wednesday, August 16, we follow a schedule of morning meetings, followed by an extensive jog-through, and after more meetings and a full afternoon practice, I figure the guys can use a break. So, when the players arrive for our team meeting that night, they walk into the room and take their seats, awaiting my next PowerPoint presentation. I start in on our objectives, review the schedule for the next day, and then flip to the next slide, which reads, "We're going bowling!" There are some shouts of surprise, but I can tell the players must have had an inkling something was up; still, it is a dramatic way to start the night. We pile into buses and head out to a local bowling alley. We divide the players and coaches into teams, making sure that the four- or five-man teams are diverse: young guys, veterans, offense, defense, coaches, players.

Kareem McKenzie, at six foot six and 327 pounds, bowls two 225 games (Kareem and David Tyree even bring their own bowling balls). I roll with Jeremy Shockey, David Diehl, R. W. McQuarters, and coach Dave DeGuglielmo. Honestly, I am not a good bowler, although I do improve from the first game to the second game. The eventual winners of the bowl-off include coach Chris Palmer, David Tyree, Michael Jennings, and Sinorice Moss, who all receive trophies from the owner of the bowling alley. The night is memorable as we laugh, joke, and down pizza and soda. We all enjoy the competition and fellowship and the time spent together. I have a blast, and I am sure the players notice.

OUR SECOND PRESEASON GAME IS against the Baltimore Ravens on Sunday, August 19. Since I have been the head coach of the Giants, whenever we fly on the team charter, the coaching staff sits in first class and the players in coach. Me? I am smack in the middle of the coach section, usually around seat 16B. Why? Sitting in the back allows me some occasional interaction with players, which I wouldn't normally have. I still do my work and study tape, and, yes, I do listen in on some conversations. Among others, Amani Toomer sits nearby. I want the players to feel—sincerely or not—that I am one of them.

Against the Baltimore Ravens, most of our starters play the entire first half. We see some improvement between the first and second games, especially on defense. Take, for example, the first quarter, when the Ravens have 1st and 10 on our 12-yard line. We force them to settle for three points; our defense is getting better. In fact, the D allows just 75 yards rushing and no touchdowns in the game and they only give up 3 rushing yards to elusive running back Willis McGahee. On offense, we still search for our groove, but Eli looks strong, going ten of thirteen for 114 yards and a touchdown while playing deep into the second quarter. The kicking battle heats up between Lawrence Tynes and Josh Huston when Huston hits field goals from 50 and 30 yards. We win the game, 13–12. There are always things to work out, and penalties are one of them. We amass twelve penalties for 111 yards. In 2006, penalties cost us too many games, and we can't allow mental mistakes to hold us back.

There are bound to be injuries in games, even preseason games, and safety Will Demps dislocates his elbow and Sam Madison pulls a hamstring on the same play. Wide receiver Michael Jennings is playing exceptionally well in place of Plaxico when, on his final catch in the second quarter, he stretches for a ball, steps awkwardly, and ruptures his Achilles tendon, though amazingly he is able to hold on to the ball. His season is over. Fellow wide receiver Steve Smith leaves the game with a concussion after getting hit catching a 10-yard touchdown pass. All of this is deeply frustrating and worrisome. The biggest question after the injuries to Demps and Madison is whether Corey Webster, Aaron Ross, and Michael Johnson will step up.

The following Saturday night against the Jets in New Jersey, the starters play into the third quarter and the entire defense again plays well—after allowing a long touchdown pass on the first snap from scrimmage, that is. After that big play, the defense permitted the Jets −13 yards of offense and zero first downs on the next sixteen plays. Defensive end Justin Tuck has a great game, recording four tackles and a sack, and David Tyree makes a few huge plays on special teams. Eli throws a perfect fade to six-foot-five Anthony Mix for a score. We are 2–1 in the preseason.

Concerns? As usual, there are many. We had the ball in the green zone three times against the Jets yet scored just one touchdown. You don't need to go far back in the 2006 season (Philadelphia in January) to identify our struggles in the green zone. All during training camp I have preached to the offense that we have to come away with touchdowns when we have the opportunities. But perhaps of most concern is the kicking game, with the situation still unsettled and our snapper now gone. Our long snapper since 2003 has been Ryan Kuehl, but Ryan injured his calf in the early days of training camp, leaving us with a big hole. Rookie Jay Alford has been handling the placekicking snaps while rookie Zak DeOssie snaps on punts. With new long and short snappers, it can take weeks, if not months, to nail down the mechanics.

Against the Jets, Lawrence misses two field goals and Josh misses one. Lawrence's first kick from 40 yards goes wide right; his second from 43 goes wide left. Was it the kicker or the snapper and holder? The mechanics between all three are proving to be more difficult to master than I expected.

As I ponder the situation, I remind myself that Lawrence is a veteran kicker who is more reliable than he has shown in the first month of camp. And I begin to wonder if the events of the summer have taken a toll.

Shortly after we traded for Lawrence in May, his wife went into premature labor with twin boys in Kansas City. He called to inform me of the severity of the situation, and I gave him my blessing to remain at her bedside as long as he needed to, which included missing minicamp in June. The twins were born in July, and after they were finally released from the hospital, Lawrence arrived at training camp. But even at training camp, his family isn't far from his mind; at night in Albany, Lawrence logs onto his computer and watches his twin sons on a Web cam. The difficult summer has not allowed Lawrence a lot of time to work on his kicking. He is a great guy who takes his job seriously, but as a coach, I have to ask myself: will he be able to regain his consistency when it counts?

AS WE APPROACH THE LAST preseason game at the end of August, we have some tough roster decisions to make, including which of our three backup quarterbacks to keep: Tim Hasselbeck, Anthony Wright, or Jared Lorenzen. Which kicker do we go with? Who will be the third wide receiver? The answers do not come from a performance in any one preseason game but rather from a cumulative and ongoing evaluation. After every preseason game, the coaches rank the players at their respective positions and an overall offense/defense/special teams rank is rendered. Jerry Reese and I discuss the players who played well and who did poorly as we try to trim the roster down to fifty-three.

It's no fun releasing players at the end of camp, especially the ones who have done everything you asked and who have showed real heart on the field. So I keep it short and simple. When it comes time to let the player go, a member of the pro personnel staff will track down the player and ask him to bring his playbook to my office. I usually encourage the player to stay in shape and remind him there are thirty-two NFL teams, so there could be another opportunity. Even so, such conversations are hard; we both know why we are there.

Our final tune-up will come against the Super Bowl favorite New England Patriots. There is a ten-day window after the game before our regular-season opener against Dallas, so I want our starters to get a fair number of reps against the Pats. Some coaches elect not to play their starters in the last preseason game every year, fearing injury and wanting one last look at borderline players. But I feel differently. Our first-teamers will play fifteen snaps or so against New England. Bill Belichick will play just one of his twenty-two starters.

Injuries to our defense before and during the game create a lack of depth, which keeps some of our defensive starters out there for most of the first half. On offense, the green zone issues continue to perplex us at times. After Jeremy Shockey picks up 20 yards on a catch to give us 1st and Goal from the 2, it takes us five plays to finally score. But at least we score a TD in the green zone with our goal line offense. Two other times inside the 25, we come away with field goals. Both defenses take a backseat in this game, with the two teams combining for 651 yards of offense as the Pats win, 27–20. We again help to beat ourselves, receiving thirteen penalties.

The biggest concerns of 2006—failure to score points in the green zone, an inability to prevent our opponents from driving and scoring, a pronounced deficiency in stopping the run, and too many penalties—

all apparently still plague us, and we don't have much time to shake them.

MICHAEL STRAHAN DECIDES HIS HEART is indeed in the game, and he arrives in New Jersey just after the end of training camp. Though I am glad he is back, experience tells me it may take close to three weeks of practice and games for him to be operating at full speed. He shows up in great cardio shape, but physical contact and game condition are a different story, and I am concerned about injuries if we move too quickly.

Coming out of training camp, I think we are a pretty good football team. We have veterans playing well and rookies learning quickly. So far, communication between me and the players seems to be improved, but we haven't faced much adversity yet to really test it, and I am not sure we have the structure in place to gut it out through the tough times and difficult issues.

That's where the players' Leadership Council comes in. It is an idea that I have been working on for months but chose not to unveil until after training camp was over and the roster finalized. Other NFL coaches have their own version of a players' leadership committee, including Andy Reid in Philadelphia and Mike Holmgren in Seattle, but I want to put our own spin on it. Even the name, Leadership Council, is unique and well thought out. Selected players will be a part of the decision-making process on some issues, and they can help the rest of the team understand my reasoning on others.

Charles Way, who is instrumental in our organization and who sits in all of our staff meetings, helps me choose the right guys for the council. We want to make sure it is a diverse group, covering all positions. There are so many players who make sense, but we can't include them all. So we come up with a group of eleven: Eli Manning, Michael Strahan, Jeff Feagles, Chris Snee, Shaun O'Hara, Antonio Pierce, Jeremy Shockey, David Diehl, Amani Toomer, Osi Umenyiora, and Mathias Kiwanuka.

In our first meeting, on September 6, we sit in a semicircle in the team meeting room in Giants Stadium. I lay out the objectives of the council and explain the process. It is safe to say that the guys aren't too sure at first what to make of it. I envision an open discussion of issues, a place where players can speak freely to one another and to me. The first issue is captainship. In all of my years as a head coach, I have never had permanent captains but rather chose captains on a week-to-week basis. I ask the players on the council what *they* want. Though they are mostly quiet as they try to feel this out, they begin to share ideas and opinions, and eventually they vote to have the entire team elect season-long captains. So the next morning, by secret ballot, the entire team decides that five guys will wear the letter *C* on their game jerseys: Manning, Strahan, Feagles, O'Hara, and Pierce.

Also in the first Leadership Council meeting we talk about what the players have for lunch on Fridays, and I ask them how they like the new schedule of practices and meetings in the mornings. The following week, topics in the forum include pregame introductions and player tardiness. As the season wears on, various issues will come up before the council: curfews, families, the Christmas week schedule, the media, and so on. To their utmost credit, this group never complains or nags; the meetings remain a productive use of our time. And our time is limited and extremely valuable.

The opening game of the regular season is just days away. Are we ready?

As a head coach, you are never quite sure but I am confident that the veterans on our team can get us through the first few games as we adjust to new systems and the rookies get a real welcome to the NFL. Training camp is over. Preseason games are in the past. Every play counts now. And with so much riding on this season, the outcome of the first game is magnified.

FOUR

● ● ● ● ● ● ●

A man can be as great as he wants to be.
If you believe in yourself and have the courage,
the determination, the dedication, the competitive drive,
and if you are willing to sacrifice the little things in life and
pay the price for the things that are worthwhile, it can be done.
— VINCE LOMBARDI

I

T'S HARD TO IGNORE THE HISTORY AND THE SIGNIFICANCE OF THE Dallas–New York rivalry in the National Football League. The teams first squared off in 1960 and haven't stopped fighting since. The great Cowboys teams of the 1960s and 1970s—coached by former Giants player and defensive coordinator Tom Landry—dominated the rivalry, with Dallas winning eleven in a row from 1975 to 1980, but the great Giants teams under Bill Parcells in the late 1980s won seven of eight. Since I was hired by the Giants in 2004, we have gone 4–2 against the Cowboys, but four of the six games have been decided by a touchdown or less, including a devastating 23–20 loss in December 2006 in the middle of our struggles.

Michael Strahan's return is great news for new defensive coordinator Steve Spagnuolo, whose unit has made progress during camp but certainly hasn't looked smooth or efficient just yet. Justin Tuck, Kawika Mitchell, and Osi Umenyiora are healthy, which is a very good sign. How Aaron Ross and Corey Webster will perform at corner come prime time is still a major question.

On offense, I feel more comfortable. We have good firepower. Our line, from right to left, consists of Kareem McKenzie, Chris Snee, Shaun O'Hara, Rich Seubert, and David Diehl, and they look solid, though Diehl has a tough new responsibility in protecting the quarterback's blind side. Left tackle is his fourth different position in five NFL seasons, but whatever we ask of David, he accepts the challenge and responds with purpose. In the backfield, we have plenty of depth. There's no way for us to know at the start of the season how big a contribution Derrick Ward and Ahmad Bradshaw will make, but with those two, Reuben Droughns, and a combination of power and size in Brandon Jacobs, we will be fine. At wide receiver, Amani Toomer and Plaxico Burress have health issues, and their status may be day to day. Some days Plaxico practices, some days he doesn't. But give credit to him: he listens and watches, imagining himself in place of his teammates and making the necessary corrections. Behind center, I have complete confidence in Eli that he can run the show and take us far. I spoke to him privately a few times in training camp, challenging him to up his game, and I'm optimistic he'll respond.

Of course, our kicking game is still a concern. We'd better get it fixed before Sunday.

THERE ARE DOZENS OF WAYS coaches prepare for games, but all of us, at some point in the process, rely on statistics and tape. Football is a game of numbers: first downs, percentages, yards, points, turnovers, time. There are more than enough numbers to prove, or disprove, a point of view, but often when it comes to tendencies, the numbers don't lie. And that's what coaches look for on stat sheets and while studying tape: tendencies. What does an opponent like to do and when?

In preparing for Dallas, the first thing we do as a staff is look at the stats. Obviously they can run the ball, but Tony Romo has added a passing dimension. There are hundreds of questions that need to be answered in a short span of time, which is why off-season game planning is critical. After self-evaluation in March, we spent a great deal of time in April preparing in-depth game plans for our first four opponents of the season, watching eight of their games from 2006. We then proceed to study the next four opponents. When all the off-season opponent study is over, we have game plans on the first four opponents and our three divisional opponents, play call lists for the next four, and for the remainder of the schedule, four games are broken down and all data is collected. In 2007, Wade Phillips took the reins in Dallas, so we go back and study tape of his defenses the prior year in San Diego to get a feel for what he likes to do. Jason Garrett is the new offensive coordinator, but there won't be much change in the Cowboys' offense. Of course, there is some tweaking to the Dallas game plan, as now we have four preseason games to study as well.

On Monday nights as we get into preparation, we self-scout. That is, staff members present tape breakdown on ourselves, noting *our* tendencies, so we know how our opponents might view us. As the hours and days progress in game planning, we study our opponents, looking for how they play. Are they physical? What is their style? What is the pedigree of their coaching staff? Then, for example, the offense takes a closer look at specific downs and distances—3rd and 1, 3rd and 2 to 3, green zone, et cetera—to identify front, stunt, coverage, blitzes.

Professional football is a cumulative game. There is no way to prepare for every scenario each week of the season, which is why things we work on in training camp help us in week twelve. As a staff, we try to be efficient with our time. We spend a great deal of time studying tape and game planning on first and second downs. Why? The numbers show that roughly 40 percent of snaps in a game come on 1st or 2nd down and 4 to 7. Third downs are approximately 12 percent of snaps, so we spend about 12 percent of our time on the field, in training camp, and in practices on third down. Goal line? Just 1.7 percent of all snaps, so we usually run just five goal line snaps on Friday afternoons in season.

In a typical regular-season week, which is how we treat the Dallas week, the players have Tuesday off but the coaches are hard at work on the game plan. From 7:30 A.M. until the early hours of Wednesday, we are planning. Early mornings are for first and second downs for both the offense and defense, though the offensive coaches split between the run game and pass game. By midmorning we are finalizing the run game and moving into gadget plays on offense while the defense focuses on reverses, halfback options, and the like. After a quick lunch, it's back to work, now focusing on first- and second-down pass, play action, screens, nakeds, and various formations. For the next four hours or so, coaches are on their own to work on scripts, Wednesday's practice, tip sheets, and any other individual duties. After dinner and a full staff meeting, it's on to third-down preparation.

On Tuesday nights, since we typically don't finish up our game planning until the wee hours of the morning, I usually take a shower in the coaches' locker room and sleep on the couch in my office. I am up by 5:00 A.M. on Wednesday and start my routine with a workout and quick breakfast. A Wednesday in-season schedule for me:

5:25 A.M.	Strength program
6:10 A.M.	Breakfast
6:30 A.M.	Review scripted tape for video scouting report
6:50 A.M.	View opponent offensive tape
	Put material in order
	Review written material for team meeting
7:00 A.M.	Review practice schedule
7:30 A.M.	Meet with individual players if necessary
7:45 A.M.	Special teams meeting/QB meeting
8:25 A.M.	Team meeting
8:40 A.M.	Offense/defense meetings
9:45 A.M.	Study and make notes of opponent two-minute tape
	Tite Green
10:15 A.M.	Study game plan book—protections

	Review practice schedule for Wednesday
	Prepare Thursday practice schedule
10:40 A.M.	Offense/defense jog-through
11:05 A.M.	Media
11:25 A.M.	Special teams jog-through
11:55 A.M.	Practice
1:45 P.M.	Phone interview with opponent media
2:00 P.M.	Offense/defense/special teams evaluate practice, corrections
2:35 P.M.	Special teams meeting (review practice)
3:00 P.M.	Offense/defense meeting (review practice)
3:45 P.M.	Tape Giants Game Plan Show
4:15 P.M.	Full staff meeting—practice critique, special teams tape, Thursday practice schedule
4:25 P.M.	Individual staff: Offense: continue third down, third/7–10, third/11+, anti-pressure, pocket, gadget Defense: continue third down
5:00 P.M.	Meet with medical staff
5:20 P.M.	Meet with offense
6:30 P.M.	Dinner
6:45 P.M.	Resume third down
7:30 P.M.	Short yardage
8:30 P.M.	Goal line
9:30 P.M.	Two-minute
TBD	Secure

When the players come in on Wednesday, we have a team meeting to introduce Dallas, their overall tendencies, and our keys to victory, illustrated, of course, by video and statistics.

Dallas is one of the preseason favorites to win the Super Bowl, and they possess a high-octane offense and a powerful defense. They are exceptionally physical. On defense, the goals are clear: the Giants have to stop the run, keep Tony Romo in the pocket and not let him buy time,

NEW YORK GIANTS

PRACTICE SCHEDULE - WEDNESDAY
(Tuesday - 9/4 - In season Weds. Practice schedule)

DATE: 9/4/2007	LOCATION:	UNIFORM: PADS
MEETING TIME: 7:45 AM - 8:25 AM	EMPHASIS: 1st/2nd Down, Fringe Red/Green,	OPPONENT: DALLAS #1
FIELD TIME: 11:25 AM - 11:40 AM	Pressure, Red/Green - Shots +-45, 35, 25	SPECIAL TEAMS: KOR/FG/PUNT

10:40 AM - Def/Off Scripted Jog Thru

11:25 AM - Special Teams - Scripted - Video Taped Jog Thru

11:35 AM - Special Teams - C-QB Exchange Run & Stretch

11:40 AM - Team Run & Stretch (Tank)

11:45 AM - Special Teams Period - C-QB Exchange

Field:		Work:		Cadence:			
Mod	Vid	Emphasis	SAF/ QB	DW/ WR	ILB/ RB	OLB/ TE	DL/ OL
1		Individual	Pride	Fund.	Core - Shoulders Ready		Technique
2		↓					Run Prep
3		Def 7 on 7					9 on 7
4		Off 7 on 7					Pressure Prep
5		↓				(Service)	*Pace Party
6		Def 9 on 7			Off Emph. Ind. 1 on 1		
7		Off 9 on 7			Def Emph. Ind. 1 on 1		
8		↓					
9		Def Pressure				(Mix)	
10		Off Pressure					
11		↓					
12		Special Teams					
13		Def 7 on 7					OL/DL PP-PR
14		Off 7 on 7					Service Def/Off
15		↓					
16		Def Team #1				(Mix)	
17		Off Team #1					
18		↓					
19		Def Team #2				(Mix)	
20		Off Team #2					
21		Red/Green	+-25 +-18/16	+-14/12			
22		Secure/Mandatory Medical Treatments					
23			3:10 - 3:50 PM - Practice Tape Review/3:50 Medical Orthopedic Appts.				
24		Thurs	7:45 Am - Special Teams KO/Punt/PR			8:25 AM Off/Def Meetings	

manage an enormous offensive line, and contain their skill players Terrell Owens, Jason Witten, and Patrick Crayton. Beyond points scored and allowed, turnover margin is the biggest difference maker in games. Just look at the statistics. When teams don't turn the ball over, they win 82 percent of the time. When they are plus-one in turnovers, they win 70 percent of the time; plus-two, 86 percent; plus-three, 97 percent. You've got to love stats.

The Wednesday practice before Dallas is typical, with position periods building into team periods. Everything—every minute, every play—is scheduled and scripted.

THE NIGHT BEFORE THE OPENER in Dallas, we gather in the banquet room of the Marriott Las Colinas in Dallas for our traditional Saturday night team meeting. The special teams meet, the offense and defense split and review assignments and key points, and then the team gathers together to hear me speak and to watch a highlight tape. In my Power-Point presentation, we decide what is most important for victory and review it. Every week, video assistant Ed Triggs and our senior director of football information, Jon Berger, help me put together the presentation, coming up with numbers, videos, pictures, and quotes to get my message across.

"What do we want people to think when they watch our team?" I ask the players. "What is our message going to be this year?" We know what the message was in 2006.

If you would have told me prior to kickoff in Dallas that we would score thirty-five points on the Cowboys on the road, I certainly would have guessed that we'd win. Reality tells us something different. We don't score *enough* points. Brandon Jacobs goes down with a sprained medial collateral ligament (MCL) in the second quarter, but Derrick Ward steps in and steps up, rushing for 89 yards. Our problem isn't scoring; it is stopping *them* from scoring. We simply make too many mistakes on defense, too many mental errors; we have too many players out of position and do not put enough pressure on Tony Romo. He throws for 345 yards, and tight end Jason Witten appears to be open all day, piling up 116 yards receiving. We give up eight big plays—plays over 10 yards on a run or 25 yards on a pass. Our special teams are just mediocre, allowing a huge kickoff return late when the score is just 38–35. Michael Strahan does not start but does end up playing more than anticipated when Osi Umenyiora injures his knee.

After the game, I am also concerned about Eli Manning, but not because of what he does on the field. With 7:20 left in the game, trailing 38–28, Eli was thrown to the turf by rookie Anthony Spencer as we attempted a two-point conversion. A personal foul should have been called but wasn't. Gibril Wilson intercepted Romo on Dallas' first offensive play after the takedown, and Eli went right back out there despite pain in his right shoulder. Starting with great field position, he threw a 10-yard touchdown pass to Plaxico. It was Eli's last snap of the night. When the deficit got to ten with just a few minutes left, and with a capable backup in Jared Lorenzen, Eli remained on the sideline. Jared came close to making plays, but we turned the ball over on downs on our last possession.

As you might imagine with us coming off the 2006 season, the media are ready to pounce. How could our defense allow forty-five points, 478 yards of offense, and six touchdowns? Do I have faith in Steve Spagnuolo and his defensive scheme? Will changes be made to personnel? We didn't keep Tony Romo from buying extra time, Dallas had too many big plays on us, we had too many coverage breakdowns . . . and the list goes on.

On top of the critical questions about the defense come the never-ending queries about Eli, whose bruised shoulder becomes the front-page story as we prepare for Green Bay. The words "crisis point" even appear in print—after *one* game.

For us, there is no panic after the loss to Dallas. The outside world thinks the season is about to cave in, but we don't. We know we played well in some areas and need to improve in others, but it was the *first game*, especially for a defense playing a new system. In the locker room, there is no finger-pointing, no dissolution of the unity we built in training camp. I am confident we are headed in the right direction and I remain calm. I don't show signs of panic or of being overly frustrated, and I think that sends a message to the players and coaches. We are in this together, for better or for worse.

The day after the game, ESPN reports that Eli has separated his shoulder and is out a month, which is news to all of us. As for his playing against Green Bay the next Sunday, we will do whatever the medical staff tells us. If he can play, great. If not, we will be ready. Jared Lorenzen and Anthony Wright take the snaps during the week in practice, as Eli can achieve little motion with his shoulder.

WE ARE 0–1, certainly not the start we had hoped for. Already, just *one* game into the season, we would all be put to the test. How would our team unity hold up? Could I maintain my poise with the media despite the onslaught of negative questions? Would the pressure of needing to win in 2007 sink us? Those questions will be answered in their own time, not mine, as we look ahead to the Green Bay Packers.

Wednesday morning during the team meeting, we introduce Green Bay. The Packers have plenty of offense, just like Dallas, and we need to stop the run and disrupt the passing rhythm of Brett Favre by getting pressure. We need to stay in coverage and deny the big play. On offense, we need to control the line of scrimmage, handle the defensive pass rush, defeat press man coverage, hold on to the football, and score! Most importantly, we need to keep Green Bay and Brett Favre off the field and on the sidelines.

Thursday and Friday bring still more questions about Eli, and we don't have the answers. On Friday, he takes some snaps in practice but doesn't throw. Ronnie Barnes, our head trainer, calls in Dr. Russell Warren, an orthopedic surgeon and team doctor, to check Eli on Saturday morning, which is an unusual time for an evaluation. The swelling has subsided and Eli feels good. His strength has returned and he is confident that he can throw. It is decided that he won't be jeopardizing further injury by taking the field, and Dr. Warren clears him to play on Sunday. So the coaching staff and the players know by Saturday morning that he will play, and Eli takes all the snaps during our jog-through and situational practice. The team responds well to the fact that Eli is out there. Of course, we want the Green Bay coaches to keep guessing and preparing for multiple QBs, so we keep Eli's status unknown to everyone but us.

As I do for most home games, I head home on Saturday around 1:00 P.M. and then drive to the team hotel at 4:40 P.M. for meetings. Because we lost last week, the video staff does not put together game highlights from the Dallas loss to show during Saturday night's meeting. Instead, on this night, the video consists of scenes from the movie *Miracle*, which chronicles the incredible 1980 U.S. Olympic hockey team and its stunning upset of the Soviet Union en route to the gold medal.

"When you pull on that jersey, you represent yourself and your teammates. And the name on the front of the jersey is a hell of a lot more important than the one on the back," coach Herb Brooks reminds his team. My message is clear.

During my talk, I ask the team again: What is the personality of our team going to be? What are we most proud of? I suggest as an answer the four E's: effort, energy, enthusiasm, execution. "Twenty men of such differing backgrounds now standing as one," Herb Brooks says later in the movie. "Young men willing to sacrifice so much of themselves, all for an unknown." If we are going to win in 2007—if we are going to beat Green Bay the following day—we need to be a team in every sense of the word.

I challenge them to be great both as a team and as individuals and illustrate that point with this from Vincent Lombardi:

> A man can be as great as he wants to be. If you believe in yourself and have the courage, the determination, the dedication, the competitive drive, and if you are willing to sacrifice the little things in life and pay the price for the things that are worthwhile, it can be done.

At the end of the third quarter, Green Bay holds a 14–13 lead at our home stadium. Our offense plays mediocre football for forty-five minutes but can't get a late score for the victory. We have some dumb penalties and some costly turnovers, which don't help in a 35–13 loss. Eli, despite the nagging injury that kept him out of practice all week, makes no excuses for the offense or for himself.

In the first two games, we have allowed eighty points, the most by a Giants team since 1966. The great Brett Favre goes 29 for 38 for 286 yards, three touchdowns, and one interception. We do everything we can to get to Favre. We blitz, we send four players, five players, six players, but we just do not get to him. There are some positives on defense, including a solid run defense on first and second downs. But as happened against the Cowboys, we can't get pressure on the QB, and that is our downfall.

In the postgame locker room, I am matter-of-fact. We have made mistakes, yes, but we are headed in the right direction. There is no sarcasm, no yelling, no raised voice.

"I lose games, you guys win them," I insist, hoping it can be a positive message going forward.

As you might imagine, now the heat from the media and the fans is really on. "Pack It In for Big Blue" is a headline in the *New York Post.* The press is looking for blood—again—and folks are already looking ahead to next year, assuming that I will be long gone. But they neglect to consider that Eli hadn't practiced all week. I understand the concern. The last time a Giants team started the season 0–2 and still made the play-offs was 1934! What's more, in 2006, we might have fallen apart after the Green Bay loss. In 2006, I might have lost my composure and lit into the guys. But this isn't 2006. As chaos and panic swirl around us, we stay right on track. I don't blow my top and don't revert back to the old Tom. Am I upset? Sure—0–2 is not fun. But a season is a marathon, not a sprint, and I like this group of guys. Plus, I know we are better than we have showed against two of the best quarterbacks in the NFL.

These days test my relationship with the media. I have worked hard since the off-season to be more patient, more understanding, more respectful. That was doable when we were 0–0, but what about when we are 0–2? The questions about the defense come fast and hard and keep coming and coming and coming. And I can't blame the media for asking; we haven't been very good defensively. But I have faith. I believe the defense will come around under Steve Spagnuolo's leadership. Judy later confides in me that Steve told her that "we are going to be okay" after the 0–2 start. I believe him.

All optimism aside, our next game is on the road at Washington, a divisional game, and we need to get a win.

Though there is no panic in my mind or in my body, I am staring at an abyss that I haven't faced before. I can't let this team lose. The only way we are going to climb out of this hole is with discipline, mental toughness, and pride, values ingrained in me long ago in a small town named Waterloo.

FIVE

● ● ● ● ● ●

"I will prepare and some day
my chance will come."
— ABRAHAM LINCOLN

WATERLOO, NEW YORK, IS LIKE A LOT OF SMALL TOWNS IN America: close-knit families, a Main Street, one public high school, a place where everybody knows everybody and everybody's business. The town rests in upstate New York, about 255 miles from New York City, situated between Geneva and Seneca Falls. It used to be a factory town, where fathers and sons worked in the same building. Now Waterloo is a shell of its former self, as most of the factory jobs are gone. But the spirit and values from the 1950s and 1960s remain. In the Waterloo I grew up in, there were family, church, work or school, and athletics, and that was about it.

The Coughlins (which is pronounced "Calklins" up there) and my mother's side of the family, the Posts, had a long history in upstate New York, so much so that my grandfather helped build the Erie Canal. My father, John Louis Coughlin, was not a very big man, maybe five foot nine and 170 pounds, but you would have thought he was a giant. He was strict, he was disciplined, and in his mind there was only one way to do something—the right way. Dad had been drafted into World War II right before I was born, and after his discharge he returned to New York and worked at the Seneca Ordnance Depot in nearby Romulus before retiring at the age of fifty-nine. As for my mom, Betty, she was like many mothers of her generation, running the home front. I was the oldest of seven children; the others were Carole, John, Kathy, Patty, LuAnn, and Chris.

We lived in a fairly typical four-bedroom, one-bath house at 15 Church Street, where John and I shared a room. The Episcopal church was across the street; the Waterloo Memorial Library, an attached museum, and a Presbyterian church sat behind us. I attended St. Mary's Grammar School on Center Street, where the classes were small: just eight students in my eighth-grade class. St. Mary's was so close to our house that we would come home for lunch. In addition to school, I often served as an altar boy and the master of ceremonies at midnight Mass at St. Mary's. In those days, the clergy was the final authority on all things.

The work ethic that has made me somewhat well known was born and bred in Waterloo. My father's cousin, and our neighbor, Dan McGuane, was the manager of the Grand Union grocery store and when I was in seventh and eighth grade, I delivered groceries for fifteen cents a trip, the food stuffed into a big basket on the front of my bike. When other kids bolted from school to play, I often headed to Grand Union. No matter wind, rain, or snow, I was out there after school and on Saturdays. The delivery route provided more work opportunities, as I would shovel snow and cut lawns for older men and women in town. I didn't mind it. At a very young age, I had the discipline to work, and to work before play.

Our family didn't have a car, and we didn't own a television set until I was eight or nine. We did have a radio, and I remember settling in next to it for episodes of *The Lone Ranger.* But like most kids in Waterloo, I never spent much time inside. In the summers, we would swim in the Seneca barge canal one or two times a day, and when we weren't getting wet, we were playing sports: Little League, CYO basketball, the Youth and Rec Center. My group of friends lived and breathed sports. I would always "play up," playing with kids older and better than me—a philosophy, not coincidentally, that I still believe in.

We'd peek behind the chain-link fence on Saturday nights to watch the high school football games, and when we were old enough, my friends and I would travel on school buses to watch the Waterloo High School basketball team play. I spent many nights sitting with my best friend, Terry Manfredi, on his front porch as his father, John, tried to listen to St. Louis Cardinals games on the radio but received more static than stats.

Though my father had the most influence on me in my younger years, as I grew older the coaches in my life began to help shape what I have become. At Waterloo High School, a broken ankle sidelined me freshman year from football, which was devastating at the time. Before the start of my sophomore year, Mike Ornato took over as the head football coach from longtime coach and athletic director Russ Herrick. Coach Ornato was young, maybe mid- to late twenties, and had played football at Ithaca College. He was a tough but endearing guy. He had been in the army and often regaled us with his stories from the military.

I started as a defensive back and a fullback on a varsity football team that finished 3–5. Next, I was on to varsity basketball and coach Bill Carey, who also coached varsity baseball. He was old-school. He was five-eleven, maybe 175 pounds, with a sharp Irish tongue. Like many coaches, he was a physical education teacher, and his uniform was a gray sweatsuit with stripes down the side. Coach Carey was the kind of teacher who carried a ball in his hand and would fire the ball over the heads of students who weren't paying attention. This is the same guy who would have us raking the baseball field at all hours and who, when pitching batting practice, would throw hard and inside if you had previously hit a ball back toward the mound. As tough as he was, Bill Carey continues to be a good friend and mentor to me now, more than forty years after coaching me.

It is safe to say that my junior year in high school was a pivotal year in my life. On the football field, Waterloo went 8–0 and I scored sixteen touchdowns playing halfback. College coaches began to take an interest in me, and there were recruiting letters from big-time and small-time schools, including Oklahoma, Buffalo, Holy Cross, and Syracuse. (Future NFL coach Buddy Ryan sat in my living room as the defensive coach at the University at Buffalo.) Also junior year, I started dating my future wife, Judy Whitaker. Judy and I would often tag along on dates with Terry and his girlfriend, Elaine Robson. What started out as a friendship eventually grew into something more.

As senior year came to a close, I thought about what comes next. Some of my friends did not choose to go to college and would enter the workforce like their fathers. Some of us would go on to college, including a surprising number from the football and basketball teams. Amazingly, for such a small town, we had a large number of really good athletes. The recruiting letters kept coming. Since Syracuse University was just forty-five miles away, I had grown up a huge fan, watching the likes of Jim Brown, Ernie Davis, and John Mackey. I was such a passionate fan of Ernie Davis that my friends in Waterloo nicknamed me "Ernie." Syracuse football in the late 1950s and early 1960s was elite, always in the hunt for a national title. When Coach Ben Schwartzwalder offered me a full scholarship to Syracuse University, it was a dream come true.

The town of Waterloo, the men and women of its fabric, my father, and my high school coaches, Mike Ornato and Bill Carey, instilled in me a true sense of mental toughness, a sense that working hard is the *only* way to work, that adversity is not something to run away from but rather an opportunity to get better. More than anything, pride mattered. And I would need all of these virtues at Syracuse.

PICTURE THIS SCENE: IT IS my first day as a freshman at Syracuse University and my parents are helping me move into Booth Hall. After numerous trips, most of my stuff is in the dorm room and my parents are on their way back to Waterloo. I am waiting for the elevator. The door opens and there are two enormous human beings inside. One has to be six-three, 235, the other a bit smaller but not by much. Me? I am five-eleven, maybe 185 pounds.

"So, what do you guys play?" I ask.

"Fullback," says one.

"Halfback," says the other.

Meet future pro football Hall of Famer Larry Csonka and Ed Mantie, my new teammates and freshman buddies.

We had two-a-day practices, full pads, no water. Since freshmen were not eligible to play, we were often the scout team and went up against the varsity in camp. We scrimmaged them in famed Archibald Stadium with the varsity dressed in white, the freshmen in blue. They looked like the Roman army; we looked like, well, not the Roman army. The first play of the scrimmage, I was on the field as the left defensive halfback and they ran a toss at me. Jim Nance was the lead blocker as the fullback. Gary Bugenhagen, an All-American tackle, pulled on the play, as did another All-American, center Pat Killorin. Three-time All-American Floyd Little had the ball and they ran right at me. *Welcome to college, Tom.* I remember going low on the lead blocker, perhaps Nance, and that's all I remember.

How tough was football back in those days? During the spring practice of my freshman year, I went down in practice one day with an MCL injury. As I lay on the field, Coach Schwartzwalder walked over and said, "That's a shame. That will teach you to cut back to the inside on a screen pass" He continued practice twenty yards downfield.

Playing for Syracuse University was such an honor and privilege for me, and there was the added benefit of having my parents and siblings come to watch most home games. The same characteristics that now define me as a coach—work ethic, discipline, overachiever—were exemplified during my years at SU. During my freshman year, I watched as the varsity went 7–4. My sophomore season, I started the last two games, and I continued to make an impact over the next two seasons, in which we won sixteen games. The ball never came my way much, maybe four or five times a game, but I took advantage of the opportunities and even set a school record for season receptions with 26 my senior year. It may not sound like a lot, but considering the old record was 22, set in the 1950s, 26 is a lot for the Syracuse offense. I enjoyed my teammates and everything that came with major college football: playing against the great programs of the northeast, like Penn State, West Virginia, and Boston College, and some national powers including UCLA.

Judy and I continued to date throughout college, and in early August 1967, between my junior and senior years, we were married back home in Waterloo. Judy had just graduated from the State University of New York at Brockport and had gotten a job teaching at North Syracuse High school. We lived in a small apartment in campus housing on University Avenue, and we were on our way. The following year, after graduation, I remained at Syracuse as a graduate assistant while working on my master's degree. In 1969, I got my first paid coaching job as a young assistant at the Rochester Institute of Technology (RIT).

In early October 1969, Judy was due to give birth to our first child. On October 6, while I was getting fitted for orthotics at Strong Memorial Hospital, I received a message that Judy was in labor at Rochester General Hospital. So I flew over there and ran up and down the labor ward looking for her until someone finally told me she was not there. I called home and found out that Judy was waiting patiently for me to come and take her to the hospital. Thankfully, our brother-in-law Bob Kingston, married to my sister Carole, taught at Bloomfield High School, just five minutes away from our home, and he quickly rushed Judy to the hospital, since I was at least thirty minutes away. I nervously paced in the hospital lobby while waiting for Judy and Bob. They arrived eventually, and our daughter Keli Ann was born a few hours later.

AFTER ONE SEASON AS AN assistant at RIT, I was promoted to head coach and did everything from the laundry to lining the fields to recruiting the next wave of RIT players. I relied on *my* coaches in those early years at RIT. I thought back to Mike Ornato, Bill Carey, and Ben Schwartzwalder. What drills had they run? How had they organized practice? How had they dealt with the players? And I did everything I could to gain additional knowledge, to develop as a coach, including traveling to coaching clinics in the region to learn from the game's greatest minds.

On February 8, 1972, Judy gave birth to our son Timothy Paul, and now things were really chaotic.

We went 16-15-2 in my four seasons as the head coach, and I am still the only head coach in RIT history with a winning record. But I was looking for the next challenge. Coach Schwartzwalder retired at the age of sixty-three, and my alma mater hired the defensive line coach from Michigan, Frank Maloney. Frank had coached under Bo Schembechler, who in turn learned the game from Woody Hayes, so his lineage ran deep. In the spring of 1974, Frank went on a speaking tour to Syracuse alumni groups all around the state, and I went to hear him speak to the Rochester alums. After he finished his talk, I approached him, shook his hand, and told him that I would be interested in joining his newly forming staff.

"I don't have any openings," he replied in a football coach kind of way.

Two weeks later, while I was still unsure of what was next for me and for us, Frank called me in Rochester and asked me to interview for a position on his staff, which totally caught me off guard. The position that was open was a defensive position, so I pointed out to Frank that while I was the coach at RIT we had shut down the nation's top rushing attack in Division III, Hobart College's wishbone under head coach George Davis. Hobart had the nation's leading rusher, halfback Donald Aleksiewicz, and we stopped him. I volunteered to make a presentation on our strategy to Frank, and he agreed. We decided to meet a few nights later in Syracuse.

When the day of the interview arrived, I rushed home from RIT, showered and shaved, put on a coat and tie, and was ready to leave. One problem: I couldn't find the car keys. Judy and I looked everywhere as Keli, now four, and Tim, almost two, who had been playing with the keys, looked on. They watched us scurry around the house. We checked everywhere—the registers, the cushions, the shelves—to no avail. I finally picked up the phone and called Frank. I explained the car keys situation and said that I didn't think I would be able to make it to Syracuse in time. He agreed to postpone the interview a couple of hours, so we kept looking for the keys.

Judy eventually found the car keys in a bobby-pin box under the sink in the bathroom, where she had seen Tim playing earlier. He had taken the keys, crawled into the cabinet, and put the keys in the box. By the time we found them, I was completely soaked in sweat and thought I had blown my chance with Frank. I called him and told him we'd found the keys but I would be cutting it close in getting there for the interview. He started to laugh and said, "Hey, I've got kids, too. I know how that can be."

I met with Frank two weeks later and gave the presentation. Another few weeks went by and he finally called to offer me a job—not as a defensive assistant but as the quarterbacks/running backs coach. It turns out that during the two-week delay before my interview, Frank had shuffled the staff a bit and now wanted me on the offensive side of the ball. I like to think that young Tim Coughlin changed the course of New York Giants history.

MANY YOUNG MEN AND WOMEN don't know what they want to do with their lives; I was one of the fortunate ones. Ever since my junior year of high school, I knew that I wanted to be a football coach, and here I was at twenty-seven with four years of coaching experience. But to excel in a chosen profession you need to challenge yourself and your ideas, and returning to my alma mater, I did just that. I was thrilled to be back on top at Syracuse. But as much as I loved coaching, as much as I looked forward to Syracuse, I learned a very traumatic lesson: coaching football is a business—a business that gives leniency to no one.

As I've noted, Frank Maloney was a disciple of Bo Schembechler and Woody Hayes, so during my seven seasons as his assistant, I really felt that I was learning from Bo and Woody as well: the organization, the detail, the toughness. Coaching at my alma mater was certainly different from playing, but despite the coaches' and players' best efforts, we never had a breakout season. In 1977, I was promoted to offensive co-ordinator, the same year Judy gave birth to Brian Thomas on July 17, and I thought things would be better. But in 1980, after a 5–6 mark, Frank Maloney resigned. When the assistants received word of the resignation, I was a bit naïve and not sure what was going to happen to the staff. I didn't know if I would be asked to stay or not. I did know that I was a good football coach, and I also knew that I would continue to work hard until someone told me to stop.

When we finally did receive the news that we wouldn't be back, I will never forget Keli and Tim running to me crying when I came home, as they had heard the news on the radio. Judy and I decided right then we would never again let the kids find out about a job change before we had the chance to tell them, but for right now it was too late. I explained to them what had happened and what I thought might come next, even though I had no idea.

I have never been a "phone coach," never great at networking or keeping an eye out for jobs and such, so when I was out of work, I suddenly had to call people I knew, hat in hand. The paychecks from Syracuse would stop in March and I had a family to support. To top it off, Judy had not been feeling well. We presumed it was the flu, but no, it turned out to be the first sign of the coming of our fourth child, Katie Elizabeth, who would be born on September 11, 1981. We had been very fortunate in that my first two jobs, at RIT and Syracuse, were within an hour of Waterloo, so the kids could be around their grandparents, aunts and uncles. But what now? Where were we headed? I thought about leaving the coaching profession to find a more stable career and even considered selling insurance, but Judy pressed me to follow my heart.

There was an opportunity to join Frank Kush in the Canadian Football League, but Canada was not too appealing for us. I also interviewed at Boston College with Jack Bicknell, and after Jack offered me a job, we accepted and made the decision to move away from upstate New York to the big city of Boston.

The spirit and enthusiasm of Boston College were like nothing I had ever known. The athletic director, Bill Flynn, was an amazing administrator whose passion and love for the school was evident in his every word and action. The college is deeply rooted in the Jesuit tradition with a strong balance among mind and body, service to community and God, and athletics, and everyone on campus was involved in some sort of sports or exercise. It was routine to see professors out for walks or, in the winter, ice skating. The spirit on campus was infectious.

Early on, before my family even moved to Boston, I stayed with the other coaches in a hotel before moving to a monastery across the street from the campus. The rooms were small, but at least we did have our own priest on Sunday mornings.

Toward the end of the spring of 1981, after I had been on the job just a few months, we had to make some decisions about recruits. Assistant Barry Gallup had led the effort to recruit a young, fiery quarterback, a five-foot-nine player from Natick, Massachusetts, whom only BC and Dartmouth were recruiting. As the quarterbacks coach, I was involved, but Jack made the final decision to offer Doug Flutie a scholarship.

Doug started out as the seventh quarterback on the depth chart but moved up quickly. Some veteran players got hurt or hadn't gotten it done, and Doug kept improving and advancing. Finally, in the fourth game of the season on the road at mighty Penn State, Doug entered the game in the fourth quarter, led us on two outstanding drives, and threw a touchdown pass. The next morning back in Boston, Jack came into the offensive staff meeting and asked, "What are we going to do? We've got these veteran QBs and this freshman."

"Coach," I told him, "we have to play this freshman."

In those days, Bill Flynn was not shy about scheduling the college football powers, and we always played a tough schedule against the likes of Clemson, Alabama, Texas A&M, and Penn State. Doug Flutie was a gamer every time out. He and I grew close, thanks to a mutual love of the game and a burning desire to win. Doug was the kind of guy who would play touch football with young kids on the stadium field or suit up for intramural hockey in the winter. He just loved competition, and his passion tended to raise the level of play of everyone around him. When he was on the field, he was like a little boy, and his attitude was contagious. He would throw a touchdown pass and then smile and laugh, but it didn't mean he wasn't a ferocious competitor. He was a doer, not a talker.

Boston College was wonderful in so many ways. Jack Bicknell was so great to work for, and the entire coaching staff was fun to be around. Jack could be tough when he needed to be, but he had a calm demeanor around the players, which they were receptive to, in stark contrast to the coaches that I had known.

In three years at Boston College, we won twenty-two games, and I loved the college and the city. But I wanted to be a head coach by the time I was forty-five, and it became clear to me that I needed NFL experience on my resume, a different path from what I had envisioned.

Ron Meyer, the head coach of the New England Patriots and a friend, recommended me to Philadelphia Eagles coach Marion Campbell at the Senior Bowl. Marion had taken over for Dick Vermeil the year before and was now looking for a "young, smart, aggressive coach" to work with the wide receivers. After I interviewed Marion, he offered me the position. It was an opportunity to coach alongside and against the greatest minds in football, including Tom Landry, Joe Gibbs, and Bill Parcells, and my salary would almost double. Although it was extremely difficult to say goodbye to BC and to tell Doug Flutie I wouldn't be with him in his senior year, the opportunity was too great to pass up.

Working in Philadelphia was certainly an adventure. Ted Marchibroda, the offensive coordinator, and Marion Campbell taught me a lot about both sides of the game as did quarterback coach and Hall of Famer Sid Gilman. It was eye-opening to work with All-Pro players who, despite their stature, worked every day to get better. In Philly, I had the privilege to coach outstanding wide receiver Mike Quick. We never won big, though, and my stay in the City of Brotherly Love lasted just two years, until new owner Norman Braman fired the coaching staff.

Next stop was Green Bay, where I had the opportunity to coach Hall of Famer James Lofton. What an experience it turned out to be. I knew a little about Green Bay from reading about the life of Vince Lombardi. It's an amazing small town where everyone lives and breathes Packers football and where hard work and pride are valued above all else—my kind of town. My stay there would be a short one, however. Though I enjoyed working for Forrest Gregg during the 1986 and 1987 strike season, he left suddenly to become the athletic director at Southern Methodist University. At the time, I wasn't sure whether or not the incoming coach, Lindy Infante, would retain me. As it turned out, he would not.

So just to recap: I was let go from Syracuse, I was let go from Philadelphia, and I was let go from Green Bay, none of which was due to my performance, or so I believed.

AS MY CAREER MOVED ALONG, and as my family just *moved*, I never lost touch with my roots. As often as I could, I would return to Waterloo, but even those weeks and months when I could not pay a visit, my family was never far from my mind.

Growing up in Waterloo, there were two professional football teams to root for, the Cleveland Browns and the New York Giants, so you can imagine the thrill when Bill Parcells offered me a chance to join a staff that had just won the Super Bowl in 1986. It turns out that Bill was a very personable guy. He loved to joke with his coaches and talk about a variety of interests from boxing to baseball to horses. But don't let that fool you. He was demanding. He ran a tight ship, and with leaders such as Phil Simms and Lawrence Taylor, the team rarely strayed from Bill's message. In fact, I felt as if his team assumed his personality.

More than anything, Bill knew how to win. Winning meant having an organization that, from the top down, did the things that needed to be done. He was always very consistent in how we practiced and how we played. His emphasis on solid defense and limiting turnovers remains a hallmark of our Giants teams today.

In 1990, things were rolling along and we were on our way to perhaps the Super Bowl when I received a call in October: my sixty-nine-year-old father had had a heart attack.

It happened to be a bye week for the New York Giants, so Judy and I and Brian and Katie drove up to visit Dad in the hospital. We were going to spend Saturday and Sunday with him, but he looked so well and healthy during our visit on Saturday that I suggested we head back to New Jersey early Sunday morning. Judy convinced me otherwise.

The following Saturday, as we prepared to play the Redskins in D.C., I called home to check in with my mother, and my father answered the phone.

"Dad, what are you doing home?" I asked.

He had been cleared by doctors to return home, back to his normal life. I was relieved.

Four days later, Wednesday, October 17, I was sitting in a players' meeting in Giants Stadium when Whitey Wagner came in with "not good news." My father had walked into the bathroom, started to make his way back to the kitchen, and collapsed with another heart attack. He was gone.

We drove up to Waterloo on Thursday night for a private family viewing. As you might expect, it was emotional. My siblings were wrecks, and though I was crushed inside, I attempted to stay composed to be strong for my mother. Friday would be the wake, Saturday the funeral. The lines were out the door of the Doran Funeral Home as hundreds came by to pay their respects to a longtime Waterloo resident and a good man. I remember standing at St. Mary's Cemetery as they lowered my father into the ground. I remember experiencing a true soul-searching moment. *Is this all there is to life?* I wondered. My father had spent his whole life working hard, raising a family; he was tough but fair, honest, and righteous. He had retired at the age of fifty-nine and then for ten years battled health issues, never really having an opportunity to enjoy his retirement. And then *boom*—life is over.

I wish it could have been different.

IN LATE NOVEMBER 1990, JACK Bicknell was fired as the head coach of Boston College, and I was offered my first major head coaching job by athletic director Chet Gladchuck. At the time, the Giants were in the middle of an incredible run and I didn't want to leave. But after BC agreed to let me finish out the season with New York, I decided to return to Chestnut Hill. I knew that I could handle both jobs in the interim, though it was a difficult balance. But the Giants kept winning, and the BC program started anew. Sure enough, we won the Super Bowl, and the very next day, after we landed in Newark, a car was there waiting for me to hit the road recruiting.

At this point in my career, I had been coaching for close to twenty years, and I had full confidence in my ability to be a head coach. I was forty-five years old, had coached at the college and NFL levels, and brought a wealth of experience to the job. And Boston College was a great place for my first head coaching job, as I already knew the school so well, including the key alums and the school president, Father Donald Monan. We went right to work.

Installing a new sense of discipline with an emphasis on academics, we built the program one day at a time. Our first season in 1991, we went 4–7, and in 1992 we won eight games against a difficult schedule, including a victory over number nine Penn State. During that season, the New York Giants reached out to me about replacing head coach Ray Handley, but I knew in my heart there was still work to be done in Chestnut Hill. I graciously declined.

Our third year at Boston College opened with two losses. There were some rumblings about where we might be headed, but I knew we had a good football team. In fact, we ran off seven straight wins and sat at 7–2 heading into our annual showdown with Notre Dame. Now, the year before, the Irish had imposed their will on us, winning 54–7. That was a Lou Holtz team that featured Jerome Bettis in the backfield. They led big at halftime, and early in the second half they executed a fake punt, adding some salt to the wound. Despite the bait from reporters after the game, I never publicly complained about the trickery, but I—and my team—remembered.

In 1993, Notre Dame had beaten top-ranked Florida State the week before our match-up to take over the top spot in the country. I have to imagine they viewed us as nothing more than a bump in the road to a national title. We jumped out to an early lead in Notre Dame Stadium, but the Irish battled back to go ahead. In the closing minutes, we drove down the field and called a go screen, a screen often used when anticipating a blitz, and our quarterback, Glenn Foley, got the ball to Ivan Boyd, who set up a 41-yard field goal attempt for our kicker, David Gordon. We called time-out with five seconds to play, trailing 39–38.

David was one of the hardest-working players I had ever coached, the kind of player who would be out on the stadium field in the middle of winter, shoveling snow off the turf so he could practice kicks late into the night. Before he jogged onto the field at Notre Dame, I told him one thing: "Just strike the ball solidly."

We knew that the rush would be forceful, so our protection dug in. As the lines clashed, David kicked the ball just over the reach of the Irish chargers. Now, from where I was standing, it looked like the ball was going to be outside the uprights. But the screwball kick suddenly started to curve in. The kick was good. You have never heard eighty thousand people so quiet. It was an important lesson: for as long as there is time on the clock, you must believe that you have a chance to win.

As our players erupted in celebration, I jogged to midfield. Lou Holtz was gracious in defeat. When I was done with an NBC postgame interview, I ran to the locker room to talk to the team. One problem: there was no team. Apparently they were all still on the field celebrating and didn't want to come in. It was just me in there at first. Father Monan followed shortly thereafter, and then Glenn Foley came in. It was just the three of us before the rest of the team filed in.

We flew back to Boston, where an impromptu celebration was under way with thousands of students outside the stadium. Boston College was back.

OPPORTUNITY SURE SHOWS ITSELF IN funny ways.

In February 1994, one of my former players called the Boston College football office and left word that he'd like me to be a reference for a job he was going after. When a call came through from a guy named David Seldin, all I heard was the word *Jaguar*, and I figured he was a car dealer looking for a reference for the former player.

"Who is this?" I asked again.

"David Seldin, the president of the Jacksonville Jaguars."

It took me a minute to figure out what this call was about.

"We are conducting a search for a head coach, and we wanted to know if you would be interested," David asked.

Wow. It had come truly out of left field. Jacksonville wasn't even on my radar screen at the time. I didn't have much time to think, but I did know that I didn't want to be involved in a long drawn out process.

"If there are five people you're considering, then I'm not interested," I candidly told David.

He asked if he could possibly call again in a couple of weeks.

He did call when it was down to just two candidates, and after a series of meetings in Providence and in our home outside of Boston, I accepted the offer to become the first head coach of the Jacksonville Jaguars. It was an extremely difficult decision to leave Boston College. But in Jacksonville, I would be responsible for building a franchise from scratch. I would hire the coaches, the personnel department, the video staff, the trainers, and all departments dealing directly with the players. That also meant I had full control over our roster, which most NFL coaches didn't have. I was excited to get down there and get started.

Patience is a virtue. I mean, we had more than a year and a half before we ever played a game that mattered, so we could systematically plan and build our franchise the right way. But that didn't mean things went smoothly that first year.

The day I arrived to start work was a wet one in Florida. The area around the office was covered in mud. Now that I think about it, though, *office* is a kind word. Really, it was a trailer sitting next to the old Memorial Stadium and near the ongoing construction of what is now Jacksonville Municipal Stadium. On that day, there were rivers flowing around the trailers. I walked in the trailer door and saw six people, including the owner, Wayne Weaver, and David Seldin. I was the seventh employee.

I thought, *What have I gotten myself into?*

I knew that the possibility of success rested on preparation, and I went to work right away on an organizational chart. *Whom do I hire first? How many trainers will we need? How many scouts?* I started hiring personnel people first, including Ron Hill as the head of pro personnel and Rick Reiprish as our director of college scouting. We needed to build a team from nothing and had to evaluate everyone in college and the pros, even though we wouldn't face a draft until the following spring and wouldn't start playing until the fall of 1995. In the spring of 1994, we did a mock draft. We watched tape on prospects, did our research, and met for days as if we really were picking. Think of it as a full dress rehearsal. We would not only get familiar with the players but also perfect the process. And we did something else unique for a staff without a team: we game-planned. We set up a mock schedule, including our divisional foes, and spent hours studying tape, figuring out how we would play each opponent. We even made up game plans and play call sheets for every team. When the fall of 1994 rolled around, we would evaluate talent in the early part of the week and game plan in the latter part of the week, then hit college games on Saturdays and NFL games on Sundays. It was a grueling schedule, but the preparation was invaluable.

Judy and I lived with Brian and Katie, in Ponte Verdra Beach, Florida, about fourteen miles from Jacksonville. Shortly after starting work in Jacksonville in 1994, I'd received a call from a retired insurance executive named Ernie Bono. Pat Martin, who had coached Ernie in high school and whom I had gotten to know as a scout, had suggested Ernie call me to offer our family assistance with the move to Jacksonville and to help answer questions we might have about schools, places to live, churches in the area, and so on. It had nothing to do with football. Ernie is a character. A five-foot-two Italian Catholic from Philadelphia, he has a zest for life and for his faith. Over the years we have become close friends with Ernie and his wife, Rita, and their family remains a big part of our lives. We take trips together, we share wine together, and we occasionally play golf together. It was good to make friends in a new city because I would need them.

On February 16, 1995, we drafted players in the expansion draft. The NFL mandated that every team had to make five players available for the expansion draft who passed physicals. Well, as you might imagine, they didn't offer up any All-Pros. No, these were guys who might struggle to make a roster, had injury concerns, or were on their way out of the league. We were able to identify some talented players who could help us build a solid foundation. There was still the possibility of free agent signings for us in 1995, but we didn't dip our toes too much in the market. In the 1995 NFL college draft, when we were given multiple picks, we chose tackle Tony Boselli from USC with our first pick, second overall. Tony would be the cornerstone of the franchise. We also executed a trade for Green Bay quarterback Mark Brunell the day before the NFL draft. Shortly after the draft, we finally moved into our new offices in the stadium, which was on track to be ready for the preseason opener in August.

We had an off-season program, and I'll be the first to tell you that it was demanding, as was our first training camp, in Stevens Point in Wisconsin. Steve Beuerlein started at quarterback for us, but it wasn't long before Mark Brunell took over behind center. And Jimmy Smith, who had been released by Philadelphia and who had suffered an illness and a temporary lack of confidence, was in the mix at wide receiver. In 1995, we won four games, including two over the Cleveland Browns. We didn't win on talent; we won on heart, effort, and above all toughness.

The following year, in 1996, we signed some free agents, including Leon Searcy and Keenan McCardell. We caught fire late and went on a five-game winning streak, earning a play-off berth on the season's last weekend when Atlanta's Morten Andersen slipped while trying to kick a game-winning field goal. In the first round of the play-offs, we had numerous players come up with big plays in a win against Buffalo, and in the Divisional Play-off Game for the AFC Championship Game, Mark Brunell ad-libbed an incredible scramble and hit Jimmy Smith on a fade late in the game to help us advance on the road against John Elway and the Denver Broncos.

On a dark and cold game day in New England, however, we simply didn't play our best football in the AFC Championship Game, and we lost to the Patriots, 20–6. Still, for a second-year franchise to reach a title game is an impressive feat.

Over the next three years in Jacksonville, we won thirty-six games but lost in the play-offs to Denver and the New York Jets in 1997 and 1998, respectively. In 1999, we went an impressive 14–2 during the regular season, with our only losses coming at home and on the road to the Tennessee Titans, who were led by Steve McNair and Eddie George. We beat Miami in the Divisional round of the play-offs, 62–7, but as fate would have it, we lost to Tennessee again in the AFC Championship Game. In all three of the losses, we had our chances to win but couldn't make the necessary plays when the game was on the line.

Despite our incredible stretch of five years, a perception had developed in the media about me: that I was cold, distant, aloof. Maybe it was because I wasn't overly friendly with the press; maybe it was the tough training camps; maybe it was the rules.

After winning fifteen games in 1999, we were poised for a run at the Super Bowl in 2000. But injuries, beginning in training camp, took their toll, as did our inability to make the plays needed for victory, and we won just seven games. We were shocked. And the ultimate responsibility fell on me as the head coach.

In 2001, things had to be better, I thought. But before we could find out, tragedy struck.

I NEVER BELIEVED IN CELL phones until September 11, 2001.

By the fall of 2001, Judy, Keli, and I were in Jacksonville, Brian was in law school at the University of Florida, Katie was at Boston College, and Tim and his wife, Andrea, were living in Hoboken, New Jersey, as Tim was working for Morgan Stanley in 2 World Trade Center, the south tower, in lower Manhattan. When the first plane hit the north tower, I was in meetings and Judy was on her way to the dentist. Keli heard about the attack first and immediately called Judy and then called me at work. Mike Perkins, our video director and a longtime friend, came into a meeting to tell me what was going on. I rushed from the game plan room to my office and tried to reach Tim on his cell phone, but there was no answer. By that time, word had spread throughout the family, and we were all calling Tim and trying to make sure he was safe. We decided that just one of us should keep calling, and all agreed it would be Brian, but I admit I asked my assistant, Nancy Hoey, to keep calling every ten minutes. That's the father in me, and I can't really apologize for it.

While that was happening, Tim, whose office was on the sixtieth floor of the south tower, made his way down to the lobby on the forty-fourth floor, where hundreds had gathered. Security officials told workers that it was okay to return to their offices if they chose. Five minutes after that, another plane hit the south tower. As Tim describes it, the building felt like it was picked up five yards and put back down. The second plane hit between the seventy-eighth and eighty-fourth floors. Unbelievably, the lobby on the forty-fourth floor had flat-screen televisions, so those watching could see the plane hit their building. At that point, everyone rushed to the stairwells.

As Tim made his way down the stairwell with thousands of others, Brian finally got through to him on the twenty-ninth floor and quickly passed on word to all of us that Tim was okay. Brian told him that these were coordinated attacks and the explosions were commercial jetliners.

I got through to Tim near the ground floor as he was about to exit the stairwell.

"Get out of there as fast as possible," I told him.

I believed in cell phones now.

"It looks like Beirut," I remember Tim saying.

He would tell me about the heroic men and women, NYPD, Port Authority, and FDNY, who were running up the stairs into 2000 degrees as he and others were walking down. At the time, Judy and Keli were sitting on the floor in Keli's townhouse watching the television coverage and crying.

Tim and his Morgan Stanley colleagues made their way to the company's contingency site on Varick Street. As they were walking, the tower collapsed. There were working phone lines at the Varick Street office, and he called and left Judy a voice mail at 10:36 A.M., letting her know he was fine but that he was worried about his friends. Because of the attacks, many of the phone lines in the New York region were out and

Tim's wife, Andrea, could not get in touch with him. Judy and Keli finally got through to tell her that Tim was safe.

Judy just wanted to get on a plane immediately to see Tim and give him a hug, but all flights were shut down for days. Later, Judy told me that during the events of the day, Katie, whose birthday is September 11, told Judy, "Mom, this is my worst birthday ever, but I received the best present ever, Tim."

Tim lost close friends in the attacks of September 11; it was simply impossible for any of the rest of us to comprehend what he and thousands of others had gone through. But two days later, he and his coworkers were back at work at a secondary site in Jersey City, across the Hudson River from Ground Zero.

The Holy Spirit took Tim by the hand and guided him out of the building. While we rejoiced in Tim's safety, we pray for the families who had loved ones who did not survive that fateful day.

Like a lot of families, our family grew closer because of 9/11. We were always close, but now we swore we would never take anything or anybody for granted. We give more hugs; we say "I love you" more often. None of us could shake the terrible reminder of just how precious life is.

And I would never be without a cell phone again.

IN 2001 AND 2002, THE Jaguars won just six games each season, but we were so close in '02. In fact, we lost five games that season by a combined ten points. Not surprisingly, the media began to beat the drum of change. The owner, who had been good to me for so long, began to worry about community relations and attendance. Wayne Weaver had told me that I was the guy to build the franchise back up again, but perhaps he was having doubts. We still weren't adding players—in fact, we were subtracting them to get under the cap, and I didn't even know if we would be able to have a full fifty-three-man roster in 2002. Guys who had built the Jacksonville franchise were let go. I remember walking across the street from our house to sit on Tony Boselli's front porch in

2002 to let him know that we were making him available for the Houston expansion draft for cap reasons. Tony was the quintessential football player and the guy with whom we'd started the franchise, and here I was telling him he was out. I still believed that I would be coaching the Jags in 2003.

In our last game of the 2002 regular season, we faced Peyton Manning and the Indianapolis Colts. We played well but still came away with a loss. Immediately after the clock hit 0:00, I jogged to midfield to shake hands with Colts coach Tony Dungy. Tony grabbed my hand and leaned in close.

"Keep your head up," he said, and reminded me he had been in a similar situation when he was at Tampa Bay. Colts president Bill Polian told me I was a "great coach" and encouraged me to stand tall.

The next morning, less than sixteen hours later, I was called into a meeting with Wayne Weaver and told I was no longer the coach. I knew things weren't going well, but Wayne had indicated earlier that we would have the time to rebuild. Now, obviously, we wouldn't. I called Judy and all of the kids to let them know. They seemed less surprised than I, mostly because they had been reading the papers and listening to the radio and had a better sense of the climate.

Despite how things ended, I was proud of what we had done in Jacksonville. The Jacksonville Jaguars were the most successful expansion team in the history of the NFL. We had built an NFL franchise from the ground up—just as I had done once upon a time at RIT—and we had competed in two AFC Championship Games. We had done things the right way and planted the foundation for the future, all while exemplifying toughness. We made many great decisions in drafts and free agency.

But it never stops hurting when you have been fired. Your pride is bruised, your ego battered. I took responsibility for what had happened, but this was *my* team.

Now what?

I made the decision shortly after being let go by Jacksonville that I was going to take advantage of the situation, even though for the first few months of 2003 I felt a black cloud hanging over me. There were a few offers to join other staffs, but at that time, in that place, I wasn't ready to jump back in as an assistant. It looked like it would be the first time in almost thirty-five years as a coach that there would be no spring drills, no training camp two-a-days, no daily tape breakdown, no practice, no seventy-thousand-seat stadiums filled with fans. Frankly, I didn't know what to expect. I knew I couldn't just sit around—that's just not me. I also knew that Judy would get sick of me fairly quickly.

I believed that I would coach again in 2004—I just didn't know where yet. With that in mind, I committed myself to coaching a team right then and there: a team with no owners, no players, and no assistants. I would, in essence, be the head coach of a nonexistent team.

As February turned to March and then April, coaches and GMs around the NFL hunkered down to study tape on college prospects in preparation for the draft, and I did the same. When the league converged in Indianapolis for the NFL Combine, I stood alongside my colleagues with a stopwatch in hand. When training camps started up in late July, I graciously accepted the invitations of friends in the profession, including Bill Parcells and Dick Vermeil and Dom Capers and Jim Haslett, to visit camps to observe, to learn something new, to stay involved in the game. Judy was so thankful that I was busy that she sent a fruit basket to Dom Capers' staff thanking them for taking me. And all went well until kickoff of the regular season.

How in the world would I spend my Sundays?

I decided to spend them as most football fans spend theirs: locked in a room with a remote control in hand. Every Sunday, I would get up bright and early, go to church, then come home and watch football until the last snap of the last Sunday night game. I took notes, of course, and studied the schemes and the personnel. I did this because I knew my time would come again.

In the meantime, we had much to be thankful for. Our first grandchild, Emma Rose, was born on August 13, 2003, up in New Jersey to Andrea and Tim. Our second grandchild, Dylan, was born a few weeks later, on September 2, to Katie during a time when she was living with us. The timing of these two miracles could not have been mere coincidence. I would have time to visit Emma in New Jersey and time to be with Dylan. Little Dylan was a big part of my daily routine while I was out of coaching—a saving grace during a difficult time. We would play together in the mornings, and he would often just sit and smile while I made phone calls and worked in my office.

Hiring season, which typically lasts from December until mid-January, approached. I had made it clear to my agent and those around me that I wanted back in. It just so happened that the New York Giants, for whom I had worked in the late 1980s and early 1990s before leaving for Boston College, needed a new football coach. Jim Fassel had been let go, a decision announced two weeks before the end of the regular season. I knew all about the Giants and they knew all about me. After discussions with general manager Ernie Accorsi and John Mara, a few days before Christmas in 2004, I met with them once again in early January and was offered the job. What a twist of fate.

It was no secret what the team needed to improve on: they needed to turn the ball over less, collect fewer penalties, be better on special teams, and improve the play of the lines. Of course, all of those areas come back to discipline, something I had always emphasized. At my introductory news conference, I was nervous, but much more I was excited—both to be coaching again and to be part of the New York Giants.

"What we must be all about right now," I said, "immediately, is the restoration of New York Giants pride—self-pride, team pride, the restoration of our professionalism and the dignity with which we conduct our business. We must replace despair with hope and return the energy and the passion to New York Giants football."

Now, as you might expect, not everybody was on board with my hiring. There were those in the media who thought the Giants could have done better. And there were some feathers ruffled when I noted in the press conference that some injuries were "a mental thing." But, coming off a 4–12 year, there wasn't much room to go down. The first thing we focused on was putting together a staff and changing the attitude of the players, and that began in off-season workouts. I think it was clear to the players that things would be done differently, on and off the field. And things were different for me as well.

My mother, Betty, had been battling diabetes, and after losing her leg she was confined to a wheelchair. She was too proud to be in this state and claimed she was a burden, and so she decided to stop dialysis. She returned home and spent her last days in a hospital bed in the living room in Waterloo, surrounded by family with the noise of young children playing in the yard around her—just the way she liked it. I went up to visit her Easter weekend, and on April 11, while driving back to New Jersey with my brother, John, I received word that Mom had passed away—fourteen years after my father had died and almost thirty-six years to the day after her mother had passed away, on Good Friday in 1968. I wrote and delivered my mother's eulogy. Not for the first time in life, I worked through the grief by focusing on football.

THE 2004 DRAFT GAVE US Eli Manning, but on a personal level for Judy and me, it was a second-round player who stood out: a six-foot-three, 320-pound guard from Boston College named Chris Snee, the same guy who would soon be the husband of our daughter Katie. On draft day, I called Judy, who was still back in Jacksonville, and asked her if she was going to be okay if we drafted Chris. She was ecstatic that even more of the family would be together in New Jersey.

And still more changes were in store for the organization. You know the stories of the 2004 and 2005 seasons, but you may not know the effect that the deaths of Wellington Mara and Robert Tisch had on me and this organization. I had gotten to know Mr. Mara on my first stop in New York in the late 1980s, and I quickly learned what a distinguished and virtuous man he was. The way he carried himself, his humbleness, his charisma, his ability to move others with his words, and his knowledge of the game of football were all remarkable. Every day that I was the head coach in New York, Mr. Mara would come visit me in my office to make sure everything was okay. Whenever he had to leave town, he would come down and tell me face-to-face or send me a note. We grew close, and so I was deeply saddened when he became ill in 2005. He passed away at home on October 25. Three weeks later, his partner and good friend Robert Tisch passed away from a brain tumor. Mr. Tisch would eat lunch in my office every Friday, genuinely concerned about the coaching staff. I remember visiting Mr. Tisch shortly before his death on November 15; while mostly unresponsive, he would still roll his eyes and crack a slight smile when I would talk to him or touch his hand.

The legacies of Mr. Mara and Mr. Tisch remain with me, as do their portraits, which watch over me from an office bookshelf. I wanted them to be proud of this team, and with a difficult start to the 2007 season, I thought often of their wisdom and compassion.

We were 0–2 after losses to Dallas and Green Bay and facing a make-or-break game on the road at Washington. It was then, when everything seemed to be going against me, against us, that I summoned up the lessons from six decades on this earth: discipline, mental toughness, hard work, persistence, pride, faith, and, perhaps most of all, a belief in myself.

Little did I know that another one of life's lessons was about to enter our lives.

SIX

• • • •

Truly great teams form a bond by going through something together,
and whatever you are going through right now, no success ever comes easy.
Nothing is promised to anybody in this life, starting with tomorrow.
—LIEUTENANT COLONEL GREG GADSON, UNITED STATES ARMY

I T IS SAID THAT IN THE STATE OF COLORADO THERE WAS A MAN LOOK-
ing for gold in a place where he believed there should be a rich vein.
He tried and tried and tried to find it. He sold everything he owned and
spent millions of dollars looking for it, but he did not find it. Finally, he
became so discouraged that he gave up. A junk dealer came along and
bought all of the mining equipment and the rights to the place where the
prospector had been digging. That junk dealer took the equipment and
began to dig deeper. He dug three more feet and struck the richest vein
of gold in the state of Colorado.

At 0–2, we need to dig three feet deeper, and it is up to me to make
sure our team does. Outside Giants Stadium, target practice is under way
on both me and Eli. The head coach and the quarterback are tied together. Right or wrong, fair or not, at least in the public perception the

successes and failures of a team fall on both. So it was not surprising that when we struggled in 2006 and again early in the 2007 season, the media turned its laser on us.

In our draft meetings in April 2004, there was much discussion about our needs. Keep in mind that in Jacksonville, I had full authority to draft whom I wanted, but I was always looking for help. In New York, it was a collaborative decision. Before those meetings, we had visited a handful of top prospects to see for ourselves what we couldn't see on tape. One of those prospects was the quarterback from the University of Mississippi, Eli Manning—the brother of Peyton, the son of Archie. He had led his Ole Miss team to ten wins in the Southeastern Conference with very few pro prospects on the roster.

We flew to their hometown of New Orleans and gathered at the Saints' training facility for Eli's workout. He arrived just a few minutes before the intended start, having stopped for a sandwich. He walked onto the field, shook a few hands, took off his jacket, and started to loosen up his arm. Within minutes he was zinging fastballs to the receivers—accurately. It was one of the most impressive workouts I had ever witnessed.

Back in New Jersey, general manager Ernie Accorsi was taking the pulse of the organization. Were we ready to get our franchise quarterback, and what were we willing to give up to get him? How fast could he take us to the promised land? The entire organization believed in Eli Manning; it was a matter of getting him to New York.

In the 2003 season, the Giants had finished 4–12, the same record as the Chargers, Raiders, and Cardinals, but San Diego won the strength-of-schedule tiebreaker and we were fourth, giving the Chargers the first pick in the draft and us the fourth. They wanted a quarterback as well, and, in addition to Eli, Miami of Ohio's Ben Roethlisberger, North Carolina State's Philip Rivers, and Tulane's J. P. Losman were the top QB prospects. Leading up to the draft, Eli's representatives made it clear that they did not want him to play in San Diego and indicated that he would not sign if drafted by San Diego. Ernie tried to trade up with the Chargers, to no avail.

On draft day, San Diego took Eli. Now what? We ended up drafting

Philip Rivers with our pick, but then Ernie and San Diego GM A. J. Smith executed a trade, giving us Eli and sending Philip, along with our third-round pick in the draft and our first- and fifth-round picks in 2005, out west. It took a lot of work and a lot of conviction on Ernie's behalf to make the deal on draft day. Nevertheless, we had our franchise quarterback.

I have always admired Eli for his character and for the way he handles the pressure. This young man is playing the marquee position in the city of New York with a famous and successful brother and father, yet manages to maintain his composure. When his critics say he doesn't have the personality to lead, when they say his body language after a play isn't good, when they say maybe he isn't cut out to lead the Giants, Eli is patient, smiles, and answers the questions.

Here's what you may not know about Eli Manning. He comes in early and stays late. He is in the office on our off days, Tuesdays, looking at tape and working on his strength and conditioning. He stays after practice watching tape in the classrooms, preparing for the *next* day's presentation. He is in during the bye week and most days of the off-season. His competitive fire burns as hotly as anyone's and he desires to be the very best, a trait he embraces more than anyone I've ever been around.

Eli has always had the tools to be a great quarterback, but I think that as the seasons have turned, he has become more comfortable with himself as the New York Giants' quarterback and therefore more assertive. He has also started to trust his coaches more. Nowadays, he opens up and tells us if he is uncomfortable running a particular play in a particular situation. When things don't go right, he doesn't let it impact future performances. Chris Palmer asked Eli after a poor game if he knew what the Cy Young Award was for. Eli acknowledged he did, that it went to baseball's best pitcher. "Well," said Chris, "sometimes the best get knocked around. But by the end of the year, he's still the best pitcher." Eli understood the point.

I have a special coach-quarterback relationship with Eli, similar to those I had with Bill Hurley at Syracuse, Doug Flutie at Boston College, and Mark Brunell in Jacksonville. Maybe it is because I have aged, maybe it's because Eli has a unique personality, but I have been a bit more nurturing with him. He will often stop by my office on Tuesdays during the season, having come in to get a head start on what the coaches are thinking about the upcoming opponent. We may talk about a personal issue, but most of the time we simply talk football. I think we have developed a mutual respect for each other based on our love and passion for the game, just as Doug Flutie and I once did. Since we have such an experienced offensive staff with the Giants, I leave the techniques, the day-to-day fundamentals, and the play calling to others. Moreover, I am continually reinforcing key points, asking questions to stimulate thought and analyzing practice tape.

Every Saturday morning before position meetings, I gather with the QBs and we run through tape of selected plays from the previous week across the NFL. The agenda includes clock management plays, situational concepts, and green zone examples. The idea is to broaden the QBs' overall game management. It's like helping them create file cabinets in their brains so it is instinctive on the field.

If we're going places in 2007, we need Eli to play smart, and he did everything he could to help us win against Dallas and Green Bay, despite being injured and not practicing at all in the days before the Packers loss. His physical toughness and his resolve to lead this team bode well for the remaining games, and we need that leadership in Washington.

PRIDE IS ON THE LINE during the week of practice before Washington, and I notice Eli elevates his focus and his effort. The Redskins are 2–0, with wins over Miami and Philadelphia, and against Washington Eli will have to deal with a strong pass rush and a boisterous crowd.

On defense, we expect them to run. In their first two games, they ran the ball seventy-four times on 127 offensive plays, so we figure we must stop the run, stop the play action pass, and, because they run the ball so much, keep their receivers and tight ends, including Santana Moss, Antwaan Randle El, and Chris Cooley, in check to thwart any big plays. They also favor a lot of movement prior to the snaps, which requires immediate adjustments by our defense.

Coming out of the Green Bay game, we are determined to win the fourth quarter. We trailed 14–13 in the fourth quarter against the Packers before they scored three touchdowns to pull away. We have to finish the job.

But for all that preparation, all you really need to know about the Washington game takes place in fifty-eight seconds and in the space of three feet.

Fifty-eight seconds left on the game clock: New York 24, Washington 17. Redskins quarterback Jason Campbell has hit Antwaan Randle El on a 20-yard pass on 3rd and 13 to set up 1st and Goal from the 1-yard line. Campbell spikes the ball per instructions from Joe Gibbs, as the Redskins have no time-outs remaining and the coach wants to get his goal line package in the game.

We trailed in this game, early and often. Our offense turned the ball over, our receivers dropped balls—Plaxico alone had three drops—our defense couldn't stop much of anything, and we went into halftime trailing 17–3. But there's a reason why we play the second half.

"We are just a few plays short," I reminded my guys in the locker room. "We simply must make the plays when we need to. Let's take the opening drive and score to cut the lead to seven."

And we did just that when Reuben Droughns runs it in from 1 yard out. The defense locked down and held Washington to just 81 total yards in the second half. Our offense started to click, and Plaxico had five catches for 86 yards, including a spectacular 33-yard catch-and-run touchdown to put us ahead with just over five minutes to play. Still, despite the impressive second half and the comeback, the possibility of getting a much-needed NFC East road win comes down to fifty-eight seconds.

At moments like these, you generally don't know what is going through the minds of your players. But right now, I know I'm not alone in thinking about the words we heard last night, words that will carry us through a season—and through the next fifty-eight seconds.

I CAN STILL RECALL THE exact moment when I first met Lieutenant Colonel Gregory Gadson. It was outside the banquet room at the Loews

Madison Hotel, which doubles as our team meeting room when we travel to Washington. Greg is sitting in his wheelchair with his wife, Kim, by his side. I had spoken to him over the phone a few times, but being in his presence is something unique. His legs are amputated above the knee, and my eyes quickly go to that spot. Then they dart to his upper torso and you can tell that he is strapping and strong. One of his arms doesn't bend, so it sticks straight out. This is a man who is not trying to hide anything. I look into his eyes, see the gleam, and know that this is a real American hero.

Greg grew up in the Tidewater region of Virginia, a devout believer in his faith, his country, and football. His athletic prowess and commitment to discipline earned him a prestigious appointment to West Point. After joining the Corps in 1985, Greg's zest for life and for country roped in those around him, including his teammates.

You want to know what a born leader talks like, looks like, and acts like? Spend a moment with Greg Gadson. Though not overwhelming in size, Greg played linebacker at Army and helped lead the team to twenty-nine victories in his four-year career, including three victories in the Army-Navy classic. After graduating from West Point in 1989, he began his military career, which would soon take him to battlefields in Bosnia, Afghanistan, and Iraq. In May 2007, Greg was the commander of the 2nd Battalion, 32nd Field Artillery, based in Baghdad, a four-hundred-man unit made up of young American warriors. Iraq was a dangerous place in 2007, and every time a member of the U.S. military stepped off the base, there was a chance he or she would not return. Greg had seen the horrors of war: the arms blown off, the blood, the death. In the first week of May, Greg and many other members of his battalion bravely traveled to a memorial service outside of the city for their fallen comrades. It was on the way back, on a road south of Baghdad, that Greg's life changed forever. The armored vehicle he was riding in was blown apart by an improvised explosive device. As soon as the blast hit, chaos erupted.

The first thing this soldier thought of was his rifle. Where was it? How could he defend himself and his troops? In a flash, those men and women he had trained to win battles were at his side, imploring him to hold on to life. He remembered the helicopters flying in to take him out. The next thing the lieutenant colonel knew, he was in Walter Reed Army Hospital outside of Washington, D.C. In the ensuing days, doctors would have to remove his left leg due to extensive artery damage; shortly thereafter, against his wife's wishes, Greg agreed to have his right leg amputated as well. His life was changed forever, but not in the way you might think.

As he began to recover and started his grueling rehabilitation at Walter Reed, with his wife and children, Gabriella and Jaelen, at his side, football came back into his life. Word had spread quickly among his Army football teammates after the incident in Iraq and, unbeknownst to Greg, some had rushed to his bedside at Landstuhl Regional Medical Center in Germany, even while he was unconscious. When he was transferred back to the States, even more teammates arrived to lend their support. One of those men was Mike Sullivan.

We had hired Mike to be the wide receivers coach with the Giants in 2004, after he'd worked with us in Jacksonville. Mike graduated from West Point with Greg Gadson in 1989 and went on to graduate from the U.S. Army Airborne, Ranger, and Air Assault schools. On a trip to Walter Reed to visit Greg, Mike brought along a Giants jersey with Greg's Army football number, 98, stitched on the back and front. Before Mike left, Greg told him he would love to bring his kids to a Giants game one day.

That day would be Sunday, September 23, in D.C., just a short drive from Walter Reed and Greg's home base, Fort Belvoir, Virginia. Mike had told me about Greg a few weeks earlier, and he suggested that Greg come visit us on Saturday night before the Redskins game. Now, I had never met the man, but I trusted Mike, and after hearing Greg's story, I was confident that he had a worthwhile message. I normally do not bring in guest speakers on Saturday nights, as some other coaches do, but I felt this was worthy of exception. Greg and I traded a few phone calls, and he was receptive to the invitation of talking to the team.

So it was on Saturday night outside of that banquet room that I got to shake Greg Gadson's hand and thank him for his service to our country. As the players filed in to take their seats, Greg sat in the front corner of the room while his wife looked on.

"You have to play the game for one another," he said. "For your teammates. You have to fight for the guy on your left, the guy on your right." And later, espousing a theme of ours now about finishing, he said, "Be vigilant and fight for every yard."

As Greg spoke, the grown men before him were riveted. He went on to talk about how his Army teammates rallied around him when he most needed their support and about how we all need to appreciate the opportunities in our lives. In a nod to his audience, he told us how meaningful sports are to soldiers overseas and just how badly he wanted to get back to the war theater to be with his men.

"Truly great teams form a bond by going through something together, and whatever you are going through right now, no success ever comes easy. Nothing is promised to anybody in this life, starting with tomorrow."

Everyone took away something different from a story like Greg's, and here is what stuck with me: vigilance. He relayed the story of a soldier on patrol in a violent section of Baghdad. The soldier goes out on patrol one night and doesn't have to fire his weapon. He breathes a sigh of relief when he gets back to the base and doesn't bother cleaning his weapon for his next patrol the following night, assuming he will be safe again. But vigilance and preparation are what keeps the soldier alive. Human nature is to relax; it's not to clean a gun, not to run the extra lap, not to get up thirty minutes early to get more done. Human nature will get you beat every time.

The manner in which Greg spoke, the experience he possessed to back up the words, left an imprint on me and on the players. As soon as he was done speaking, the players and coaches stood up in unison and gave Greg a long ovation that all of the hotel guests could surely hear. I shook his hand again and thanked him for speaking. All of the players, one by one, took turns expressing their thanks and shaking his hand as well. A few, including Plaxico Burress, stayed around a little longer, perhaps in an effort to glean just one more precious lesson from Greg.

There wasn't much more to say after that. I had put time and thought into my presentation, but all I could say was, "Fellas, get a good night's sleep."

We had previously invited Greg and his family to watch the game on the field on Sunday, and now it would be even more meaningful. Something he said—really, everything he said—resonated with these Giants.

FIFTY-EIGHT SECONDS. DESPITE HAVING JUST allowed a huge 20-yard pass play, giving Washington 1st and Goal from the 1, our defense doesn't get down on itself. They will not give up.

The Redskins elect to stay in their goal line package. After spiking the ball on first and goal costs them a play, the Redskins call a play action pass on second down, a dump-off to fullback Mike Sellers. Sellers drops the ball, though Kawika Mitchell would have been all over him if he had held on. The Redskins don't huddle; instead, they rush to the line. On third down, running back Ladell Betts, in the game for Clinton Portis, runs away from Michael Strahan toward the left-middle—our right— and is stuffed by Kawika. As time continues to tick away, our defense hurries back to the line. On fourth and goal, again with no huddle, with the game on the line, Betts tries once more to score through the left, but this time Justin Tuck, with some help from Aaron Ross and James Butler, shuts him down.

The New York Giants win.

"We don't have to spot them 17–3," I tell the team in the postgame locker room. "Hell of a second half. Way to battle back. Uphill, had some things put us behind the eight-ball, fought our way back, and we got it done, a credit to all of you guys."

And it is at that moment, on that field, that our season seems to turn around. We came together to fight for the men on our right and left, and we finally found a way to finish. I know we have a long way to go, but I am excited to have our first victory under our belt.

I hand the game ball to Greg Gadson. He smiles. We are honored to consider him one of us.

SEVEN
· · · · · · · · ·

A bend in the road is not the end of the road . . .
unless you fail to make the turn.

— AUTHOR UNKNOWN

USUALLY AFTER GAMES, PLAXICO BURRESS CAN'T WALK. I MEAN, HE can walk, but very gingerly and slowly. In fact, usually he doesn't walk normally until Wednesdays after games. Against Washington, he further aggravated a right ankle injury suffered against Green Bay, to go along with his still sore left ankle. Last season, Plaxico injured his left ankle and had surgery in the off-season in 2007. Though many speculate that his new injury is a sprain, it is actually a torn ligament. Right now, we need him on the field and he needs us, but what about his ankle? Plaxico visits Dr. Robert Anderson, a renowned orthopedic surgeon in North Carolina, who lays out three options: surgery, which will end his season; playing with pain and risking further damage; or strapping on a boot and sitting out six weeks. You can guess which way he goes. I can tell you it is a selfless decision.

Plaxico has changed. He has come a long way from when we first met in 2005, when he joined the Giants from Pittsburgh. He wasn't always able to focus solely on football, and when his beloved mother passed away in 2002, a support beam of his life was gone. But one day he woke up and realized what was holding him back, and he matured into a fine young man and professional football player. He is blessed with a wonderful wife and, in January 2007, a son, Elijah. Once he became a father, Plaxico became a new man, and everyone in the organization could sense it. His decision to put off surgery to try to help the team is an underappreciated story of our season.

We need his experience and abilities to attack the Philadelphia Eagles' defense. When you play the Eagles, you know it will be tough to score. It's been that way since I have been in the league. They always are hard-hitting with a tremendous pass rush and they play pressure defense, so our offensive line needs to be up to the challenge. But Philly has added a new dimension in recent years—a powerful offense led by the dynamic Donovan McNabb. In their win the week before, they piled up fifty-six points on Detroit, and McNabb had his best day as a quarterback.

On defense, we need to be decisive and get everyone in on tackles. We know that the Eagles starting left tackle, William Thomas, is injured, so it will be up to second-year tackle Winston Justice to protect Donovan's blind side. Osi Umenyiora is eager to attack!

On offense, we can't have receivers drop balls, we need to protect Eli, and we need to run the football. I point out to the players on Saturday night that in our last four contests against the Eagles, we have gone to overtime twice with two lead changes in the final three minutes. Our theme of winning the fourth quarter, started after the Green Bay loss, will be relevant once again.

FROM THE GET-GO, THE PRESSURE on McNabb is intense. Osi continually blows past Justice to get in the backfield, and the sacks start to pile up.

One.

Two.

Three.

The Eagles, to our surprise, do not do much to help the overmatched Justice. Four. Five. Six. Osi records a franchise record six sacks, and the team finishes with twelve. The defense found itself and played a complete game for the first time all year. It's not a coincidence that Michael Strahan was playing at full speed and was in game shape; his rush, no doubt, kept the Eagles from concentrating on Osi.

The offense? Good, not great. The highlight is Plaxico outjumping Sheldon Brown and Quintin Mikell for a 9-yard touchdown pass, despite his bad ankles, and we go on to win, 16–3.

Ah, yes, the kicking game.

Lawrence Tynes misses a 34-yard field goal and an extra point. Most kickers miss a field goal every now and then, but a PAT? We have to do something. Early in my first year in New York in 2004, our kicker Steve Christie missed three field goals against Green Bay and I decided to stick with him. He went on to nail 17 of 18 kicks. But what do we do now?

What we do is bring in two kickers for a tryout: Josh Huston, who had lost the kicking battle to Lawrence in training camp, and Billy Cundiff. We want to see who can possibly step in if we decide to make a change. And we also want it to serve as a warning to Lawrence Tynes. Not all of our kicking woes in the preseason and the regular season have been his fault, but he needs to start being consistent. We need to know that down the stretch, when the game is on the line, when the kick matters most, he will come through.

SOMETIMES THIS PROFESSION — AND LIFE in general—throws a curveball and you have to be prepared. Experience gives you the ability to make the right decisions under pressure while keeping the big picture in mind. In football, it can be a season-ending injury or a turnover on the last series that in an instant changes things. But in today's NFL, it's not just on the field where things can change in a moment, and leading up to the New York Jets game, our team learned that lesson well.

When I was with Jacksonville, playing the New York Jets on the road was always difficult. The fans were loud and the team physical. So those memories stick with me as our 2007 team prepares to host the Jets at the stadium we share in New Jersey. It is Saturday night, October 6, Keli's birthday. Our meetings have gone well and we are focused. We review our keys for the game, which include expecting the unexpected on special teams, converting on third downs, and holding the Jets to seventeen points or less. I point out that we are 2–2 and there are eleven teams in the NFL with better records. There is a huge difference between being 3–2 and being 2–3.

Sunday morning, when my focus should be on the New York Jets, it is pulled away onto one of our players. It comes to my attention that rookie Aaron Ross has broken a team rule. To his credit, he owns up to it, apologizes, and is willing to take whatever punishment we dole out. I am disappointed but also encouraged to see how quickly he realizes that he has let himself and his teammates down. He will be fined and suspended for the first half of the game against the New York Jets. *What* he did isn't as important as *how* he responded.

I realize that this is an issue I need to connect with team leaders on, so on Sunday morning at breakfast, I pull aside the defensive captains, Michael Strahan and Antonio Pierce, and inform them of the situation. It seems to me that they have complete confidence in the decision, which is encouraging. They understand that rules are in place for a purpose.

The players should not confuse my new willingness to open up with a relaxation of discipline or rules.

The NFL itself has a bunch of rules. The league has rules about practice, about how to wear a uniform on Sundays, about when and how to speak to the media. But we have additional rules with the Giants, and I never saw what was such a big deal about having rules covering conduct, travel, and professionalism. I don't have rules for the sake of having rules—I have rules because it keeps our players disciplined and focused, which makes us a better football team.

Most of the fines that our players incur are due to tardiness to team activities or unexcused absences, with the fines ranging from $100 to $8,000, while a missed day in training camp can result in a fine of up to $14,288 per day. There are rules against dirty play, the use of motorcycles during the season, inappropriate wardrobe, visitors to a player's hotel room, public criticism of team or coaches, and gambling, among other things.

So yes, there are fines for certain violations, but as I tell the players, if they worked at IBM and had missteps, they would be out the door.

Society has rules, such as criminal statutes and traffic laws. They keep us safe and create order. Well, football organizations need those same parameters. Rules help us focus, help us prepare, keep us together, keep us healthy, and otherwise ensure that the work needed to win games in the NFL is done.

As coaches and players we must learn to deal with the unexpected and with adversity even if we bring those on ourselves. Turns out, Aaron Ross has a pretty good football game even for a guy who only plays one half. After sitting out the first thirty minutes against the Jets, he has two interceptions in the second thirty minutes, and they will prove crucial.

On offense, it is a tale of two halves. In the first, we gain 97 yards and score seven points. Eli's passer rating is 0.0. Toward the end of the first half, we have 1st and 10 from our 21 with twenty-eight seconds left. I realize that in this situation, most coaches would run out the clock. Instead of taking a knee or running the ball, we decide to be aggressive and take a shot downfield, hoping at least to get into field goal position. Eli throws down the middle to Amani Toomer but is picked off by Jonathan Vilma.

The Jets lead 17–7 at the half.

In the second half we turn to the run and Eli plays spectacularly. In the fourth quarter, he picks up a Jet blitz and spots Plaxico one-on-one with cornerback Andre Dyson. Eli throws a bullet to Plaxico, who stiff-arms Dyson along the sideline, then sprints past him for a 53-yard touchdown that gives us a 28–24 lead with just under eight minutes to play. With our backs against our end zone, Ross snatches a lob away from Jerricho Cotchery at our own 2. Later in the fourth, he seals the win with another pick, stepping in front of Cotchery again but this time returning it for a touchdown.

As he jogs off the field I run down to him. "Great job," I say.

"Thanks, Coach," he says.

And we embrace.

FIVE WEEKS INTO THE SEASON, we are happy to have an extra day to prepare for our Monday night game against the Atlanta Falcons—and an
extra day to nurse any nagging injuries back to health, including
Plaxico's ankle, Derrick Ward's ankle, and Osi Umenyiora's knee. Steve
Smith won't play against Atlanta due to a scapula injury. At this point in
the season, we continue to look for players who have the potential to
break out and who can help us down the road.

To keep the win streak alive by beating Atlanta, it is clear we need
to start fast and maintain our poise in the loud Georgia Dome. Keeping
third downs to manageable distances and being wary of defenders strip-
ping the ball will be critical on offense, while rattling Atlanta quarterback Joey Harrington every time he drops back to pass will be just as
important on defense.

When we play a Monday night game, the coaching staff uses Monday morning of game day to start work on the following week's opponent, in this instance San Francisco.

Like in many of our games in the 2007 season, we have to come
from behind against the Michael Vick–less Falcons. We battle back from
3–0 and 10–7 deficits, including seventeen unanswered points from the
second quarter on, and win 31–10. We dominate the time of possession
and our ground game is clicking, as Brandon Jacobs rushes for 86 yards
and Reuben Droughns adds 90, including a 45-yard run. Derrick Ward
gets into the act, scoring a touchdown. At times, Eli plays strong at quarterback, completing twelve straight passes during one stretch. He also
hits Plaxico on a beautiful 43-yard pass play deep down the middle. Still,
Eli is plagued by interceptions, this game throwing two, one late in the
first half, one late in the third quarter. He also fumbles the ball on a sack.

Fortunately, our defense responded, and the Falcons score zero
points off the turnovers in our territory. The best way to summarize the
game is to look at how the Falcons' drives ended. After scoring a field

goal and touchdown on their first two possessions, their last eleven drives ended like this: punt, missed field goal, punt, punt, interception, punt, punt, punt, punt, turnover on downs, end of game. That is something for our defense to be proud of.

IT IS TUESDAY, OCTOBER 17, and I pick up the phone to call Brockton, Massachusetts, as I do every October 17.

You have probably never heard of Jay McGillis. Neither had I until I arrived at Boston College in 1991. Jay was from the south side of Brockton, one of six children in an Irish Catholic family. He loved three things: his family, his teammates, and his sports. Though undersized for football at just five feet nine inches, he had earned his way onto the Boston College football team. Coaches loved him, teammates loved him. Jay was a scrappy safety, the kind of kid who played above his ability and who worked hard to gain everything that came to him.

After redshirting his freshman year, the season before I arrived as head coach, Jay became a major contributor to our defense as the starting strong safety. He was always extremely positive, trusting in his coaches and teammates. Anything you asked him to do, he did it, beyond your expectations. I admired his heart and discipline but never had a relationship with him beyond coach-player. Late in the fall of 1991, we went to Syracuse, where we lost 38–16, and returned to Boston looking to right the ship. On Sunday, Randy Shrout, our head athletic trainer, told me that he wasn't sure if Jay could play the following Saturday against number one Miami at home. Apparently, Jay's glands had swelled under his armpit and ear, and the medical staff was concerned.

The athletic trainers sent him to Cardinal Cushing Hospital for a mononucleosis test, which came back negative. He went next to St. Elizabeth's Hospital for additional tests, one of which revealed a high white blood cell count. The next day, a Wednesday, we learned Jay McGillis had leukemia.

The word *leukemia* is terrifying and devastating, and does not discriminate against the young and the old. I will never forget the emotional task of telling the team before practice on Thursday that Jay had leukemia. He was such a popular player, best friend to really every one of his teammates. Jay was immediately admitted to St. Elizabeth's, where he began chemotherapy. When the cancer would not go into remission, Jay was moved to the Dana-Farber Cancer Institute in Boston and began receiving heavy doses of radiation and four blood transfusions.

As you might imagine, his parents, Pat and John McGillis, were blindsided by the diagnosis and the impact of the strain financially, emotionally, and psychologically would eventually take a toll. They were a close-knit family before Jay's illness, and the adversity brought them even closer together. His sister, Kathy, gave up an internship at a prestigious law firm in Washington, D.C., to basically move into the hospital with Jay. Through it all, the McGillis family displayed amazing strength and courage.

As for me, it was like I was continually being punched in the stomach. Why was this extraordinary young man entering the prime of his life, suddenly struck down with a debilitating and often fatal disease? I decided immediately after the diagnosis that I would be there for Jay and his family. He would not have to ever feel that he was in this battle alone. I tried to visit Jay almost every day. Graduate assistant coach Dave DeGuglielmo would take my car keys and pull the car up outside the office at 11:30 A.M., and we would make the roughly fifteen-minute drive to Dana-Farber. Dave would sit in the car and I would run up to see Jay for thirty minutes or so. We would talk about sports and about Boston College spring practice, whatever might be on the agenda for the day. And in concern for his strength and stamina, I would always ask him, "How's your appetite today?"

Our players, who also continually paid visits to Jay, wanted to do something more. They knew they couldn't help ward off the leukemia, but they could do something to make the process easier on the McGillis family, as the financial toll was beginning to set in. Led by Mike Panos, the BC players decided to raise money through a liftathon in the spring, and went into the community gathering pledges for every pound they would lift. During halftime of our spring football game, we presented the McGillis family with a check for $50,000.

Jay's condition worsened in the late spring of 1992. A cord-blood transplant from his brother, Michael, in May 1992 was a last effort to save his life. I received word that the transplant had failed, however, and soon after that I got a call from Jay.

"Coach, do you know?" he asked in a now weakened voice.

"I know, Jay," was my reply. "Promise me you'll keep fighting."

"I will, Coach, I will."

The fact that he felt he had to call me and tell me indicates everything you ever need to know about Jay McGillis.

Jay returned home for the last few days of his life, passing away on July 3, 1992.

Jay and his family's courageous battle left a lasting impression on me. Maybe it was the way in which they kept fighting; maybe it was the way his family showed what family means; maybe it was because as his coach, I felt like I could or should have done more. I made a promise to myself that Jay's memory and spirit would live on, and so would my relationship with his family. I call Pat and John McGillis at various times throughout the year and always on July 3rd and October 17th.

Having seen up close what the crushing blow of a child with leukemia had done to the McGillis family, I vowed to help other families in similar situations. I knew it would be called the Jay Fund, to keep the name and spirit of Jay McGillis alive, but I just didn't know how to make it work and how to raise the money. In 1994, after we moved to Jacksonville, we officially established the Jay Fund. When I hired Fran Foley and brought him to Jacksonville, I told him my vision of the Jay Fund and I asked him if he would help me establish the foundation.

It wasn't until after our first official season in 1995 that things picked up steam. We now had the momentum of an organization behind us and players and coaches to help. We partnered with Dr. Michael Joyce, the director of the pediatric transplant program at the Wolfson Children's Hospital in Jacksonville, who worked with so many ill children. Social worker Helena Richards, who herself lost a child to leukemia, helped us and Dr. Joyce identify those families in need. We wanted to provide emotional and financial support to families who incurred great medical debt or who were threatened with home foreclosure. That took money, so in the spring of 1996 we held our first golf tournament, which raised close to $30,000. Our daughter, Keli, got involved in 1998 and eventually became the executive director of the Jay Fund in 2004.

The grants that we provide are to help with so many things, including water and electric bills, mortgage payments, food and car payments, and even funeral costs. We also help pay for umbilical cord blood transplants, which can cost up to $24,000 and which insurance carriers won't cover. They are generally a last resort for sick children. To date, we have given out $2,078,032, raised through private donations, golf tournaments, wine tastings, and other special events.

Over the years, the Jay Fund has hosted ice cream socials and holiday and Valentine's Day parties for pediatric cancer patients, their siblings, and parents. It is rewarding to do something special for the children, to bring smiles to their faces, and add a little joy into their lives, if only for a few hours.

Perhaps the most important event we hold every year is also one of the toughest.

The World Golf Village in St. Augustine, Florida, is a beautiful, sprawling resort—not exactly the place where you would expect to find twenty or so grieving families. But every year, in conjunction with the Nemours Children's Clinic, we invite families who have lost a child to cancer to come for a Remembrance Weekend. Trained psychologists and counselors are on hand, and families rely on one another to continue the healing process. There are also fun activities for the families, including putting together scrapbooks or golf-putting tournaments. On Sunday, the weekend concludes with a memorial service. Parents and siblings stand in front of the group one at a time and speak about their loss and their loved one. These are devastated families with the courage and strength to want to help themselves and help others keep the spirit of their child alive. This religious service is one of the most moving ceremonies I have ever had the privilege of attending.

It's not just the money that we raise that is important to the cause, it's the time we spend with the young patients. On bye weeks in Jacksonville, I would often go over to the hospital, put on a gown and gloves, and visit the kids in the bone marrow transplant unit; occasionally I'd visit them in their homes.

In 2002, I found out about a two-and-a-half-year-old girl on the south side of Jacksonville who was sick with leukemia and near death. Her father was a Florida State Trooper and had moved his family to Jacksonville so Lyla could get treatment. I called my good friend Ernie Bono, who is on our board and who is a big part of the Jay Fund, and asked him if he'd meet me at the home of Ryan and Sarah Burchnell early one Saturday afternoon after practice.

We met out front and knocked on the door. Inside, Lyla's younger sister, Kate, was playing on the floor; Ryan, Sarah, and Lyla sat on the sofa. It was a normal Saturday afternoon—but Lyla was dying. Ernie and I had brought a bag of candy for Lyla and her sister, and Kate dug right in. Lyla was sick and listless and not interested.

Lyla said, "Don't worry about me Mommy, I will be okay." Here sat a young child near death trying to comfort her mother, understanding that death was near.

I got on my hands and knees trying to get Lyla to laugh or at least share a smile, but it was difficult.

After the forty-five-minute emotional and heartbreaking visit, Ernie and I stood by the car crying and hugging. We felt so helpless. I drove home and gave Judy a big hug, and I would later find out that Ernie had done the same with his wife, Rita. The next day, we were hosting the Cleveland Browns in a divisional clash. That morning when I got into the office, I listened to my voice mail. Lyla had passed away at 5:37 A.M. To realize that this struggling young family had just lost their young daughter was almost too much to bear.

What is great for me is not only being able to help out those in need but also watching some of the youngsters survive and flourish. Alex was four or five when I first met him in Jacksonville, diagnosed with a brain tumor. The outlook was not good. One day, I received a small package at my office in the mail. Alex had found a rock and thought I might like it, and his mother passed it on. While I kept that rock on my desk as a source of motivation and inspiration, Alex had the brain tumor removed. He is now close to sixteen. He still attends many of the Jay Fund events, an example of survival and strength. There are many other success stories as well.

No matter what was thrown his way, Jay McGillis kept his spirits up and his attitude positive. He was always concerned about others, not himself, constantly asking me during our visits how his mother and father were doing. Such strength. I think of him often, most notably on his birthday, October 17, and I continue to draw strength and inspiration from his spirit.

THE WIN STREAK IS AT four and the Giants defense is playing well. San Francisco is coming to town and we have a chance to go 4–0 in what I like to call the "second season"—the one that began after we started 0–2. In hopes of encouraging the team, I devote a great deal of time in my Saturday night talk to recapping the incredible finish accomplished by baseball's Colorado Rockies. On May 21, the Rockies were in last place in the National League West, seven games behind the Los Angeles Dodgers. By September 15, they were six and a half games behind the Arizona Diamondbacks and four and a half behind San Diego in the Wild Card race. Twelve days later, with three games to play, Colorado had won eleven straight games and had closed the gap to just two behind Arizona and, along with the New York Mets, were just one game behind San Diego. With two games to play, they were two back from San Diego. The Rockies won their last two games, San Diego lost their last two, and in a thrilling, thirteen-inning marathon, Colorado clinched a play-off berth with a 9–8 win over the Padres. They had won thirteen of their last fourteen games. But they weren't done. They swept the Phillies in the Division Series and Arizona in the League Championship Series before losing to the Boston Red Sox in the World Series. The Rockies had started slow and finished fast. The analogy is obvious.

On Sunday against the 49ers, the defense continues its dominance, registering six sacks on Trent Dilfer, forcing four turnovers that lead to twenty-four points and holding the 49ers to just 103 yards rushing and

164 yards passing in a 33–15 win. Osi Umenyiora is completely healthy and has a big game, hitting Dilfer from the blind side in the third quarter, scooping up the loose ball, and running 75 yards for a touchdown. Just as important, the defense gives Eli and the offense great starting field position at the 49ers' 27, 30, and 5. Amani Toomer scores early in the game, giving him the franchise touchdown-receiving record of 49. Our kicking game is efficient on field goals, with Lawrence Tynes converting field goals of 29 and 39 yards but—much to our disappointment—missing another extra point.

San Francisco could have been a "trap" game. They came in at 2–3 and our players might have been caught looking ahead to the London trip we will take the following week. Instead, we remain steady—a good sign of our maturity and indicating that our veteran leadership has shaped our team.

"We talked about turnovers being the key and our defense got four of them," I told the team in an excited postgame locker room. "We always have work to do. We will improve, we will improve. We are five and two, only four teams with a better record in the whole NFL. Ten A.M. tomorrow. Keep climbing is the key, keep climbing is the key. Don't be satisfied with winning. The challenge is to be as good as we can possibly be." The self-analysis continues.

We are 5–2, which is where we were in 2006. But there are some big differences. First, we are still pretty healthy. Second, the attitude and outlook of this group are much more positive; collectively, we refuse to let a negative hang around too long. And remember, the 2006 team was coming off an 11–5 season and they were expected to be 5–2; the 2007 Giants are the surprise of the NFL season so far. Now we are about to take the long-awaited trip overseas to play at Wembley Stadium in the first regular-season NFL game ever played abroad.

The distractions and media attention will be enormous. Are we mentally tough enough to stay focused? Do I have the patience to deal with what is likely just ahead? We must keep our eye on the prize.

EIGHT

• • • • • • • •

Great champions have an enormous sense of pride.
The people who excel are those who are driven to show
the world and prove to themselves just how good they are.
—NANCY LOPEZ, LPGA Hall of Famer

WELLINGTON MARA AND ROBERT TISCH ALWAYS STOOD FOR WHAT is right in the game of football. They understood that what was best for the NFL was best for the New York Giants, and vice versa. Though they made changes at a conservative pace, they made sure the franchise adapted as the game evolved. As the marquee franchise in the media capital of the world, the Giants have been asked many times by the NFL to lead the league. So when the possibility of playing a regular-season game overseas was first tossed around in 2006, with the promise of a bye week to immediately follow and the assurance that we would be the visiting team so as not to lose a home game, the sons of Mr. Mara and Mr. Tisch, John and Steve, thoroughly analyzed the league's request and decided to accept the historical challenge.

After months of discussions and negotiations, the NFL agreed to play a regular-season game in London, England, in an effort to spread the NFL brand. Sure, there had been NFL Europe before it disbanded, but to have two real NFL teams playing a meaningful regular-season game overseas would be big. In January, we learned that the Miami Dolphins would be one team, and they agreed to give up a home game for the experience. But there were still details and negotiations to be worked out on just who their opponent would be. Finally, on February 2, the NFL announced that Miami and the New York Giants would play October 28 in London. The media blitz began immediately. In the first three days after the announcement, there were over half a million requests for tickets. In the first ninety minutes after tickets went on sale in May, forty thousand were gobbled up. The frenzy and buildup surrounding this game is similar to a Super Bowl.

As an organization, we left little to chance before flying over to London. Jim Phelan, our director of administration, made multiple trips to England along with other staff members in the months leading up to the game to explore everything from the practice fields and the driving route to the hotel to customs at the airport. The players and coaches, many of whom had never traveled outside of the United States, started applying for passports as early as March. In May, representatives from the Giants and the Dolphins met in London to talk about logistics, media, and marketing. To make the trip as smooth as possible, we even found an upscale hotel that was as American in nature as a British hotel could be.

As you already know, I am a stickler for routines and schedules, and so you can imagine that the thought of traveling overseas in the middle of the season with all of the hoopla was a bit worrisome to me. I worried about the practice schedule, the travel plans, the temptations, the weather, the stadium locker rooms, and just about everything else. And this was in February! But as we began to hash out our plans, I came to realize that this was a good thing for the Giants and for the NFL. A flight from New York to London was really just a bit longer than a flight from New York to Seattle. And we decided we wouldn't fly over until the

Thursday night of game week, so it would not even be a full week of distractions. As the months went by, the plans were refined again and again until they were just right.

BECAUSE WE ARE TAKING SUCH a long flight and passing through five time zones, we are concerned for the players' health, particularly dehydration and fatigue. We consult a variety of experts on how best to keep the body in prime condition while traveling by air. Particularly useful is Lawrence Segrove, who works with athletes from the world of track and field, who routinely fly around the globe between competitions.

Many things are out of our control, including the length of the flight, airport customs in England, and traffic—all things that had been discussed and prepared for. Earlier in the week, as we were putting the finishing touches on the London schedule, I spoke to the coaches in our staff meeting about the need to stay patient throughout the trip. "We all need to take our patience pills," I remarked. I will need them the most.

Well, the next day, as I began to conduct the staff meeting, I noticed a jar of jelly beans sitting in the middle of the table in the staff room. On the side is printed, "Patience Pills: Take as Needed."

I grinned and asked, "Who did this?"

Silence.

These coaches know me.

As the trip approaches, some decisions still need to be made. And that's where the Leadership Council comes into play. In discussing curfew for the trip, the players ask that they not have a curfew on Friday and Sunday nights. I think it is a dangerous idea, especially when it comes to Friday. Not that I don't trust the players, as they are grown men, but the later they stay out, the less likely they will be focused in practice and meetings on Saturday morning. As I have often told our own children, "Nothing good ever happens after midnight."

But the players on the council make rational arguments about why lifting the curfew makes sense, and eventually I see an opportunity to enhance leadership, and I agree to no curfew. Beyond that, I'm glad to see that the veterans have empowered themselves to take ownership of the rules. We represent the NFL and the New York Giants, and we want to conduct ourselves in the most professional manner possible.

Another issue that comes up in the council in the weeks leading up to the game is my insistence that we practice shortly after landing in London on Friday. With the five time zone changes and overnight flight, we will be arriving just before we would normally meet on a Friday and I want to stick to the routine. Experts had already told us that after flying to Europe, it's best to try to stay awake and have a normal day. I explained to the eleven players on the council my rationale for getting right to work, and though they all don't agree, they at least understand why I made the decision. That reasoning will then be passed on to the rest of the team. Lastly, I remind them once again that we will need patience, as there will be issues that are out of our control. I am reminding myself as well.

DURING A TYPICAL WEEK AS the visiting team, we review the previous day's game on Monday; the players have Tuesday off and practice Wednesday, Thursday, and Friday, and then we conduct a jog-through before flying to the game site on Saturday. For the London week, we give the players off on Monday and practice Tuesday through Thursday before flying, in order to install all of our game plan before we leave the States.

Finally all of the preparation, the months of planning and worry, are behind us as we board the charter flight on Thursday, October 25, at Newark Liberty International Airport. Though this is a business trip—we are going over there to win a football game, after all—I sense a new kind of excitement from the players. We know that we are in this together; as one, we are sailing uncharted waters. Instead of heading home individually after practice or meetings, we will be together in an unfamiliar city. It is a chance to further cement what we talked about way back in June; it is a chance to grow as a team.

We depart Newark at 6:00 P.M. and arrive in London around 6:00 A.M. local time. We are tired and a bit bleary-eyed from the long flight. We pass through customs, which takes some time (something I had warned the Leadership Council about), and we board buses to head to the hotel, which is located on Park Lane across from Hyde Park. Because of traffic, that bus ride takes over an hour. Most of the guys have brought handheld camcorders to record everything on the trip, but many are simply too tired to use them to shoot out of the bus windows. After arriving at the hotel, the players have ninety minutes before the offense and defense meetings begin at 9:30 A.M. Then there will be a team meeting concerning security on our trip, then a one-hour lunch, then tape and dress time. By 11:30 A.M., we are back on the buses.

Our practice site is about thirty miles from the hotel in Cobham, the training facility of the famed Chelsea FC soccer club in England's Premier League. The more the bus rolls along, the farther out into the country we seem to get. Fittingly, the bus ride lasts longer than planned. Patience pills, anyone? Of course, there isn't much I can do about it and I remain calm, figuring that the players will take their cues from me. When we pull into the facility, the bus drives right past the press area, where we are scheduled to meet with reporters, so when we finally do get off the bus, those of us asked to talk to the media cram into a shuttle to drive back to meet the press. When we get off the shuttle, the media, especially the foreign media, are ready to pounce. Most of the questions for me have to do with how the players are acclimating with the overnight flight and little sleep. I make clear that only time will tell. We take a picture with Avram Grant, the new head coach of Chelsea.

For all the initial chaos at Chelsea, the facility is spectacular: beautifully groomed fields and well-finished exercise rooms and locker rooms. Practice goes well. Afterward, we are swarmed once again by the media, and this time we do separate interviews with many of the reporters. When we finally get back to the hotel, we split into offense and defense to review practice tape. Come 3:30 P.M., the players are on their own until Saturday morning. Now, keep in mind that the Leadership Council has decided, with my approval, there will be no curfew tonight, so this will be a big test of our responsibility and accountability. As for me, I go to dinner with family and friends who have made the trip across the Atlantic.

If you are a parent, then you know what it is like staying awake until your children are safely in bed at night. That is how I feel when I am back at the hotel waiting on my players. Though I trust our guys, I know that anytime young men are out and about late at night, something can happen, whether it is their fault or not. We don't have a curfew, but the players do have to check in with our security personnel stationed on their floor when they return; those men will report back to me when all is secure. At the end of the night, I am deeply relieved: everyone has checked in safely.

SATURDAY MORNING, WE ARE ALL there, ready to go, and again we keep things normal. I meet with the QBs at 8:30 A.M. and the team spends the morning in position meetings. At 11:25 A.M., we are back on the buses headed for Wembley Stadium. It is beautiful. The first thing we notice is how low the grass is cut on the field and how slick it appears to be. The players and equipment staff walk the grass judging what kind of cleat should be worn. With the expectation of rain on Sunday, we anticipate a muddy, slow surface. Despite my initial hesitancy, we take a team picture around the midfield logo after the jog-through, then we shower and head back to the hotel.

The final gathering of the entire team begins with special teams on Saturday night at 7:30 P.M., which is 12:30 P.M. in New York. An hour later, we are all together.

"This is the first regular-season NFL game played overseas and will be seen in two hundred and sixteen countries and heard in twenty-one different languages," I remind the players. "This is a chance for us and the NFL to showcase ourselves to the world."

I quickly move on to our keys to victory against Miami, with special teams up first. Our punter needs to punt the ball toward the sideline, and the coverage team has to get downfield quick and get leverage on the returner. Our punt return team needs to be penalty-free and average 10 yards a return. Our kickoff team needs to force the returner to stay between tackles, and our kickoff return needs to stay with the wedge.

For me, it all began with wonderful parents. Here are Lou and Betty Coughlin on my sister Patty's wedding day.

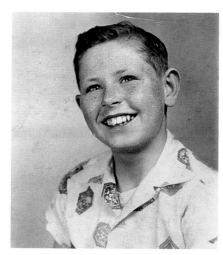

Back in seventh grade.

My sophomore year at Waterloo Central High School, I played varsity basketball for the Indians. I'm the one with the blank look on his face, wearing #40; my best friend, Terry, is front and center, #44.

In 1963, Coach Mike Ornato presented me with the Outstanding Athlete Award, which I was extremely proud to accept. Between us stands my brother, John.

Here I am in a tux for Judy's Senior Ball, with best friends Elaine and Terry.

Judy and I visited the Brockport State Teachers College in Brockport, New York, in the winter of 1966.

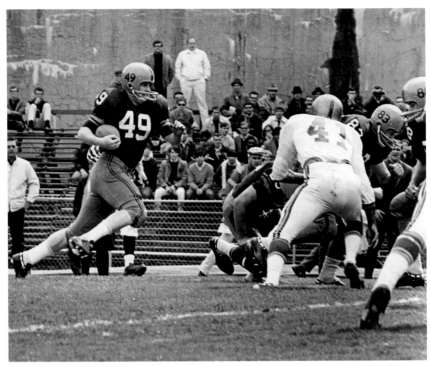

Approaching the line at Archibald Stadium in the fall of 1966. (Syracuse University)

Breaking through a hole—and trust me, it had to be a big hole for me to get through it.
(Syracuse University)

Making a cut in 1966 while Little and Csonka block—and for me that was a rare treat, I can tell you. (Syracuse University)

Prior to the 1966 Gator Bowl, Larry Csonka and I get a memorable introduction to the animal itself in St. Augustine, Florida. (Syracuse University)

One lucky man and one beautiful bride, in August 1967.

A few Syracuse teammates in the fall of 1967: Olley Allen, Larry Csonka, me, and Ed Schreck. (Syracuse University)

A group of us at the end of my career with the Orangemen: (bottom row) *Larry Csonka (#39), Jim Cheywinksi (#32), and Frank Parrish (#12); (top row) Dave Casmay (#50), Tony Karcich (#33), Steve Zegalia (#86), and me (#49).*
(Syracuse University)

In the summer of 1978, while I was working as an assistant coach, Syracuse held Family Day. Here I am with Tim, Brian, and Kelly.

The fashionable 1979 Syracuse University football staff. (Syracuse University)

In 1981 with the quarterbacks corps I coached at Boston College: Dennis Scala (#8), Doug Flutie (#22), Joe Ricca (#26), Mark Mayock (#2), John Dougherty (#7), and Doug Gwyer (#9). (Boston College/JET Commercial Photographers)

With Doug Flutie, a few years after I coached him at BC.

In 1984, I coached the wide receivers of the Philadelphia Eagles. Here I am with Mel Hoover (#85), Mike Quick (#82), Tony Woodruff (#83), Joe Hayes (#80), and Ken Jackson (#81). (Philadelphia Eagles)

1990 NEW YORK FOOTBALL GIANTS
SUPER BOWL XXV CHAMPIONS - JANUARY 27, 1991

Row 1 Raul Allegre, Sean Landeta, Matt Cavanaugh, Matt Bahr, Matt Stover, Jeff Hostetler, Reyna Thompson, Lee Rouson, Perry Williams

Row 2 O.J. Anderson, Mark Collins, Dave Duerson, Rodney Hampton, Phil Simms, Head Coach Bill Parcells, Lawrence Taylor, Carl Banks, Everson Walls, Myron Guyton, David Meggett

Row 3 Lewis Tillman, David Whitmore, Maurice Carthon, Roger Brown, Greg Jackson, Bob Abrams, Pepper Johnson, Gary Reasons, Brian Williams, Eric Moore

Row 4 Bob Kratch, Tom Rehder, Bart Oates, William Roberts, Leonard Marshall, Doug Riesenberg, John Washington, Eric Howard, John Elliott

Row 5 Offensive Coordinator Ron Erhardt, Eric Dorsey, Clint James, Bob Mrosko, Stacy Robinson, Mark Ingram, Odessa Turner, Stephen Baker, Lionel Manuel, Howard Cross, Defensive Coordinator Bill Belichick

Row 6 Offensive Line Coach Fred Hoaglin, Tight End Coach Mike Pope, Mark Bavaro, Mike Fox, Kent Wells, Johnie Cooks, Steve DeOssie, Running Back Coach Ray Handley, Defensive Line Coach Romeo Crennel

Row 7 Coaches: Strength–Johnny Parker, Special Teams–Charlie Weis, Wide Receivers–Tom Coughlin, Ass't. Video Director John Mancuso, Field Security Mgr. Joe Mansfield, Admin. Ass't. Jim Phelan, Locker Room Mgr. Whitey Wagner, Equipment Mgr. Eddie Wagner, Athletic Trainer Mike Ryan, Trainer John Johnson, Head Trainer Ronnie Barnes, Special Teams–Mike Sweatman, Linebackers–Al Groh   (Not pictured: #36 Adrian White, #57 Lawrence McGrew, #84 Troy Kyles, Video Director Tony Cegbo)

(Jerry Pinkus)

In 1994, I am awarded the Syracuse University Letterman of Distinction Award by Chancellor Ken Shaw. (Syracuse University)

My mom and me in Ponte Vedra Beach, Florida, in 2000.

The Coughlin clan at the hayride the Friday night before Super Bowl XLII.

Emma Coughlin and Dylan Snee in the hotel the night before Super Bowl XLII.

Judy and I enjoy a celebratory glass of wine in our suite after the big win.

Since Memorial Day was born in my hometown of Waterloo, it's always been an important holiday for me. Here I am, enjoying it at the grill.

Addressing the team in training camp, before we knew what exactly 2007 had in store for us. (Jerry Pinkus)

We were proud to have Greg Gadsen with us on the sideline before the play-off game in Green Bay. (Jerry Pinkus)

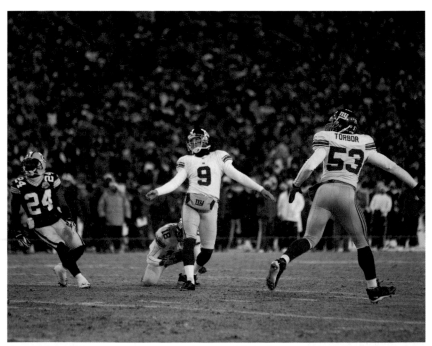

And who could forget Lawrence Tynes's incredible kick against Green Bay? (Jerry Pinkus)

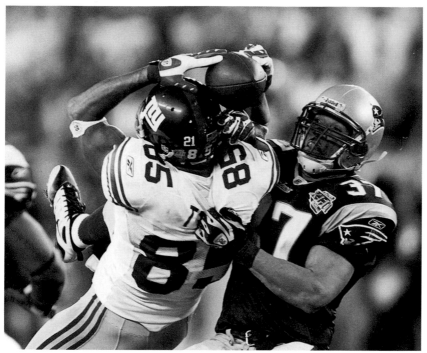

Or David Tyree's miraculous Super Bowl catch? (Dan Burns)

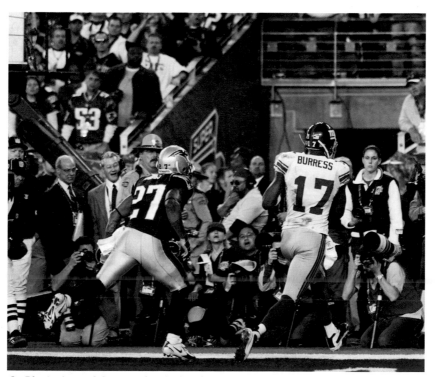

Or Plaxico's touchdown grab, which secured the win? (Dan Burns)

To the victor goes . . . . Gatorade. (Jerry Pinkus)

Without a doubt, one of my proudest professional moments: holding the Lombardi Trophy. (Larry French)

As for the defense, we need to stop the run, play physical with the receivers, pressure the QB, deny the big plays, and create turnovers. For the offense, we need to run the football, recognize the blitz, score when we're inside Miami's 20, and win the time of possession.

"Great champions have an enormous sense of pride," says LPGA great Nancy Lopez. "The people who excel are those who are driven to show the world and prove to themselves just how good they are." How appropriate on the eve of this game. On the theme of team and togetherness, I quote appropriately from "The Law of the Jungle" by Rudyard Kipling:

> *Now this is the Law of the Jungle—as old and as true as the sky;*
> *And the wolf that shall keep it may prosper, but the Wolf that*
> *   shall break it must die.*
> *As the creeper that girdles the tree-trunk the Law runneth*
> *   forward and back—*
> *For the strength of the Pack is the Wolf, and the strength of the*
> *   Wolf is the Pack.*

Finally, on top of all of the other adjustments the past three days, Saturday night just happens to be the night in England when Daylight Saving Time goes into effect, so we have to move our clocks back an hour. This has been a long weekend already, and we can use the extra hour of sleep. There is no telling Father Time what to do, however, so we do our best to roll with the punches and to remain patient.

GAME DAY IN ENGLAND. THOUGH the team's wake-up call is at 9:00 A.M., I am up at 5:00. After breakfast and brief meetings, we are finally on our way to the stadium. Prior to kickoff, NFL commissioner Roger Goodell visits with me on the field and asks my honest opinion of playing a game overseas. I tell the commissioner that there are just so many difficulties placed on the coaches and players in a short time frame that I believe a bye week following a game in Europe is necessary. But for the moment, that is neither here nor there. It is almost kickoff.

Obviously, this isn't just any regular-season game, and that point is made loudly and clearly when "The Star-Spangled Banner" is followed by a rendition of "God Save the Queen." Then, too, we are faced with classic London weather: by kickoff, the field is already a mess, and the rain continues to pour down.

Miami comes into the game 0–7 and has struggled on both sides of the ball. Still, this is football, the game of "any given Sunday," and we will have to play well to finish the first half of the season at 6–2. Weather can be a great equalizer. Miami's defensive coordinator, Dom Capers, is a good friend and a heck of a football coach, so I know it won't be easy.

As expected, the game is ugly. And I mean that in the worst sense of the word. The offenses cannot get anything going, especially through the air. The field conditions are horrid, with players spinning their wheels in the mud, not being able to cut or change directions. The 81,176 fans are having a jolly old time, as the overhangs of the stadium keep the spectators from feeling a drop of rain, but the teams combine for just 483 yards. There are seven fumbles, two missed field goals, and fourteen penalties.

Just before the start of the second half, a man dressed as an official standing by the end zone runs out to the 30-yard line and rips off his clothes, revealing a jock strap in the shape and color of a football. I must admit, it's funny. Funny, that is, until security personnel have to wrestle him into custody.

The second half continues to be sloppy and the game does not end quite the way we hope, as we pick up four penalties on one drive, Eli fumbles, and Lawrence Tynes misses a field goal. Miami's Cleo Lemon hits Ted Ginn Jr. for a touchdown after an 80-yard drive to trim the lead to three with 1:54 left, but the ensuing onside kick goes out of bounds before going 10 yards and we are able to run out the clock. We win, 13–10. The English fans boo as we kneel, and I wonder if they don't understand American football.

After the game, the players are excited in the locker room. The game wasn't pretty and the weekend had its challenges, but we got what we came for.

"We came here to win a game and we won a game," I tell the team huddled around me. "We're six and two. It wasn't pretty, but we're six and two. We are humble. It wasn't our best, but we're six and two. Let's give credit where credit is due: they played a hell of a game. They are a team obviously struggling to win, but they never quit. The people here were magnificent to us, the stadium was beautiful. We're proud to represent the New York Giants and the NFL in this game. And we won the football game. Tonight, be responsible. We've got a good thing going and we want to keep it that way."

In the postgame press conference, I try to be a good ambassador for the NFL and the New York Giants, praising our trip, our hosts, and Wembley Stadium. Some members of the press try to get me to complain about the field conditions, but I don't bite.

That night, again there is no curfew for the players, but they do have to sleep in the team hotel and check in with our security staff.

On Monday morning after my media obligations are complete, it is a beautiful, sunny fall day, and Judy wants to take a walk and show me a few of the historical landmarks nearby. She flew over on Wednesday with Keli and her husband, Chris Joyce, and had some extra time to stroll the streets of London. Quite honestly, I'm not all that interested, but I agree to go, along with Mike "Murph" Murphy and Vinnie Byron, our security personnel. It is a beautiful day and we walk down to Buckingham Palace. We stand there for a moment, then I say, "Okay, I've seen it, let's go."

On the way back to the hotel, my pace quickens, but I don't think I am in an all-out jog, the way Judy remembers it. So much for the relaxing stroll she had envisioned. By 4:30 P.M., we are wheels up, headed for home.

There are many positive results from our international trip. Most notably, we won the football game. We proved to the world that we are ready, and we proved to ourselves just how right Rudyard Kipling was. The way in which this group of players decided to approach the game, to do what was right, to accept responsibility, and to focus on what mattered most is what impressed me. The planning, the travel, the hotel, the media, the glitz—all of the things that could have gotten us off track didn't. Because of that, we are 6–2.

Then again, we were 6–2 last year.

Can we finish in 2007?

NINE

• • • • • •

If you think you are at the end of your rope, get some more rope.

—RICK MURRAY

WE ARE MIDWAY THROUGH THE SEASON, AND SOME OF THE QUES-tions we carried into training camp have still not been answered. Our kicking game, snapper-holder-kicker, is still not a smooth machine. Aaron Ross is playing well for a rookie, but what about down the stretch? And we are still worried about the health of Plaxico Burress. Plaxico isn't practicing at all, so the only time he has with Eli is on the field right before games.

We had a bye week after Miami, so the players had off Wednesday through Sunday, while the coaches took Saturday and Sunday off. In practice on Tuesday, we don't look ahead to Dallas the following week, but rather work on situations that need our attention: red and green zones, third downs, two-minute drills.

I know that we've improved since we were beaten by the Dallas Cowboys in our opener, 45–35. At the same time, we are more humble. Apparently before the first Dallas game Brandon Jacobs said that we were going to "whup their butt," and I know he won't be saying that now. In preparation for this rematch, the coaching staff studies tape of our first game against Dallas, plus the Cowboys' last four games. They, too, have improved, and Tony Romo is playing awfully well.

It doesn't take long for us to understand that. Under four minutes into the game, in fact, Romo hits Tony Curtis on a 15-yard touchdown pass. Another early deficit for us. But on our ensuing possession, Eli shows his poise and maturity and leads us on an eight-play, 67-yard drive that results in a Jeremy Shockey touchdown, one of twelve catches by Shockey on the day. We are aided on the drive by three Dallas penalties, including an unnecessary-roughness call against Bradie James. After Lawrence Tynes kicks a 40-yard field goal, leaving just one second remaining on the clock, we are tied at 17 at halftime.

Like I am during every game, I'm active in every aspect of offense, defense, and special teams. Any decisions related to strategy, time-outs, critical run/pass calls, four-down territory, kickoffs, and personnel are all on me. I typically do not get involved in the actual play calling, but I do listen in on the headset. I believe this is our game to win.

Terrell Owens and Tony Romo have other ideas. We go three and out on our opening possession of the second half and the Cowboys strike, scoring on a seven-minute drive covering 86 yards. On 1st and 10 from our 25, Romo hits a streaking Owens down the right side for a touchdown. After Lawrence kicks another field goal to pull us to within four, Romo and Owens hook up again, this time on a 50-yarder right down the middle of the field with 10:58 to play in the game. It is 31–20 and that is the end of the scoring.

"We were our own worst enemy," I admit to the team and the press after the game. Turnovers (two), penalties (eight), coverage breakdowns, and mental errors killed us. In fact, we had three delay-of-game penalties, for which I take responsibility. Plus a Brandon Jacobs touchdown run was nullified by a holding penalty early in the fourth quarter; we had to settle for a field goal. The Cowboys only rushed for 80 yards, but they threw for 243, and that was a difference. And the turnovers. And the penalties. In two games against Dallas, we have given up 76 points.

We have to put this one behind us quickly and move on, but the media continue to dwell on the loss. They are critical of Eli's performance and his apparent lack of emotion. They are quick to condemn the three delay-of-game penalties, and they are happy to remind the world of our 2006 collapse. We make no references to 2006 in any of our team meetings, in the locker room or on the practice field.

We won't panic.

I have a chance to talk to Eli during the week about ways in which he could improve. He knows how to handle the critics and the media. As for the delay-of-game penalties, those should never happen, so that week in practice we use a thirty-five-second play clock during many of our scripted periods. It's not always the quarterback's fault when you are penalized with a delay-of-game call. It could be that a player is late getting back to the huddle, the QB gets the play late from the coaches, or the wrong personnel are on the field for a particular play call.

We play Detroit on the road the following Sunday, in a game that could go a long way toward determining our play-off chances. Detroit is 6–3, and their home crowd can be loud inside Ford Field. I am also concerned about special teams, as the Lions have an innate ability to block field goal attempts and pressure the punter. On defense, we want to force multiple turnovers, especially by quarterback Jon Kitna; on offense, the focus is on tempo. We don't want any delay-of-game penalties.

"Up-tempo," I remind them on Saturday night in Detroit. "Hustle in and out of the huddle. Run to the line of scrimmage. All eleven of you on offense need to be responsible for the tempo and the forty-second play clock."

Then I offer the quote for the night: "The ultimate evaluation of a man is not that he gets knocked down, it's what he does after he gets knocked down — he gets back up with a greater purpose and is a greater fighter than before!"

AS IT TURNS OUT, WE don't have a delay-of-game penalty on Sunday, but we do have an illegal substitution, an illegal formation, an offensive holding, and a false start in the first half alone. Despite the penalties, our defense plays great, holding Detroit to just ten points—three points for the first 55 minutes of the game. Safety James Butler comes up big to get a pick, and with under a minute to go, Sam Madison grabs another interception, one of three thrown by Jon Kitna. Lawrence Tynes is three for three on field goals. We win, 16–10, and hold a two-game lead in the NFC wild-card race over Detroit.

The victory is soured by the loss of Mathias Kiwanuka and possibly that of Brandon Jacobs, who pulls a hamstring. On the second play of the game, Mathias breaks his fibula. This is incredibly frustrating, especially because he's been playing so well after switching positions in the off-season. With him, Osi, Michael, and Justin on the field at the same time, especially on third down, we present a pass rush force that is very difficult to outscheme, as opponents cannot double-team all of our players. We are forced to shift some hopes onto the shoulders of Reggie Torbor. Much to his credit, against the Lions he steps in and plays well.

SOMETIMES THERE IS JUST NO foreseeing a collapse. Such is the case on November 25 at Giants Stadium. The 4–6 Minnesota Vikings, who came into Giants Stadium two years earlier and took the ball away five times in winning 24–21, have the worst pass defense in the NFL but the top-ranked run defense, so it makes sense that we are going to throw the football. We aim for 50 percent or better on third-down conversions. On defense, we want to stay alert for play action passes and gadget plays, as they had run on their opening series against Oakland the week before.

"I am a member of a team, and I rely on the team," says soccer great Mia Hamm. "I defer to it and sacrifice for it, because the team, not the individual, is the ultimate champion."

The great former football player Jack Youngblood: "You learn that whatever you are doing in life, obstacles don't matter very much. Pain or other circumstances can be there, but if you want to do a job bad enough, you'll find a way to get it done." I do not know at the time how prophetic those words are.

In the game against Minnesota, we do throw the ball—just not always to guys in our jerseys. Late in the first quarter, with the score tied at seven, Jeremy and Eli miscommunicate on a hot read and Darren Sharper picks off the pass. (A hot read comes about quickly when the tight end and quarterback adjust the route for a quick pass when they recognize there are more defenders than available blockers.) In the second quarter, now trailing 14–7, Eli backs up, deep in our own territory, and throws off target to Plaxico. Safety Dwight Smith intercepts the pass and returns it to our 8-yard line. Early in the fourth quarter, with us now down 27–10, Eli has a wide-open Jeremy Shockey for a touchdown, but the ball is tipped at the line of scrimmage by Ray Edwards and deflects to Dwight Smith, who runs it back 93 yards for a touchdown. Just 42 seconds later, Eli again tries to get the ball to Shockey, but linebacker Chad Greenway steps in front and runs it back 37 yards for a touchdown. The final is 41–17.

We had more first downs, better third-down efficiency, more net yards of offense, one fewer punt, just one more penalty, and the time of possession was even. You've got to love statistics. The ones we didn't love are in Eli's stat line: 21/49, 273 yards, 1 TD, 4 INT, QB rating 33.8—clearly, one of his worst days as a professional. Three of those interceptions were returned for touchdowns. At halftime, when we trailed 24–7, the boos were as loud as I have ever heard. I will remember that forever. Even when we trailed late, I didn't sit Eli on the bench. What kind of message would that send to Eli and his teammates?

In the locker room after the game, we get on our knees to pray.

"We are all in this together," I say. "We won't stop being together now because of this."

Good, bad, whatever—this season, this group, is sticking together. Still, it is never easy to lose, and in the postgame media session, it is clear I am upset.

"I wish there was some simple explanation for this game, but there isn't," I say to open the press conference. "We played very, very poorly. In the National Football League, you obviously cannot wrap it up and hand it to the guy across the field, and we did. I did not, in my worst moment, ever think that I would be standing here talking about history repeating itself, but it did." I conclude the statement with, "There is no excuse for today and there is no explanation for it, and I started the year off with 'Talk Is Cheap, Play the Game,' and obviously there is not a lot to talk about here."

The week is the same: working on getting better, answering questions and criticisms. We are 7–4 and head to Chicago to play a team that was in the Super Bowl back in January. They have suffered some injuries but still possess a tenacious defense, and the game will be played on a dark, cold, wet Chicago night. We know they have a tendency to turn the ball over, so we need to get after it. Devin Hester is the most explosive kick returner playing today in the NFL, maybe in history. In the days leading up to the Sunday showdown, we work with the punt and kick teams on kicking the ball away from Hester. We have already decided to punt the ball out of bounds rather than have him run one back on us.

The message to the team is clear: we need to get back up with a greater purpose after being knocked down by the Vikings. Rick Murray had a greater purpose.

EVERY NOW AND THEN, WE come across someone in our lives who makes an impact, someone who inspires us by the way he lives—and perhaps, sad to say, by the way he dies. Rick Murray was one of those people who taught me that getting knocked down does not mean getting knocked out.

Every summer, our four children, and their spouses and children join Judy and I on a relaxing summer vacation. We take turns picking the destination and plan the trip on a rotating basis. In our sixth summer in Jacksonville it was my turn to pick, and I thought it would be great to return to the land of our ancestors. Cormac O'Riordan is a popular world history teacher from County Cork, Ireland, at the Bolles School in Jacksonville, where our two youngest children, Brian and Katie, attended high school. Cormac was putting together an educational tour of his home country, and I decided the whole Coughlin clan would venture across the sea.

The ten-day excursion took us all around the south of Ireland. Our group numbered close to twenty-five, composed of six or so families. One family on the trip was the Murrays also from Jacksonville: Rick, a retired commander in the U.S. Navy; his wife, Sherry; their son, Mark, who was a student at Bolles; and Mark's girlfriend. As the trip commenced and we began to get to know one another, I discovered that Rick was always talking football and knew an incredible amount about our team and the NFL. As we spent more time together, I realized he was much more than a football fan. He rode a Harley-Davidson across the prairie, played tennis, loved the Naval Academy in Annapolis, and was a lifelong Navy fighter pilot. And he also had his spirited side, evident when he and my two sons hopped over the bar in a small Irish hotel and started pouring Guinness when no bartender was in sight.

On the last night of the trip, Rick and Cormac put together a wonderful farewell dinner in Killarney. Rick was the master of ceremonies and said the nicest things about everybody, including the Coughlin family. By the end of the trip, he had become a good friend. It was sad to say good-bye to our new friends, but we promised to stay in touch.

In the following months, Cormac and others who had been on the trip told Judy and me that Rick suffers from amyotrophic lateral sclerosis (ALS), also known as Lou Gehrig's disease. The normal life expectancy is three years after diagnosis. Rick was never shy about his disease and would often speak at public events to raise awareness, including on Lou Gehrig Day at the Jacksonville Suns minor-league baseball park. He also lobbied Congress to increase funding for research on ALS. We both lived in Jacksonville and we stayed in touch through visits and phone calls. He always had a great sense of timing, a knack for getting in touch with me right when I needed a lift.

When we moved to New York in 2004, Rick could no longer walk and was in a wheelchair but had full use of his mind and speech. As the disease progressed, Rick became more frail, and he spent his days in bed or in a wheelchair with a breathing tube through his nostrils. Frustration set in when he could no longer talk. He had a small computer and a television near his bed, and he loved keeping up with the latest news in the world and in the NFL. E-mail was his new method of communication. Rick also published a book full of the lessons of life that he had learned, entitled *Rick's Reflections.* Among them is this: "If you think you are at the end of your rope, get some more rope!" Many of his friends used the rallying cry, "Don't ever quit—Rick won't."

By June 2007, Rick Murray had survived seven years with ALS, but finally he lost the battle on June 13. He never gave in to the disease. The burial was at Arlington National Cemetery. Even though I was consumed with preparing for the season, it hit me hard. He was so full of wisdom, so positive in his approach to life despite the terrible disease he was forced to endure. The man's spirit moved people. Rick showed me that when the odds are against you, when you are knocked to the ground, you don't stay down—you get up and fight. And that's just what we will do in Chicago.

IT HAS BEEN RAINING IN Chicago all day, and the grounds crew struggles just to get the sidelines in good enough shape to stand on. The rain breaks for a while but begins again shortly after kickoff and becomes heavy in a short period of time. After a nice kickoff return by Reuben Droughns gives us the ball at our 38, Eli hits Plaxico for 12 yards and Derrick Ward picks up 19 more on successive runs. But on 1st and 10 from the Chicago 31, Eli's pass, intended for Jeremy Shockey, is picked off by Brian Urlacher at the 20-yard line. Yet another turnover, this one in the green zone.

Chicago QB Rex Grossman, who himself has heard his share of criticism, promptly drives the Bears 79 yards and finds Desmond Clark on a 1-yard touchdown pass. I guess it just wouldn't be the 2007 Giants if we didn't trail early. The teams trade punts on four straight possessions. On the last one, David Tyree breaks free and gets a piece of the ball and it only travels 31 yards to give us great field position at the Chicago 32. On the very next play, Derrick scampers 31 yards down to the Chicago 1. Lovie Smith challenges the ruling, insisting that Derrick stepped out of bounds, but the call is upheld. Three plays later Derrick scores five minutes into the second quarter. By halftime, we trail 13–7, as we forced the Bears to settle for two field goals when they had the ball on our 17- and 28-yard lines in the second quarter.

Our backs are against the wall, and we need to dig down deep.

"The most important play in the game is the next one," I tell the team in the locker room at halftime. A football cliché, for sure, but appropriate nonetheless.

It would be fair to say that up until this point, we haven't had a very good offensive game. We've fumbled the ball once and Eli has been picked off once. But the team never looks back, Eli included. The only scoring in the third quarter comes on a Bears field goal by Robbie Gould. Starting on our second possession of the fourth quarter, we make the decision to go rally, which is no huddle outside of two minutes. On 3rd and 2 from Chicago's 27, Derrick picks up 4 yards for a first down but is injured on the play. We don't know how severe an injury it is. Soon after, as we're facing a 3rd and 6 from Chicago's 6 after starting on our own 25, Amani Toomer makes a remarkable diving catch in the end zone for a touchdown.

But wait: the officials rule it incomplete.

Our coaches upstairs quickly watch a replay and call down that we should challenge. After much discussion, the head referee, Walt Coleman, overturns the ruling on the field and we are back in business, trailing just 16–14 with under seven minutes remaining.

The defense stops the Bears on three straight plays and forces them to punt on 4th and 12 from their own 38. Eli confidently jogs out on the field, into the cold, wet night and leads a drive that helps propel our season. Running without a huddle, Eli marches the offense downfield. At one point, the drive is saved by Reuben Droughns recovering his own fumble at our own 40; at another, Chicago begins to use their time-outs, sensing that we are on our way to the end zone. During the last drive, David Tyree's perseverance as receiver comes through as he makes two huge catches to keep the drive going. Then, on 2nd and 10 from Chicago's 17, Eli hits

Plaxico to take us down to the Bears' 2-yard line. The replay booth upholds the catch. So we have 1st and Goal on the 2 with just over 1:30 left.

Now, some coaches—take me, for example—believe that on 1st and Goal, you call plays to score in this situation and don't concern yourself with how much time you will leave for your opponent. Other coaches would have purposely used more clock so that after a score—if you do score—the opponent doesn't have much time to work with. Chicago has the number one goal line defense in the NFL, and in the third quarter it took us three plays to score from the 1! It was foolish for me to think that we could dictate when we wanted to score. We go for it and Reuben scores with 1:37 remaining to give us our first lead, 21–16. Now we have to kick to Devin Hester. He returns the kick 19 yards to give Chicago good field position at their own 41. There is 1:28 on the clock. Playing out of a no-huddle offense in shotgun formation, Rex Grossman tries to move his team downfield. He faces a 4th and 15 with the game on the line. He hits Muhsin Muhammad on a 20-yard pass play and immediately calls time out. The Bears now have 1st and 10 from our 28. We had the game in our hands and let them remain alive. But we don't panic. We keep an eye on the next play. A field goal doesn't help them; they need a touchdown. Grossman's next three passes fall incomplete and time runs out. We've won on two fourth-quarter touchdown drives.

Bouncing back from the Minnesota loss is just as important as winning at Washington was following the 0–2 start; it shows the resiliency of this team. I told the team at the midway point of the season that I believe ten wins will get us into the play-offs; now we have eight, with four games left: Philadelphia, Washington, Buffalo, and New England. So after all our ups and downs, we are knocking on the door.

PLAYING IN PHILADELPHIA IS NEVER easy. It is tough to find a more vocal fan base, and it is always difficult for visitors to win. You walk out onto the field before kickoff and the verbal spears being thrown at you are hard to ignore.

The Eagles are very good on third down, so we make it a point of emphasis during the week to buckle down on defense on those conversion attempts. We also want to challenge their wide receivers on every play. Offensively, staying with blocks, handling the defensive pressure and the blitz, and, of course, finishing drives seem the keys to victory number nine.

Top kick returner and running back Brian Westbrook is back on the field for the Eagles, healthy and ready to go; Westbrook didn't play in our first meeting. He scores on an 18-yard pass from Donovan McNabb to give the Eagles a lead just over three minutes into the game. But Lawrence Tynes kicks two of his three field goals in the second quarter, and we are right in this game. We fumble the ball to start the second half, and Philadelphia kicker David Akers makes us pay with three points. Later in the third quarter, Eli recognizes an all-out blitz and throws a perfect pass to Plaxico for a touchdown, and the game is 16–10 Giants heading into the fourth quarter. Akers kicks another field goal with 8:31 left, and it is clear the game will come down to the very last minutes. Starting at his own 11, McNabb hits Reggie Brown, Greg Lewis, and then Brown again to cover 50 yards in forty-one seconds to set up a 57-yard field goal attempt by Akers with five seconds left. I am thinking, *There is no way Andy Reid really believes his guy is going to make a 57-yard kick, does he?* The snap and hold are good, and Akers just drills it. The ball explodes off his foot. The ball might have gone 10 yards past the goal posts, which is extraordinary. But it doesn't. It hits the right upright midway up and falls to the ground. And we win.

"Nine and four, baby, nine and four!" This is all I can muster to begin my postgame speech. "Great heart, great heart. We played our asses off and we never thought of anything but to win, and we kept playing and we got it done. There were all kinds of obstacles out there and you overcame every one of them."

We were knocked down by Dallas. We were knocked cold by Minnesota. But we rose to our feet in a big way against Chicago and now against Philadelphia. We haven't collapsed, like so many people believed we would. We got up with greater purpose in our hearts. We have three games to play and need to win one to reach the magic number ten.

Washington at home, Buffalo on the road, and the undefeated New England Patriots in Giants Stadium to close the regular season. Will we get one?

TEN

· · · · ·

There will come a time when you believe everything is finished.
That will be the beginning.

—LOUIS L'AMOUR

WITH A WIN AT HOME AGAINST WASHINGTON, WE WILL CLINCH A third straight play-off berth, so as I have continued to do throughout the season, I let the team know matter-of-factly where we stand. Win, we're in. I know the questions about the play-offs will be coming from reporters, so in Wednesday's meeting with the team we talk about it and afterward, I don't want to hear another word about it. We have one game to worry about.

Then, all of a sudden, we have something else to worry about. Saturday night looks like it is going to be a normal pregame night, but unfortunately it turns out to be a far cry from that. As the offense and defense meet in the hotel, Charles Way receives a call from Leilah Tyree, David's wife. David's mother, Thelma, has died unexpectedly in Florida. Leilah insists that she be the one to tell David, so after Charles informs me, we have no choice but to wait for her to arrive.

Here I am, standing before the team, including David, knowing what I know. My heart is empty and I am sure I am a bit flustered as I talk about finishing strong. I show them a picture of Greg Gadson, reminding them that we initially met our new teammate before the first Washington game—the goal line stand. As the highlight video plays, Charles comes into the meeting room to get David; Leilah has arrived.

When the meeting is over, many of us walk outside the room. David is sitting in a chair by the elevators and can't hold back his emotions. He is in shock, sobbing uncontrollably. We take turns holding him, hanging on to his arm. As word spreads among the players, one by one they come over and embrace David. One of our chaplains, George McGovern, goes home with David and Leilah. David would miss the next two games, with memorial services for his mother being conducted in Florida and New Jersey.

Despite the tragedy, the players have regained their focus Sunday morning, and many of them want to win for David. Todd Collins will be making his first start in ten years as the quarterback for Washington, with an injured Jason Campbell watching from the sidelines.

Strong gusts of wind play a role. In fact, gusts up to 55 mph took down our practice bubble outside the stadium on Sunday morning and averaged between 20 and 30 mph during the game. Yet Eli throws the ball a lot, mostly because we were playing catch-up. Our receivers drop twelve balls, five of them by Brandon Jacobs. Our rush defense, which has been playing well as of late, allows Clinton Portis to rush for 126 yards. We trail at halftime, 16–3. Jeremy Shockey breaks his fibula in the third quarter. There will be no comeback on this day. Eli throws a TD pass to Kevin Boss late in the game to cut the lead to twelve, but we lose, 22–10.

Our season hangs in the balance. What do I say to the players? How do I react after a poor performance with so much on the line? I am disappointed. This game, at home against a team without its starting quarterback, was our best chance to seal a play-off spot, and we let it go. In past years, I would have exploded. But this year is different. This year *I* need to be different. In a calm but authoritative voice, I lay out for the team what we have to do. We have to go on the road and win at Buffalo because common sense tells us we have a better shot at defeating Buffalo than at the New England Patriots, who are 14–0. We have won nine games, and to get into the play-offs, we had better settle it now. I don't explode. I don't point fingers. I stay true to the way I have approached the team all season long.

As for the loss of Jeremy, I am concerned. First of all, I'm concerned for his well-being because of the severity of the injury. He knew when the trainers came onto the field that it was broken. He is a strong football player, so for him to be injured takes a great deal of force. My second concern is for the future and whether or not rookie Kevin Boss will be able to fill in on a regular basis. During the season, Kevin added ten pounds of muscle weight and slowly began to be utilized in multiple tight end formations, but he has yet to be asked to be the starter.

Daunting as the task at hand might seem, playing on the road is no obstacle for us based on our results in 2007. Heading to Buffalo, we have won six of seven road games and have been nicknamed "Road Warriors." We seem to relish the challenge of going into a hostile environment and relying solely on one another. Perhaps it is because we only have each other; perhaps it is focus born of the challenge of staring down the opposition, the crowd, and the score.

Buffalo is 7–7 but has played much better than their record would indicate. Their coach, Dick Jauron, is a good friend whom I first got to know in Green Bay and later Dick was our first defensive coordinator in Jacksonville. The Bills lost to Denver at home 15–14 to open the season, and weeks later they lost to Dallas at home in a miraculous comeback by the Cowboys, who scored late, recovered the onside kick, and won the game on an ensuing field goal. We were taking nothing for granted.

Buffalo will be another tough road test, and in late December in western New York on Lake Erie, you are almost assured of bad weather.

Despite the forecast in Buffalo, the weather in New Jersey is a balmy 40 degrees with plenty of sunshine, so we have a solid week of practice.

As we board the buses at Giants Stadium for the ride to the airport on Saturday afternoon, two players are late: Plaxico Burress and Gibril Wilson. From the time we jogged off the practice field at 11:20, Plaxico and Gibril had almost fifty minutes to be on the bus on time. Despite their play this season, despite the newfound togetherness of this team, and despite my new openness toward the players, rules arc rules. On Monday, after the game, the players are fined. I don't fine players; players fine themselves. They are not happy, but their teammates realize it is team above self. But unlike in previous years, when a few voices might have cracked the team, when all is said and done, the sum understands why the parts are fined.

On Saturday night in our team meeting after we arrive in Buffalo, we review the keys to victory. In addition to the usual—no turnovers and stop the run—there are keys unique to Buffalo. They are physical and play great on special teams. We have to punt the ball deep and out of bounds to avoid the dangerous Roscoe Parrish. We have to harass and contain QB Trent Edwards. We have to get red zone stops and scores in the green zone. And we have to produce superior execution.

The season is riding on it.

DRIVING RAIN, SLEET, ICE, SNOW, 50-mph wind gusts—it is some of the craziest weather I have ever experienced during a game. At kickoff, it is 52 degrees, but the temperature drops to the low thirties midway through. It feels like the ice and sleet are coming from the ground and not from the sky. The wind is so ferocious that both teams can only throw the ball in one direction.

The Bills jump out to a 14–0 lead, scoring through the air on their first two possessions. We don't score until the second quarter, after Chase Blackburn recovers a fumble by Bills punter Brian Moorman on their 23-yard line, giving us great field position. Brandon Jacobs runs it in a few plays later, and we are down by just a touchdown. After we hold Buffalo on downs, we get the ball back and can't do much with it, but are fortunate when Buffalo's Donte Whitner is called for roughing Jeff Feagles, giving us a first down from Buffalo's 43 with 8:41 in the half. The very next snap, the right side of our line, anchored by the talented tandem of Chris Snee and Kareem McKenzie, creates a hole for Brandon. Shaun O'Hara again takes care of his assignment, and the always tough

Rich Seubert pulls from the left side. David Diehl, who covered the backside as if he had been playing left tackle for years, protects from behind as Madison Hedgecock leads the way. Brandon runs forty-three yards for a touchdown to tie the game, a credit to the offensive line, whose personalities compliment one another.

Lawrence Tynes kicks a field goal with 2:40 remaining to give us the halftime lead, 17–14.

The precipitation and strong wind play a huge role in what both teams do in the second half. When you have the wind at your back, you'd better put points on the board. And you'd better be careful when throwing the ball. On our very first play of the second half, Eli attempts to hit Plaxico but is picked off by Keith Ellison, who returns the ball to our 31. Two plays later, Marshawn Lynch scores to give Buffalo the lead back. We have the ball going against the wind so this time we run. Then we run some more. We chew up over eight minutes of game clock and move the ball down to Buffalo's 1-yard line. Reuben Droughns is tackled for a loss on 4th and 1. Even so, I don't regret the decision to try for a touchdown. I want to send a message to our team, which just produced a clutch drive. We chewed up over nine minutes on the drive, which kept the ball out of Buffalo's hands in a quarter in which they scored no points with the wind at their backs.

Early in the fourth quarter, with Buffalo facing the wind, Kawika Mitchell intercepts a Trent Edwards pass intended for Lee Evans at Buffalo's 20-yard line and runs it in for a score. 24–21 Giants. After the teams trade three punts, Eli is intercepted by Terrence McGee at midfield. But our defense picks him up by forcing another Buffalo punt, pinning us on our 12 with just over six minutes left. Eli takes the first snap, turns to his right, and gives the ball to seventh-round pick Ahmad Bradshaw. Ahmad explodes through a hole and doesn't stop running until he reaches the end zone. The 88-yard run is the third longest in Giants history. Two plays later, Corey Webster intercepts Edwards and runs it back for a score. The eventual final is 38–21, and we are on our way to the postseason. I am showered two different times with icy Gatorade after the final whistle.

Strange a game as it was, this is a thrilling win. We won a major test under horrible conditions. The weather was so bad, we chose to pass the ball just three times the entire second half. But the fundamental values that we believe in—"Talk Is Cheap—Play the Game!" and "No Toughness, No Championship"—have never rung more true than they do today. With the win, we know that we are in the play-offs. We will play the Tampa Bay Buccaneers. But first, our regular-season finale is against the New England Patriots, who by the end of the night are 15–0. On the plane ride back from Buffalo, as I sit among our players, I start to think about how we'll have to be at our best to win. And being at our best means playing our starters. By Monday afternoon, I am convinced. You play to win the game. You fight until the last breath, and you show courage in the face of adversity.

ELEVEN

● ● ● ● ● ● ● ● ●

To every man there comes in his lifetime that special moment when
he is figuratively tapped on the shoulder and offered the chance to do a
very special thing, unique to him and fitted to his talents. What a tragedy
if that moment finds him unprepared or unqualified for the
work which could be his finest hour.

— WINSTON CHURCHILL

EVERYONE IS CALLING FOR TICKETS, AND I MEAN EVERYONE: FAM-
ily, friends, former teachers, and relatives we did not know we had.
It turns out our last game of the regular season is a pretty popular one.
The mighty New England Patriots are coming to town with a 15–0
record, and football immortality is on the line. The game is so big the television networks decide to share the game which, in this league, doesn't
happen too often. The Patriots are a draw, but in a way, so are the New
York Giants. By that late December day, we are 10–5 and the play-off
picture for us is set. But a question remains: With no play-off position
to play for, should we risk injury to our starters and play them? Should
we concede the football game to the Patriots and to history? Now, many

coaches in the NFL bench their star players in the same situation. Yes, it is a bit unusual to have an undefeated team as an opponent. Even so, it is a difficult decision. It becomes clear that the media and fans care more about a play-off game and therefore don't want our first-teamers to play. But I feel differently.

The game against New England is on a Saturday night, so we have one less preparation day during the week. That means that Christmas Eve and Christmas will have to be workdays for the coaches and the players. I already have discussed the matter with the veterans and the Leadership Council, explaining my reasoning about why we must work on Christmas Day. We did set the schedule so meetings wouldn't start until early afternoon.

"Merry *&%#$@ Christmas" is the players' Tuesday greeting for me when I start the team meeting, a stunt orchestrated by Antonio Pierce. This team has earned the right to have fun, and I have earned the right to take it in stride. They don't want to be in here working on Christmas as their families gather together, and neither do I, but we all understand why. Working on holidays through the years has never been easy, especially for Judy and the kids.

IT IS SAFE TO SAY that Judy and I do not have a typical marriage. Not because of how we treat each other, but because of how little we see each other. For a great part of our marriage, we have just a handful of hours, once a week, to sit with each other and talk. She runs the household, I coach football. For the first ten or fifteen years of our marriage, she really never shared the burdens and issues taking place at home, and I guess I just assumed we were like the Brady Bunch all of those years. I figured that we had great kids and I knew they would make it to baseball practice on time, would be decent students, and wouldn't give Judy much trouble. I have since learned that things were never that easy.

Now at this stage in our lives, we share a true partnership. Our duties and responsibilities within the family are clear, but as the forty-one years have gone by, we have grown closer. We have shared in the joys of watching our children grow, succeed in their careers, and marry wonderful people. We have been blessed with five grandchildren and have another on the way. It may not be a typical marriage, but I like to think that our commitment to each other and to our family is, in its own way, extraordinary. Judy was given a plaque back in the mid-1970s that read, "We interrupt this marriage to bring you the football season." How appropriate.

Discipline, morality, and integrity are all things that Judy and I cherish and strive to represent. Our faith, our belief in a Higher Power, guides us through our daily lives and we always try to show compassion and understanding for others. They are values we hope we have passed on to our children. A football coaching career does not always lend itself to a close father-child bond, but I am proud of the relationships I have with our four children. Whether it was cleaning out the garage or getting ice cream from the ice cream truck, the moments were always cherished.

I like to think that Judy and I have not changed over the years. I like to think that we still have our priorities straight. For a good portion of our marriage we did not have a lot of money, and I think it's telling that we haven't changed our approach to life now that we have more than most. Our kids, too, will tell you the value of hard work and family, and for that I give all of the credit in the world to Judy. She has been my life partner and raised four wonderful kids, mostly on her own—while moving every few years.

So she understands when, on Christmas Day, I leave the family to drive to work.

HERE WE ALL ARE ON Christmas Day, gathered for our team meeting to begin our preparation for the Patriots. I know what the plan is, and it has nothing to do with conceding.

"We are going to play our starters and we are going to play to win this football game," I bellow to the players and assistants seated before me. "We will gauge our team against supposedly one of the best teams in the history of the league."

To my mind, we have worked too hard, come too far, not to play our best. The players are behind the decision. Antonio Pierce, for one, is forceful in his opinion that we play to win. Besides, how am I supposed to sit starters for fear of injuries? What does that say about everyone else? That *they* are expendable?

Our theme for the week is "High Energy, Extreme Focus, and Great Competition." We have a great opportunity to play a football game against the best of the best. And we have everything to gain and nothing to lose. I tell our guys that. This is a game all about positives for us. This is a historic game for the National Football League. A team is looking to go 16–0, yes, but how will history record *our* team and *our* effort? Why not us?

Of course, not everyone is happy with my decision to play our starters. Tampa Bay coach Jon Gruden, the head coach of our first-round play-off opponent, doesn't play his starters the last *two* weeks of the season to get them rest and to avoid possible injuries, and there are those in the New York media who criticize my decision. It is *the* hot topic on the regional sports radio stations, I am told. No matter, we will do what we believe is right and what I have always done throughout my career: we will compete on every play of every game.

We have already played the Patriots this season, at the end of the preseason, but neither team played their starters the whole game and New England didn't even dress Tom Brady. You don't get to 15-0 by being deficient in any one area of the game. They possess so many weapons on offense, like Brady, Randy Moss, Wes Welker, Donté Stall-worth, Kevin Faulk, and Laurence Maroney, and they love to use four wide receiver sets. On defense, Asante Samuel, Rodney Harrison, Richard Seymour, Tedy Bruschi, Junior Seau, Vince Wilfork, and Mike Vrabel lead the way. Beating the Patriots would not be easy, but we identify some specifics that we believe can lead us to victory.

On defense, we need to be both opportunistic and disciplined. In New England's win at Baltimore on December 3, they converted two fourth downs on defensive penalties on the game-winning drive. We also must get pressure and hits on Brady and challenge his receivers on every play. On offense, it goes back to our weekly goal, scoring in the green zone and winning the battle up front, which in turn will allow us to chew clock and convert third downs. Of course, turnovers will be crucial. I point out to the players that the Patriots were a mediocre 11–12 in the last five seasons when they lost the turnover battle.

The night prior to game day, our video staff shows the team great plays from the Buffalo win, but they add something else. They show clips from 1998, when a 13–0 Denver Broncos team came into New York and lost to the Giants late in the season. The montage is preceded by the words "Why Not Us?"

I again reveal the quote I used before the Miami game: "The people who excel are those who are driven to show the world and prove to themselves just how good they are." This was another chance to do just that.

And this one, from the great Winston Churchill:

> To every man comes in his lifetime a special moment when he is tapped on the shoulder and offered a very special job, fitting and unique to his talents. What a shame and tragedy if that moment finds him unprepared or unqualified for the work.

ON SATURDAY, WHEN WE ARRIVE at Giants Stadium, the parking lots are jammed and the festivities are under way. Inside the stadium, while I walk the field during team stretch, I can sense a new excitement in the air from our fans. Whether or not they wanted us to play to win earlier in the week, they all now want to win as badly as we do, and they will do whatever they can to help.

We win the coin toss and elect to receive. Brandon Jacobs gets the call on the first play from scrimmage, and on the second Eli drops back and hits Plaxico in stride for a 52-yard catch, setting up 1st and 10 at New England's 18. Just under four minutes in, Eli finds Brandon out of the backfield for a touchdown, and we are leading the game in the first quarter—a welcome change for us. The drive took seven plays, covered 74 yards, and took just over four minutes. It gives our offense confidence that we can move the ball against the great New England defense.

New England responds with an eleven-play drive in which Brady throws the ball eight times, but our defense holds on 3rd and 8 from our

19, forcing New England to settle for a field goal. After we punt on the next possession, New England starts with great field position at midfield, and Brady hits Moss on a short touchdown pass on the first play of the second quarter. Moss is so excited that he is flagged for unsportsmanlike conduct after the catch.

But of course, we have taken body blows before in 2007, and in most cases we have responded. On this night, Domenik Hixon responds in a big way. He runs the kickoff back 74 yards for a touchdown on a very well-executed return and we find ourselves ahead again, this time, 14–10.

New England kicker Stephen Gostkowski kicks two field goals later in the second quarter, and the Pats lead 16–14. Eli and the offense have 1st and 10 on our 15 with 1:54 remaining in the half. Working in our two-minute offense, out of the shotgun and in no huddle, Eli finds Kevin Boss on a 23-yard pass play to move the ball up to the 28. In fact, Boss, now the starting tight end, has a huge game. But on the play, center Shaun O'Hara is injured and comes out of the game, to be replaced by Grey Ruegamer. Eli manages the clock, the time-outs, and the field superbly, and with eighteen seconds left he connects with Kevin again, this time on a 3-yard touchdown. We go into halftime leading the undefeated Patriots, 21–16.

At halftime, the locker room is upbeat, as you might expect, and we emphasize that we have momentum on our side, having just scored before the break. "We expected to be ahead, and we expect to win the game," I remind the players before we head out to the field. "We kick off, so let's get a stop and score again."

And that's just what we do. The Pats pick up just three yards on three downs and are forced to punt on the opening drive. We then drive down the field from our own 40 and score as Eli rolls out to his right, pump-fakes, and throws a 19-yard touchdown pass to Plaxico, who somehow manages to drag his feet in bounds on the right side of the end zone. The crowd in Giants Stadium is louder than they have been all season, as we now lead by twelve, 28–16.

Though we are excited, we know how quickly Tom Brady can strike. He marches them down the field with his arm, but it is the legs of Laurence Maroney that carry them to seven points, running in from the 6-yard line. Our offense, which was exceptional the first half, sputters after Plaxico's touchdown, and we punt on two straight possessions. We simply wanted to do something with the ball to take time off the clock, but we couldn't. New England, meanwhile, wastes little time early in the fourth when Brady hits Moss for 65 yards and a TD. The Pats go for two and convert, retaking the lead, 31–28.

The next time Eli stands over center, we are in a hole. On the ensuing kickoff by the Pats, Amani Toomer is flagged for a personal foul, costing us 15 yards. Amani is on the sideline when a Patriots player gets knocked to the ground near our bench. When he gets up to return to his sideline, he trips—on his own—but an official believes Amani has tripped him on purpose. The official who throws the flag doesn't even see the play. The penalty backs us up from the 38 to the 23. I am furious at the call, and the old Tom makes a brief appearance as I let the ref know my feelings. Two plays later, Amani is called for offensive holding, costing us another 10. And then, on 2nd and 6 from our 27, Eli tries to hit Plaxico again, deep on the right, but is picked off by Ellis Hobbs.

Nothing but positives will come from this game. This game was ours just minutes ago. Can we regroup? Starting from midfield, the Patriots drive 52 yards, Maroney runs the ball in from 5 yards out, and suddenly we are down 38–28 with just over four and a half minutes to play. Though I am disappointed, I am confident that Eli will bring our team back. He spreads the ball to Steve Smith, Brandon Jacobs, and David Tyree and even scrambles for 2 yards to put us at 3rd and 3 on New England's 3 with 1:03 left. Eli dumps the ball to Plaxico, who scores. The score is 38–35.

Everyone in the stadium knows what is coming next. We do, the Pats do, the referees do, the fans do. So Lawrence Tynes lines up to try an onside kick. The ball doesn't pop high enough, and Mike Vrabel smothers it on the ground. After Brady takes a knee, I use our last time-out, but the game is essentially over.

In the postgame locker room, we are positive and proud, although we take no solace in playing well and losing. We hate to lose, but we have proven something to ourselves—that we can play with the best. We were able to drive the ball down the field and score at the end of both halves against a superb New England defense. But there is a lesson we seemed not to have grasped yet in 2007: when it is your game to take, you'd better take it. We were up 28–16 and 28–23 and could have finished strong, but we allowed them to come back and win. There comes a time in every game when a few plays win it or lose it, and we have yet to recognize when those moments are upon us and seize them. As Winston Churchill would have put it, we were tapped on the shoulder but we didn't come through—this time.

On top of the loss, we suffered injuries in the game. Shaun O'Hara and Kawika Mitchell both suffered sprained knees, and we won't know if they can play against Tampa Bay for another few days. Craig Dahl and Sam Madison also came out, Craig with a knee injury and Sam with an abdominal strain late in the game.

As the wild-card game looms, only eight days away, we know this: we are a good football team who just played a pretty good football game. And I know our defense is better than the thirty-eight points we gave up to New England. Eli played well against the Patriots. I'm confident our team will learn from the loss in our preparation for Tampa Bay.

The next morning, I listen to a voice mail from legendary coach and broadcaster John Madden:

> Just called to congratulate you and your team for a great effort last night. Not good, but great. I think it is one of the best things to happen to the NFL in the last ten years, and I don't know if they all know it, but they should be very grateful to you and your team for what you did. I believe so firmly in this: that there is only one way to play the game, and it is a regular-season game and you go out to win the darn game. I was just so proud being a part of the NFL and of what your guys did and the way you did it. You proved that it's a game and there's only one way to play the game and you did it. The NFL needed it. We've gotten too much of, "Well, they're going to rest their players and don't need to win, therefore they won't win." Well,

that's not sports and that's not competition. I'm a little emotional about it. I'm just so proud. It's something we all need to thank you for, and I believe the NFL needed that.

But now it is on to Tampa Bay, who will come into the game well rested. And Super Bowl winning coach Jon Gruden knows what I know: getting to the play-offs is one thing, but advancing is something else altogether.

TWELVE
● ● ● ● ● ● ● ● ● ●

A person's greatest fear is the fear of extinction,
but the worst thing is extinction and insignificance.
—PAT RILEY, NBA coach

IN 1997, A BOOK WAS RELEASED THAT REINFORCED THE VALUES I have always believed in. The legendary college basketball coach John Wooden, whom I had always admired, had written a book called, simply, *Wooden: A Lifetime of Observations and Reflections On and Off the Court.* It was a small hardback book, blue in color with yellow writing, not coincidentally the colors of the UCLA Bruins. Throughout my life, I have devoured books on coaching and leadership, so I was a bit skeptical that this book would be different, other than the fact that the greatest coach of all time had written it. In 201 pages, Coach Wooden shared his wisdom and principles from his lifetime on values, friendship, family, work, fairness, and every other aspect of life. He kept it simple, as life should be. He is more philosopher than coach.

After I finally put down the book, a new wave of energy came over me. I was more motivated, more convinced than ever that doing things the right way was the only way. That blue book has been a part of me for the last ten years. It sits just a few feet away on my desk in my Giants Stadium office, and I refer to it almost daily.

Behind the book is the man, and I have been honored to know him. We first spoke when I was still in Jacksonville; I remember the conversation clearly. I was extremely nervous. Here I was, an NFL head coach who had coached in the AFC Championship Game, and I was nervous talking to someone over the phone, probably because I admired, respected, and idolized him so much. But within seconds, Coach Wooden put me at ease. He and I have spoken by phone over the years, and each time I come away more inspired and enlightened.

The Pyramid of Success is a John Wooden trademark, revered by many. It encompasses fifteen virtues that one needs to possess in order to achieve success and greatness. At the top is competitive greatness: "perform at your best when your best is required." Below it are ideas such as poise, confidence, alertness, loyalty, and enthusiasm, characteristics learned over time. All virtues are defined the John Wooden way.

I pass the framed pyramid in my office dozens of times a day but don't often stop to think about it. But as we began our preparations for Tampa Bay, I thought about how far we had come since the tumultuous off-season. I thought about what we had left to accomplish, and I thought about Wooden's pyramid. So I put together our own pyramid, though the only thing it has in common with the Pyramid of Success is its shape.

At the bottom of our pyramid is the off-season strength and conditioning program. On top of that are the nine organized team activities, rookie minicamp, and the rookie/veteran minicamp. The next level in the pyramid is training camp, below the regular season, which is below the play-offs. Finally, the pyramid is capped by the Super Bowl. We have accomplished so much, but there are still more steps to climb.

We have two themes heading into the Tampa Bay game: "Road Warriors" and "Let's Keep Playing," alluding to the fact we are having fun and playing well and don't want it to end with a loss. Tampa Bay finished the regular season 9–7, but remember, they rested their starters the last two games. They have played great on special teams and have the best pass defense in the NFL, and their team speed is overwhelming. Veteran quarterback Jeff Garcia has been completing a high percentage of his passes in their short-passing offense, and he is good on the move. Also, he has won play-off games before, including the 2006 play-off win over us when Garcia was with Philadelphia. There is no doubt the Bucs will be healthy and ready to play.

There are several keys to victory for us against Tampa, but I really could give the team just one. In games in which play-off teams do not turn the ball over, they win 87 percent of the time. It is as simple as that. But, of course, there's more.

On special teams, we want to pin them inside their 10 on punts to make them drive the length of the field, and we need at least one momentum play from our special teams. On defense, we aim to hold them on third downs, contain Garcia, deny big plays to Joey Galloway and limit Tampa Bay to seventeen points or less. When we have the ball, we have to score touchdowns in the green zone and finish our blocks against a very fast defense.

Like we do during all road game weeks, we pump in loud crowd noise during practice on Thursday and Friday. I do talk to the team about the anticipated heat in Tampa (78–80 degrees) and I encourage them to get their rest, stay hydrated, and watch their diet in the days leading up to the game. That's all I say about the heat. We can't control it. Some reporters wonder if we will be bothered by the high temperatures. If the environments in London and Buffalo didn't bother us, a little heat in Tampa won't, either.

Ronde Barber, Tampa Bay's All-Pro corner and Tiki's twin brother, stokes the pregame fire a bit with this quote: "Of course we want to play the Giants. They [win] ugly, Shockey's hurt, and Eli has been inconsistent." The New York papers see it as trash talk, and it becomes the story of the week. We post it in the locker room, but our players don't bark back in the media. After all, this team knows our motto: "Talk Is Cheap—Play the Game." And nobody knows that motto better than Greg Gadson.

Many of the Giants players and coaches have stayed in touch with

Greg throughout the season, and unbeknownst to them, we arrange for Greg to fly down to Tampa to surprise our players at the team hotel. Since we last saw him, he has been fitted with prosthetic legs, and as the players walk off the bus at the hotel, they smile in amazement and surprise as Greg stands on his own, with the help of crutches, in front of them. They each eagerly shake his hand and give him hugs. The players also learn that Greg will be on the sideline with us on Sunday.

On Saturday night, I remind the players that five wild-card teams in NFL history have won the Super Bowl: Kansas City (1969), Oakland (1980), Denver (1997), Baltimore (2000), and Pittsburgh (2005). How about us?

Lose and it's over; the 2007 New York Giants would simply be a memory.

"A person's greatest fear is the fear of extinction, but the worst thing is extinction and insignificance," says Pat Riley.

THROUGHOUT THE SEASON, PLAYERS HAVE stepped up when they are called upon. Shaun O'Hara is unable to play because of the sprained knee, so Grey Ruegamer will start. Corey Webster, who in his two years has played both brilliantly and not so brilliantly, will replace Sam Madison and is charged with shadowing star receiver Joey Galloway. Kawika Mitchell will not start, so our starting linebackers will be Gerris Wilkinson, a six-three, 231-pound linebacker in his second year, Antonio Pierce, and Reggie Torbor. Will Grey, Corey, and Gerris rise to the challenge with the season on the line?

As you might expect, we fall behind in the first quarter. We give Tampa Bay great field position, and Jeff Garcia drives them to a first and goal from the 6. Earnest Graham scores two plays later, and we trail 7–0. But we respond. In the first five minutes of the second quarter Eli hits Brandon Jacobs for a 5-yard touchdown, and six minutes later Brandon runs one in from 8 yards out to put us in the lead, 14–7, which is how it stands at halftime.

Despite the Bucs having such a great pass defense, we were able to get 100 yards through the air and Eli was eleven for fourteen in the first half. Tampa put eight in the box, so our receivers had room to work. It is something we will keep in mind.

We kick off to start the second half, and Micheal Spurlock looks to have a huge return when Tank Daniels hits him, knocking the ball loose. An alert Corey Webster picks it up and we have 1st and 10 on Tampa's 30. It is a huge special teams play. A false-start penalty and one for delay of game hamper our drive, and we settle for a field goal to extend the lead to ten, having again relinquished a chance to score seven deep in our opponent's territory. On the ensuing Buccaneer possession, Corey makes another big play, this time intercepting a pass intended for Galloway in our end zone, resulting in a touchback. Eli continues his stellar play from the New England game and leads us on a fifteen-play, 92-yard scoring drive capped by a TD pass to Amani Toomer. Though Tampa will cut the lead to ten late in the fourth, our defense clamps down, and R. W. McQuarters picks off Garcia with 2:00 remaining. Can we finish? After we punt, Tampa has one more play, but they're down by ten with :07 on the clock, so it doesn't matter. We are moving on.

Eli finishes 20 for 27, with 185 passing yards and 2 TDs. More important, no turnovers. Grey Ruegamer played at a high level in filling in for Shaun, and Corey Webster shut down Galloway, who finished with just one catch for 9 yards. Gerris Wilkinson had five tackles. All three stepped up and helped us win.

The media and fans are surprised that we won a play-off game, but we aren't. Second-stringers stepped up big in place of starters; our quarterback was playing his best of the year. Nobody gave us much of a chance, but that's just the way we like it.

NEXT UP ARE THE DALLAS Cowboys, a team that beat us by a combined score of 76–55 in two games in 2007. We have seen enough of Tony Romo and Terrell Owens to know what is coming. And really, it is not often in the National Football League that two teams square off three times in a season. In Jacksonville, in our memorable 1999 season, we finished 15–3 and all three losses were to the Tennessee Titans. But it is not easy to beat a team three times, and we prepare as best we can to eliminate the errors that plagued us in the first two games. Keep in mind that we had our chances in both losses in 2007; it's not as if we were dominated. Also, we went on the road in 2004 and 2006 and won in Dallas. We know about Texas Stadium, the great atmosphere, the crowd cheering right on top of you, and we'll be ready.

"Momentum, Power of One, Collective Will." Those are the themes I present to the team on Wednesday. We have so much momentum from the way we are playing that I would pick us against any opponent. We introduce Dallas to the team for the third time this season, even though our players are very familiar with our divisional rivals. Terrell Owens has been nursing a sore ankle, and though media reports out of Dallas indicate he might not play, I know all along that T.O. will be on that field on Sunday. Defensively, we still needed to find a way to get in the backfield to Romo. We make some subtle adjustments in practice after studying their protections and schemes, and will try to get more favorable match-ups inside for Justin Tuck. In our two meetings this season, Dallas had ten drives that included a play of more than 20 yards, and the Cowboys scored touchdowns on nine of them. The bottom line is that we must win the one-on-one pass rush battles if we want to keep Romo from getting into his rhythm and leading Dallas to touchdowns.

As for the offense, it is all about controlling the line of scrimmage and finishing the blocks. It will give our backs some holes and give Eli time to make plays downfield. Our goal on third down conversions is 50 percent, which will allow us to maintain possession and keep their explosive offense off the field. On special teams, we have to get our return game going to give our offense better starting position and our tackling on punts and kickoffs has to be superb. I remind the team that in our season-opening loss to the Cowboys we gave up a 46-yard kickoff return when we trailed by just three, 38–35.

One of the days before the Dallas game, Chris Palmer and I are talking about the match-ups and Chris surprises me with this: "If we play

Green Bay next week, we match up very well." Now, normally, like most coaches, I wouldn't give such a comment much thought, as we still have to get by Dallas. But this time the words sit in the back of my mind.

In the meantime, this match-up is made for the media. Rivals. Revenge. Trash talking. Dallas wide receiver Patrick Crayton accuses our players of talking too much to hide our fear of the Cowboys. And we get word on Sunday morning at the hotel that Dallas owner Jerry Jones, who is a sharp and energetic businessman, left two tickets to the NFC Championship Game in each Cowboy's locker on Friday. We don't need extra motivation, but the Cowboys find ways to further fire up our guys.

As game time approaches, a familiar face is absent in Dallas. Greg Gadson is unable to travel due to yet another surgery. But he is with us in spirit. And I use something that Greg told me in a phone conversation earlier in the week during our team meeting Saturday night at the Dallas–Fort Worth Lakes Hilton: "It's a real struggle and things are tough for me right now. But I think of you guys, I think about how hard you guys are gonna fight on Sunday, and it helps me push through it all."

THREE MINUTES INTO THE NFC Divisional Play-off Game and we have the ball 1st and 10 from our 48. Amani Toomer and Plaxico Burress are lined up wide. Eli throws to Amani on a curl route. Amani catches the ball at the 39, makes a nice spin move to the outside to avoid tackles by Greg Ellis and Anthony Henry, and bursts down the field into the endzone, beating a sprinting Akin Ayodele. We are ahead in the first quarter. Can you believe it? The score remains 7–0 until the first play of the second quarter, when Tony Romo finds Terrell Owens, who beats Corey Webster on a fade from 5 yards out. It didn't look as though T.O. had both feet in bounds, according to our coaches in the press box, and we challenge the ruling on the field of a touchdown. But the call is upheld and we are down a time-out. The game is tied 7–7. On Dallas' next possession they drive 90 yards on twenty plays over 10:28 and score when Marion Barber appears to cross the goal line for a 1-yard touchdown. The replay officials in the booth want to review it. Again, they uphold the field ruling, and we now trail 14–7.

With forty-seven seconds to play in the half, we are not content to just run out the clock. Remember against the Jets back in October when we were aggressive and went for it at the end of the half instead of taking a knee and it cost us three points after Eli threw a pick? Well, we aren't going to change our philosophy now. Eli hits Steve Smith on two consecutive pass plays for 22 and 11 yards, Dallas' Jacques Reeves gets a 15-yard face mask penalty called against him, and suddenly we find ourselves with a 1st and 10 on Dallas' 23 with twenty-eight seconds left. We went 49 yards in just nineteen seconds. On 3rd and 10 from the shotgun, with three wide outs, tight end Kevin Boss catches a pass to give us 1st and Goal from the 4-yard line with eleven seconds left. On the next snap, Amani runs parallel to the goal line and fights off Ken Hamlin to make the catch and score a touchdown. Our aggressiveness pays off. It was so critical for us to respond and regain momentum. That's a different team from September.

It's 14–14 at halftime.

The Cowboys use over eight minutes of clock on a fourteen-play, 62-yard opening drive, but we force them to kick a field goal after they had 1st and 10 from our 14. During the drive, Aaron Ross tackled Marion Barber and reinjured his shoulder; though we can hardly afford it, he won't return. We are down to just three cornerbacks: Corey Webster, R. W. McQuarters, and rookie free agent Geoffrey Pope, recently activated from the practice squad.

We are forced to punt after getting one first down on our first possession of the second half, and our special teams contribute when we force Dallas to punt on 4th and 13 from their own 17. Mat McBriar's punt goes 45 yards to our 38, where it is fielded by R.W. He explodes for a 25-yard return before being pushed out of bounds, giving us great field position at the Dallas 37. One of our goals was to make a momentum-changing play on special teams, and we just accomplished that. On 1st and 10, Amani picks up 13 yards on a boundary catch, and two plays later, Kevin Boss picks up four more. On 3rd and 6 on the first play of the fourth quarter, Steve Smith runs a great curl route and catches the pass, giving us 1st and Goal. Ahmad Bradshaw follows Madison Hedgecock's block to get down to the 1, and Brandon muscles it in to give us a 21–17 lead early in the fourth.

Our defense continues to play exceptionally well, considering the injuries and the great field position the Dallas offense starts with. We stop them on two consecutive series. They stop us two straight times on downs.

I am thinking we are putting too much pressure on our defense to win the game. We are asking the defense to do a lot, and we should end the game with the ball in our hands.

We are backed up in our territory when Eli is sacked, so Jeff Feagles doesn't have much room to work with. His punt and the ensuing return by Crayton give Romo a 1st and 10 on our 48 with 1:50 to play. After a run and catch by Barber, Romo hits Jason Witten down the middle for 18 yards. We take a time-out with thirty-one seconds left. Witten catches another pass for 4 yards, and Dallas uses their last time-out. They have 2nd and 11 on our 23, with a trip to the NFC Championship Game on the line. Romo's next two passes, one to Witten, one to Crayton, are incomplete. In the defensive huddle, Antonio Pierce rattles off what *they* have been saying about us all year. That we can't win. That we can't get a stop. That we're not good enough. I am sure the Washington goal line stand crosses their minds. On 4th and 11 with sixteen seconds left, Terry Glenn is in the slot and runs a post route against two-deep coverage. Romo looks across the middle in the end zone for Glenn, but R. W. McQuarters comes down with the ball to seal the win, his second straight play-off game with a key interception. We are moving on.

"We've got two to go," I remind a jubilant locker room. "We're going to Green Bay next Sunday afternoon at five-thirty."

In the mix of the celebration, Chris Palmer and I hug, and I whisper in his ear, "We're going to find out if you are right or wrong."

FINAL 4

WIN ONE GAME.

That's what it says on the video screen in the team meeting room on Wednesday morning. "We are one of four teams still playing," I note to the players. "We need to win *one* game." My speech is short and matter-of-fact. We do not talk about the Super Bowl; we don't have to. We played the Green Bay Packers in week two and were in the game for the first three quarters. This is a different Giants team than the one in September. Then again, this is a different Packers team, too. After we landed in Dallas on the previous Saturday, we were able to watch a good portion of the Packers' game against a very good Seattle Seahawks team. Green Bay totally dominated and did whatever they wanted to do on all three sides of the ball.

But what we have been through, what we have accomplished, has made a team out of a group of individuals. The workouts back in March. The OTAs in May. The casino night, the bowling night, training camp, Greg Gadson's inspirational talk, the goal line stand, London, Chicago, Buffalo, New England—it's all been part of the journey. We are *this* close to the Super Bowl, and a pyramid, starting with the Buffalo game and our weekly themes, puts it into perspective.

But the story line in the media isn't about how far we have come or what a tremendous job we have done this year. No, it is about how far the mercury in Green Bay will drop. Forecasters have predicted that game-time temperatures will be in negative territory, and with windchill added, it will feel like 30 below. Ours is the late afternoon game, so temperatures will be dropping during the game. But if there is one thing that I know I can't control, it is the weather, and I won't let our team focus on it, either. We talk about it once as a team during the week and that is it. When reporters ask me or ask the players, we say it is out of our control. As a coaching staff, we prepare contingencies for the game plan in case the weather impacts our strategy, and our equipment staff, in charge of keeping us warm, does a lot of preparatory work as well.

There are other issues and questions from reporters, as the media contingent following the Giants multiplies. On January 17, there is one particular query that catches my ear:

"Lawrence Tynes hasn't attempted a game-deciding kick this season," Tara Sullivan from the *Bergen Record* asks. "Are you comfortable with him if that situation presents itself, and what is his range?"

"I'm very comfortable with his ability in any kind of clutch situation to be productive," I instantly reply.

Whether I am or am not, no coach worth his salary would ever publicly say he didn't have confidence in his kicker. That would be the kiss of death. Beyond that, I'm lucky because I *am* confident in Lawrence. Good thing, too, because I'll be forced to prove it in dramatic fashion.

Maybe Green Bay is looking ahead to the Super Bowl. Maybe they think that since they beat us once, they can do it again. Brett Favre will still be Brett Favre, and we expect him to be on the move. In the backfield, Ryan Grant, a back we traded to Green Bay for an undisclosed draft pick in training camp due to sheer numbers, is carrying the load for coach Mike McCarthy. Their defense is physical and their corners are aggressive, so there might be an opportunity to beat them deep.

We fly into Green Bay late on Saturday afternoon and take a bus to our hotel in Appleton, Wisconsin. I look out the window of my hotel room and I can see the cold. It's not every day that you can *see* cold. Even Green Bay residents, who are about as tough as they come, are running to get inside.

Despite the expected cold, many family and friends arrive in Green Bay. Judy flew out with the team; Brian, Keli, and Chris are flying up from Jacksonville; Tim and Andrea came in from New Jersey along with Katie; and even my sister Carole, her husband, Bob, their kids, Kyle and Kevin, and Kevin's wife, Jolene, will be in Green Bay. Though later I will learn that Judy and the kids will watch the game from a heated suite, I am impressed that they are willing to brave the cold and even more impressed that a pregnant Jolene will be sitting in the cold with her husband and in-laws.

The night before the game, the video staff puts together clips of broadcasters picking against us on the air the previous two weeks, along with highlights of the Dallas win, pictures of the Halas Trophy, and the words "New York Giants . . . NFC Champions . . . Feel It . . . Believe It."

There is one key to victory that hasn't been talked about much during the season in our Saturday night talks: penalties. I don't hesitate to point out that we were sixth in fewest penalties in the NFL during the season and Green Bay was twenty-ninth. We haven't been hurting ourselves the way we were earlier in the season. Let's not revert back now.

This will be a game for the mentally and physically tough, and I remind the players that in the NBA, teams that don't rebound don't win titles, and in the NFL, teams that aren't tough don't win championships. I bring out the trusted pyramid and finish with two thoughts from military men who are a part of what this 2007 team has become. Lieutenant General Ray Odierno, the commander in Iraq who so graciously wrote me a note of encouragement back in training camp, emphasizes "team and mission above everything else." Greg Gadson, our honorary cocaptain for the game along with Harry Carson, said this to us when he spoke in Washington in September: "If I could be in Iraq leading my soldiers, that's where I want to be."

JUST BECAUSE THIS IS A play-off game doesn't mean that my game day rituals will change. I wouldn't say I am superstitious, but I am definitely a man of routine. I always leave my hotel room at the exact same time to go down to the pregame meal. Our security personnel, Mike Murphy and Vinnie Byron, wait outside my room on game day and get me at the exact same time. I always travel on the first bus that leaves the hotel for the stadium, thirty minutes before the other buses. When I arrive at the stadium I put on a gray T-shirt and a New York Giants plain blue jacket. I never put on the game day clothing until closer to kickoff. And I always join our early birds in warm-ups on the field.

On this particular day, because of the frigid temperatures, Joe Skiba, our equipment director, lays out a well-thought-out wardrobe for the coaches. There is a tight bodysuit, thermal stockings, layers of sweats, and heat pads for my gloves and shoes. However, when I jog onto the field at Lambeau, all I've got on my head is a Giants baseball cap that I normally wear on game day. Bad idea. Within a minute, I can feel my ears begin to freeze. The top of my ears feel like they are going to break off. I wonder if my ears will last until the pregame routine is complete and I can get back inside the locker room.

At kickoff, temperatures are hovering below zero and the windchill is −23. There is little escape, and it shows. After forcing the Packers to punt on their opening series, we go to work from our own 18. Players' hands are exposed only between snap and whistle. Otherwise, they keep them tucked into their hand warmers. On our first play from scrimmage, Brandon Jacobs picks up 5 yards before a hellacious collision with Charles Woodson to set the tone for the day. In a classic 2007 Giants drive, Brandon, Eli Manning, and Plaxico Burress lead the way deep into Green Bay territory. With just under six minutes to play in a scoreless first quarter, we have a 1st and 10 at the Packers' 11. Brandon is cut down for no gain by a strong tackle by Brady Poppinga. On second down, Eli's pass to Kevin Boss comes up short. On third down, his pass to Steve Smith across the middle is knocked down by Cullen Jenkins. The decision is field goal. On fourth down, Lawrence Tynes puts the first points on the board. He converts a 29-yard field goal, which is an amazing feat in this cold. It is an impressive drive, but I am concerned, as I have been all year, that we didn't come away with seven points inside the opponents plus 20-yard line.

The cold begins to hamper the offenses, to the benefit of the defenses but not to the benefit of my face. Unbeknownst to me, my cheeks are turning bright red, and the television cameras can't get enough of it. Friends and family call and text message Judy and Katie, imploring them to tell me to cover my face. I won't even notice until after the game.

Early in the second quarter, we have the ball 1st and 10 on Green Bay's 17, but a false-start penalty moves us back and a few incomplete passes force us to settle for another field goal attempt, this one from the 19. Lawrence nails it again. Two trips to the green zone, six points. Not good, but I'm glad we're two for two on field goals. After the kickoff, on Green Bay's first snap, the Packers line up with two wide receivers and a tight end. On a play action pass, Favre finds Donald Driver on the sideline; he is wide open because Corey Webster slipped on the frozen turf. Driver sprints 90 yards for a touchdown. There is no panic on our sideline; it is one play. The Packers add a field goal with 1:34 to play in the first half, and we have one more chance to get points on the board with just one time-out. We move the ball from our own 23 to Green Bay's 34 and face a 3rd and 8. Already, I am thinking field goal, which impacts what play we call on third down.

I find Lawrence Tynes and ask him point-blank, "Can you kick a forty-nine-yard field goal?"

He looks me right in the eye and, with body emphasis, says, "Absolutely not!"

I like honesty in kickers. I'd rather have him tell me he can't make a kick than call for a field goal when he has no shot. We had already decided in pregame that the 30-yard line was our cutoff for field goals.

We run a short passing route on third down and Eli is sacked on fourth. The half ends with Green Bay up 10–6.

Neither team was efficient on third downs, going a combined one for thirteen. But surprisingly, despite the cold, we gained 70 more yards through the air than on the ground, and the Packers had just 11 yards rushing. The stars of the first half for us were the entire defense and Plaxico Burress, who, despite not practicing, caught seven passes for 102 yards in the first half.

In the locker room, players get warm as quickly as they can. We are doing some things well—stopping the run, keeping the passing game in check, not turning the ball over, and, perhaps most important, maintaining possession of the ball and keeping Brett Favre off the field. We will be receiving the second-half kickoff, and it is imperative that we drive and score, something I let the team know before heading back onto the field. Now, can we score touchdowns instead of kick field goals?

Five plays into the second half, on 3rd and 9 from our 43, Eli's pass attempt to Plaxico is intercepted by Al Harris. But Harris is flagged for illegal contact, and our drive continues; Green Bay is penalized three more times in the drive. With 3rd and 1 at the Green Bay 2, Brandon Jacobs fumbles, and in an instant the game begins to slip away. But Kevin Boss alertly recovers the ball, giving us a first down at the 1. The drive lasts 7:04 and ends with a Brandon touchdown run to give us back the lead, 13–10. We did what we needed to do: drive and score a touchdown to start the half. Our offensive line has been playing tremendously all season, creating holes for our backs and protecting Eli. But the lead doesn't last long.

On the ensuing kickoff, Tramon Williams returns Lawrence's kick 49 yards before being forced out of bounds at our 39-yard line by Chase Blackburn. With great field position, and helped by an unnecessary-roughness call on Sam Madison, the Packers quickly reclaim the lead as Favre hits Donald Lee for a 12-yard touchdown with just over five minutes remaining in the third quarter.

Will we respond?

On the kickoff, Domenik Hixon runs the ball back 33 yards, and Eli and the offense start on our 43. We move the ball into plus territory, and on 2nd and 10 from the Packers' 36, Eli launches a ball to Amani toward the sideline, and Amani once again makes an incredible toe-tapping catch at the Packer 12. Green Bay challenges the ruling that his feet remained in bounds. The play is upheld. Two plays later, Ahmad Bradshaw starts left, then cuts up the middle and scores from 4 yards out to give us back the lead, 20–17.

We have battled back. We are fifteen minutes from an improbable trip to the Super Bowl.

To start the fourth quarter, R. W. McQuarters has an interception deep in our territory, off a Favre pass intended for Koren Robinson. However, after snatching the ball, R.W. takes off running and is hit by Ryan Grant at the 19, and the ball comes loose. The Packers' Mark Tauscher recovers and now Green Bay has 1st and 10 on our 19. To our defense's credit, we force Mason Crosby to kick a 37-yard field goal with under twelve minutes to play in the game, and this classic postseason battle is tied at 20–20. Our team continues to play well, and with different players stepping up in different games to complement one another.

Here we are, in the fourth quarter of the NFC Championship Game, and I can tell you that Eli is the man I want out there. He works the clock and the field and puts us in good field position at Green Bay's 25, setting up a 43-yard field goal attempt for Lawrence Tynes with the game tied. The kick is no good. He is two for three.

As Lawrence jogs off the field with his head down, I tear into him a bit, as I cannot contain my frustrations. With a few choice words and a stare that could have melted Lambeau Field, I imply that we are all counting on him to make the kicks. But, of course, it doesn't change the score.

Both sides trade punts, but not without a close call. With 2:30 left and facing a 4th and 10 on their own 17, Packer punter Jon Ryan punts a ball as hard as a rock to R. W. McQuarters, who catches the ball at Green Bay's 48. R.W. picks up ten yards when he is hit by Tracy White and fumbles again. Just as Green Bay is about to scoop up the ball, rookie Michael Johnson makes a heads-up play and knocks the ball away, and Domenik Hixon recovers on the 48. We have dodged a bullet. Green Bay would have had great field position and time to move the ball. So now, with 2:15 on the clock, it is our turn again. On 1st and 10 from Green Bay's 48, Ahmad Bradshaw blows through the line and scampers all the way in for a touchdown. Our sideline explodes, but I see the yellow flag on the field, in an area that usually indicates offensive holding. Sure enough, the TD is called back. After the two-minute warning, on 2nd and 15, Eli hits Steve Smith for 15 yards, giving us a first down. Or so we think. The replay official rules Steve was down before reaching the first-down marker, setting up 3rd and less than 1, which Bradshaw easily converts. Eli manages the clock like the pro that he is and sets up our field goal unit on the Packers' 18-yard line. With no time-outs, a third down, and time ticking away, Eli did the job. Five seconds remain, and it will be a 36-yard attempt from the right hash for Lawrence to win the game and send us to the Super Bowl. Here is our chance to prove to everyone that yes, we can.

The Green Bay fans, who by now are warm from cheering, do what they can to distract Lawrence. Lawrence has hit this kick plenty of times this season, but never in this situation. Only a handful of kickers ever have the opportunity to win a game on the last play, and here is a chance to advance his team to the Super Bowl.

The snap from Jay Alford is high, the hold isn't clean, and the kick is a knuckleball that is no good, wide left.

The only one who talks to Lawrence after this second miss is Jeff

Feagles, who tells him that he'll get the ball down on the field next time and Lawrence should just worry about the kick.

The tension in the stadium is palpable as we go into overtime. A trip to the Super Bowl may rest on the flip of a coin, as the first to score wins. Green Bay wins the toss and elects to receive. Lawrence jogs back onto the field. His kickoff is returned by Koren Robinson to the Packers' 26. Any wrong move, any silly penalty could cost our team a shot at the Super Bowl. We're thinking, *How do we stop Favre?* On the first play, Ryan Grant gains 2 yards off the left side. On the second play, Favre drops back and spots Donald Driver toward the right sideline. But Corey Webster plays it perfectly and steps in front to intercept the pass, returning it 9 yards to Green Bay's 34. Remember how Corey had slipped and was beaten by Driver for a touchdown earlier in the game? He is now looking ahead, not back. Corey immediately runs off the field and heads right to Greg Gadson, who is sitting in his wheelchair on the sideline. Greg was supposed to be seated in a heated skybox but refused, not wanting to leave his teammates on the sideline. Corey gives him a hug. Then he gives him the game ball.

Now we are in the driver's seat: 1st and 10 from Green Bay's 34. A field goal wins it. But Lawrence has missed his last two, and don't think those misses aren't on my mind, even if one of them was not his fault. Our kicking mechanics of snapper-holder-kicker have been an issue since July and apparently have still not been resolved. Throw in the −24-degree windchill and the ball being hard as a rock, and nothing is certain. The best our offense can do is move the ball 5 yards, setting up a 4th and 5 on the Packers' 29—a 47-yard field goal attempt. Remember, our pregame decision was to try field goals from the 30-yard line and in.

In an instant, I have to make a decision: should we go for it on 4th and 5 or try a field goal, knowing that Lawrence missed from 43 and 36? Then, too, he told me in the first half he couldn't make a 49-yarder! So here I am, looking for some sign, some indication of what Lawrence thinks his chances are of making the field goal to send his team to the Super Bowl. Jeff Feagles thinks we are going to punt and looks for the go-ahead. I look onto the field, and there is Lawrence Tynes running to start his prekick routine.

The sight of him heading out there tells me everything I need to know.

"Field goal!" I yell. "Field goal!"

The unit runs onto the field.

The coaches up in the coaching box are in my ear telling me, "No! No! Coach, don't let him kick again!"

How many times in a career does a kicker who has missed a big kick get a chance to redeem himself in the same game? Here is a guy who, if we lose the game, will be known as the goat in New York for years, perhaps decades, to come. He will forever be the guy who missed the kick. The pressure on coaches is immense, but the pressure on field goal kickers, with so much on the line, is almost unbearable. Then again, that is their job. This kick is Lawrence's job.

By the way, no opposing kicker has ever made a postseason field goal of more than 40 yards at Lambeau.

But the way Lawrence runs onto the field tells me he is going to make it.

As the field goal team settles into place, my heart is racing. I have a perfect view of Jay Alford's snap. Feagles snatches it out of the air at the right moment, places it on the ground and points the laces toward the goalposts. Lawrence connects with a thump on the frozen ball. It travels for what seems like minutes and miles, but once it leaves his foot, I know it is good.

My first thought as the ball sails through the uprights is that we are headed to the Super Bowl.

Immediately, we go wild. Cold? What cold? Lawrence runs right to the locker room, and I hug whoever is closest to me, as players are jumping and hollering all over the field. In a classy move, Green Bay equipment manager Red Batty tracks down the game-winning ball and gives it to Lawrence.

The locker room is sheer chaos. My whole family is in there, including Judy, who has never before been in a postgame locker room. Wellington Mara's widow, Ann, is celebrating with us along with her sons John, Chris, and Frank, as are Steve and Jon Tisch and their mother, Joan, and sister, Laurie. The Fox Sports camera crews are doing interviews. Because of the nature of the locker room, there is no way we can huddle as a team, and I am sorry for that. I would like to tell my players how proud I am of all of them. Antonio Pierce comes up to me in the locker room saying, "Don't believe in us yet. Not yet. One more game." Plaxico is walking around holding up one finger proclaiming, "One more game. One more game."

The hero is Lawrence Tynes, but it is also Eli Manning and Plaxico Burress and the defensive line and Corey Webster and Brandon Jacobs and the coaches and every other guy in uniform. Even the trainers and equipment guys are heroes, as they kept the players hydrated and, more important, warm. When players came off the field, the equipment guys were right there with heavy warm coats and heaters on the benches.

We held the ball for more than forty minutes; we limited Green Bay to just 28 yards rushing; the Packers went one for ten on third downs; we amassed 377 yards of offense. And we only had six penalties.

But above all, we have lived to fight another day. This team faced extinction and said no, not yet.

THIRTEEN

• • • • • • • • • • •

I hope you have the time of your life.

—Green Day

ONE MILLION THINGS ARE RUNNING THROUGH MY MIND ON THE
flight home from Wisconsin. I am in my usual seat in coach, and
the cabin is louder than usual. I overhear Michael Strahan and Amani
Toomer talking about how excited they are to be headed to the Super
Bowl again. I have to smile. Without the knowledge of the players, of
course, we had quietly prepared a practice and travel schedule if we
should play in the big game. What time should we require the players to
come in on Thursday? How late should meetings go? When should we
start installing the game plan in practice? What day and time should we
fly to Phoenix?

By the time we arrive back at Giants Stadium it is close to 2:00 A.M.,
and with so much to do on Monday, there is no point driving home. As
I have done many nights this season, I lie down on the leather couch in
my office around 4:00 A.M. and get three hours of shuteye. When I wake
up, I get right to it. First, I check the dozens—hundreds—of voice mails,

text messages, and e-mails from family, friends, and colleagues. It really is overwhelming, and I don't even attempt to respond. Among those who reached out are Jon Gruden, Lovie Smith, and Tony Dungy.

After the Green Bay win, I spoke with Andy Reid and Tony Dungy to see how they had handled Super Bowl week and asked if they would change anything about the schedule. I consulted Charles Way and asked the assistants for their thoughts before coming to a final draft, something I probably wouldn't have done in the past.

The New England Patriots are the envy of every NFL franchise, the winners of three Super Bowls since 2001. They have one of the all-time great quarterbacks in Tom Brady, and they have Bill Belichick. Bill and I became friends in the late 1980s when we served together under Bill Parcells here in New York. I coached the wide receivers, Bill coached the defensive backs, so we were always going up against each other in practice. Was it competitive? You bet. We are both tough competitors. But it never got personal. In fact, I learned a great deal from Bill about football, especially defensive schemes. His Patriots were beyond good in 2007.

How good? Heading into the Super Bowl:

- NFL record 18–0
- Outscored their opponents 641–306
- Number one offense in the NFL for points scored, yards, first downs, passing yards, and turnovers
- Averaged 147 yards rushing in the play-offs
- Defense ranked in the top five in number of points allowed, average yards allowed per pass attempt, rushing attempts, rushing touchdowns allowed, and total number of yards allowed
- On special teams, kick returners averaged 25.2 yards per kickoff return
- Kicker Stephen Gostkowski was twenty-two for twenty-six on field goals
- Laid waste to Dallas, Indianapolis, and San Diego along the way

Were they the greatest team of all time? Hard to say. I know the Chicago Bears in 1985–86 were an excellent football team, and the undefeated 1972 Miami Dolphins, with my college teammate Larry Csonka, lay claim to greatness as well. All of that said, the only thing we can control is us.

"Will the NFC Champion New York Giants please stand up?" is how I start our Monday meeting, followed by the Lord's Prayer, which we didn't have a chance to recite on Sunday.

"Who lost the Super Bowl two years ago?" I then ask the sixty-one players seated in front of me. Silence. Seconds go by. Players look at one another. Finally from the back of the room comes a very tentative "Seattle?"

"That's my point. Nobody remembers who lost Super Bowls; they only remember who won."

I ask Michael Strahan to speak, as a captain, as a longtime veteran, and as a player with Super Bowl experience. Michael makes two points very clear. First, he and his teammates have to get rid of the distractions while the team is still in New Jersey. Tickets, hotel rooms, travel plans for family—they all should be dealt with *before* we leave for Arizona. Second, and more important, Michael attempts to convince the team that the Super Bowl, when you strip away all of the hype, is just a football game, plain and simple. He talks about waking up the day after Super Bowl XXXV, looking at a newspaper, and wondering, *Did we already play the game?* He says it was an almost surreal experience.

I echo both sentiments. I have been through the Super Bowl experience before, and I know that taking a business trip approach is the only way. I, too, insist the players take care of all of the "peripherals" *before* we touch down in Arizona. And the message isn't just for them. Believe me, Judy and I have a lot to deal with on our end as well. Our children and grandchildren will be coming to the game, along with my sisters, in-laws, cousins, nephews, and good friends. We have seventy-five tickets to distribute, and Judy handles all of that stuff.

For the most part, we keep things as normal as can be here in New Jersey. The players have three days off, and the coaches are able to go home for dinner on Monday and Tuesday nights. On the field starting on Thursday, the week of practice is productive. We install 90 percent of the first- and second-down plays on Thursday, 90 percent of the third-down plays on Friday, and 90 percent of the goal line, short-yardage, and red and green zone plays on Saturday.

I try not to be reflective—there is a time and place for everything—but I am very proud of this entire group of men. However, there is one more game to be played before the mission is accomplished.

As the home team, the New England Patriots have been given first choice in many selections in Arizona, such as hotels, practice times, and Media Day order, but we will make do. Our practice times will be in the afternoons, which is not how we worked during the season, but as I tell the players, at least our practice time will be closer to the time of actual kickoff.

We are the underdogs, the afterthought. No one is giving us a chance. A 19–0 season sounds good to a lot of people. Not to us.

ON MONDAY, JANUARY 28, IT is time to fly to the desert. Before we board the buses, a reporter from the *New York Post* asks Plaxico if he is ready to make history.

"You better believe it," he responds, and shortly follows up with a prediction of 23–17 when he is asked what he thinks the final score will be. When I get wind of the exchange, I do not have a problem with Plaxico or any player predicting we will win; we expect to win every game. I do have an issue, though, with giving out a score, for anyone in the media can perceive it as a guarantee, and that is not in the best interest of the team.

The first bus leaving for the airport, at 11:00 A.M., carries all players with five years' experience or less; the second, leaving fifteen minutes later, carries players with six years or more, as well as the coaching staff. For the trip, we require everyone to wear a coat and tie, dress slacks, and socks and shoes, normal New York Giant travel attire. After all, this is the Super Bowl and it is a business trip. On the flight to Phoenix, I take my usual seat in the middle of the players and I do some work. We land around 3:15 P.M. local time and are greeted by members of the Super Bowl Committee and the media. As the buses make their way from the airport to the hotel in Chandler, Arizona, I smile more broadly the farther and farther we get away from all of the hubbub. The location is perfect. The hotel, the Sheraton Wild Horse Pass Resort, on an Indian reservation, is also perfect. We have our own entrance, and we have plenty of space for travel meetings, treatments, and meals, plus our temporary offices are located right next to the entrance and exit. We are away from the public areas of the hotel and from much of the nightlife scene. So much so, in fact, some of our players simply decide not to travel out from the resort to go out to eat after the first few days.

As the Leadership Council discussed, there is no curfew that first night in Arizona, but I am not worried. This team has come too far for one or two players to ruin it all with a silly mistake.

It's not a mistake but rather an accident that may cost us. On Tuesday morning while in the shower, Plaxico slips and injures his knee, to go along with his lasting ankle injury. He receives treatment for the knee, but I will not be informed until Wednesday, when Plaxico's pain could become an issue.

Tuesday is Media Day, and, in any other year I might be dreading the impending onslaught. But I have evolved over the past twelve months in my patience and attitude. I have tried to make the best of the give-and-take with the press. Besides, I am having fun and enjoying the Super Bowl experience, and Media Day is a part of that experience. On the bus over to the stadium, I think about my approach. I want to maintain a presence and want the press to feel like they can ask me anything. When it is over, I want to be able to say that I have been cooperative and patient. Of course, redundant questions might not be met with as much enthusiasm as original ones. And reporters will have plenty of shots at me: every day of Super Bowl week, I meet with the media.

They organize Media Day by seating the coaches and players on stools up on small platforms, with the assembled media packed in around them. I felt like I was sitting in a dunk tank. As the head coach at Boston College, I *did* sit in a real dunk tank for charity one spring and got pelted by my players, who were more than happy to give up some money if it meant a chance to dunk me. So here I am at the Super Bowl and the media have their chance. But there isn't much negativity. There are questions for me from Boston reporters, many of whom I know from my BC days, and a few ask me to reflect on my years in Chestnut Hill. More than usual, I enjoy the repartee with the local, national, and international press, even cracking a few jokes during the process.

However, it is clear from the questions that nobody—and I mean nobody—is giving us a chance in the game.

As for the players, the only thing they have to do on Tuesday besides deal with the media is to stroll around the field. I want them to walk the field and get a feel for the grass and a sense of the stadium. I have already decided not to do a Saturday jog-through at the stadium, which is more than thirty minutes from the hotel, so this will be the players' last chance to be on the field before game day.

We work hard to keep the routine. Typically during a game week we have two full team meetings, as well as the Saturday night pregame talk. In our team meeting on Wednesday, we introduce the team to New England. That is, we *reintroduce* them. Of course, we played them in late December, and we went over much of the information last week, during our preparations in New Jersey. Still, I want this game week to be normal, so we go back to introducing the Patriots. We show a PowerPoint presentation on their team and individual players. We also show a highlight tape, as we often do in those Wednesday meetings. This one includes highlights from past Super Bowl games involving the Giants, including the 1986 and 1990 champions. I also reveal another pyramid. It has every game, starting with the Buffalo win and going through the NFC Championship Game. At the top of the pyramid is the Super Bowl logo with pictures of the Lombardi Trophy on both sides. We also bring out signs from our locker room at Giants Stadium: "Team First" and "Penalties Lose Games."

By Thursday's practice, we still do not know if Plaxico will be able to play on Sunday. Since he doesn't normally practice anyway due to his ankle, no one outside of a select few even is aware of the knee. But we do have protocol: the NFL mandates that teams release injury information in the days leading up to the game, and though Plaxico is on the list because of his ankle, we haven't yet added the knee. After talking with Ronnie Barnes and Pat Hanlon, we decide to let the news out but do not reveal how he injured the knee.

Friday morning is the main news conference downtown. I am dressed in a coat and tie, and follow Bill Belichick into the room. Typically at the Friday coaches' press conferences, the Lombardi Trophy and team helmets sit in front of the podium. Pat Hanlon has warned me beforehand that reporters will try to get me to touch the trophy, a cat-and-mouse game played out every Friday of Super Bowl weekend. Coaches are a bit superstitious, so most don't want to touch the trophy. Before photographers and reporters even have a chance to bait me, I immediately pick up the Giants helmet and hold it under my arm.

At Friday's practice, away from the stares of the media, Plaxico attempts to run a slant route at three-quarter speed to test the knee and ankle. He can't do it. Tests have ruled out a torn ligament or serious damage, but the pain appears to be too much. If he can't go, Sinorice Moss will get the call. Also on Friday David Tyree, who mainly has been a stalwart on special teams and has yet to break into the group of top receivers, drops easily catchable balls at practice. Come Sunday, we may need David to fill in.

Later in the day, I meet with the Fox broadcast crew back at the hotel: Joe Buck, Troy Aikman, Pam Oliver, producer Ritchie Zyontz, and director Artie Kempner for forty-five minutes or so. When I first sit down, Troy asks me if I picked the hotel, noting its distance and seclusion from most anything or anybody.

"No," I reply, "but I would have."

Troy and Joe look at each other and smile.

"This is a Tom Coughlin hotel," Joe adds.

In answering their questions, I am honest but not too revealing about our game plan on Sunday. I am a football coach, after all.

THE PLAYERS' FAMILIES FLEW IN on a charter on Thursday, and Friday evening, the Giants host a family barbecue for all Giants employees on the Indian reservation. It is great to see the players and coaches having so much fun with their families. And it is special for me as well. Judy, all of our children, and all of our grandchildren are here. My sister Chris and her children, Caitlyn, Kevin, and Cara, are with us, as are our good friends from Jacksonville, Jane and Mike Lewis. We take a hayride out to the barbecue location and listen to music and chase the grandkids around. Normally during the season, Friday night is "date night" for Judy and me: we go out to dinner or just stay home and have a glass of wine and catch up. This Friday night, we steal a few minutes later on and share a glass of wine with Jane and Mike.

On Saturday Pat Hanlon tells me about something special happening in Rochester, New York. More than thirty-five of my former players at the Rochester Institute of Technology traveled back to upstate New York to watch the Super Bowl together. Guys like Mark McCabe and Dave Pierson and Dave Mick and Mike D'Avanzo traveled from far and wide to watch as a team, their first reunion since leaving school. And former RIT coaches came in as well, including Bud Sims, Gary Fredericks, Greg Connor, and Russ Romano. The news gives me chills: it has been more than thirty years. I am honored.

It is the day before the game and you can sense that kickoff is nearly upon us. There are more serious looks on the faces of players and coaches, but we are all calm and collected. The players are at peace with themselves and their teammates. We do a late morning jog-through at the Arizona Cardinals' practice facility, our home for the week, reviewing situations such as first and goal on the 4-yard line with no time-outs and 42 seconds on the clock, as well as special teams. We arrive back at the hotel around 1:00 P.M. and, as typical on Saturday afternoons, the players have free time. We aren't sure what they are going to do with their five-hour break, but it turns out that many of them hit the hotel swimming pool with their kids or just spend time with their families.

More of our family and friends have arrived in town, and I work until 2:00 P.M. or so in my office in the hotel and then head upstairs to our suite to spend time with the family before I go back downstairs at 6:45 P.M. for the coaches' meeting.

The game is almost upon us.

IT IS JUST UNDER TWENTY-ONE hours before kickoff in Glendale, and I look around the team meeting room at the Sheraton Wild Horse Pass Resort. I can see the faces of players who wonder what destiny has in store for them. Sure, they believe they *can* beat the mighty New England Patriots in Super Bowl XLII, but it's just about impossible not to wonder. The video staff plays a highlight reel of some of our memorable plays and moments from 2007. The accompanying music? "Good Riddance" by Green Day. It is the chorus that sticks with me: *I hope you have the time of your life.*

Just as we did before the previous nineteen games, we review our keys to victory. On our punts: pin them down inside the 10, be physical in our protection. On our kickoffs: be wary of their wedge, and get multiple guys in on tackles. On defense: pressure and hit Tom Brady and stop the run. We led the NFL in sacks with fifty-three during the regular season, and New England allowed only twenty-one—something has to give. On offense: score touchdowns in the green zone and control the time of possession to keep Tom Brady off the field. In the AFC Championship Game against New England, San Diego had the ball three times in the green zone but came away with no touchdowns, and in our week-seventeen loss to New England, they held the ball for more than thirty-five minutes. Finally, as is my custom on Saturday nights, I emphasize the importance of turnovers, pointing out that the team that wins the turnover battle in the Super Bowl wins 91 percent of the time.

I share a quote from former St. Louis Rams running back Marshall Faulk, who summed up the meaning of the game:

> The ring is everything. There are so many guys who play this game that have never gotten the opportunity to play in a Super Bowl, let alone win one. There's no sense in playing if you can't ever get the

feeling of standing on top of the mountain and saying, "I'm the king of the hill."

As you might expect, we invite Greg Gadson and his family to join us in Arizona. He has become one of us, and his words have driven us forward. I didn't ask him to speak to the team in Tampa Bay or Green Bay, but this game is different. When I am finished with the keys to victory, I turn to Greg and say, "You're up!"

Greg looks up at this team that he is now a part of, and speaks.

"Back in September when I first had a chance to address you all as a team, I was an outsider and I wasn't one of you. I have the opportunity to speak to you tonight, and I really feel like I am a teammate and I am a part of the New York Giants. I want to thank every one of you right now for allowing me the chance to talk to you before this really important game.

"There are three things that we used to kind of rally around. Our cries that we used to rally around when I played football—I used them throughout my Army career. There are three words and I am going to go through them real quick. They are *pride, poise,* and *team.* I am going to talk about that, and I have added an ingredient.

"Pride. You have to have a lot of pride in yourself. That is the base of what you are all made of. You all have some pride, pride that has been instilled into you from day one by your parents and everything you have been a part of. If you don't have pride in yourself, you could never have pride in what I am going to talk about, and that is pride in your organization. The New York Giants. The New York Giants, one of the original teams in the NFL. A lot of history. You guys are one victory away from making history and putting yourselves in that position, you have to understand that. Prior to all the work, all the hard work, all the sweat that you guys have put into this, and all the tears, don't forget that. Hold your head high. I even got interviewed this week and I got tired of people asking me if I thought the Giants were going to win. I was like, 'What are you? Crazy? Damn right they are going to win.' "

Greg goes on to talk about having poise on the field, no matter what the opposition throws at you. He then concludes with what I believe is the central story line for the 2007 New York Giants.

"Team. I spoke to you back in September and I talked about how there will only be one 2007 New York Giants. Well, this is it, gentlemen. This is the 2007 New York Giants. I take great pride in being able to talk to you all again. But here we are, the last chapter, and your mission won't be done until we come off the field with a victory.

"Those are the three words that we rallied upon during my four years at Army, and I have added one for myself. Just kind of talking with Coach Coughlin, it is *belief.* It is friggin' belief. I believe that you are going to win and I believe we are going to do what it takes to win. We have the heart. They beat us the first time, so they know, or they think they know, that they will beat us again, but they don't have it here. It is our time to bring something to the battlefield here for the last month. The most important thing I am going to tell you is that if I was going to battle, there is not one of you here I would not take with me. I swear to God, I would take every single one of you. I believe that. Belief is that powerful. When I was lying down and those guys were doing all the things, I never believed that I would not live. And that is what belief will do for you if you really believe. You guys know it and you guys understand. That is all I've got."

If a feather were to drop in this room, you'd hear it. The players and coaches have been hanging on every word. How am I going to top that? I had put thought into what I was going to say, as I never speak to the team without purpose and preparation and this week is no different. How do I wrap up the season and put this game in perspective? It was on a walk with Judy around the hotel grounds when it hit me: just tell my own story.

"I want to leave you with one thing tonight: I hope you have the time of your life. I hope you have the time of your life because you have earned it. . . . Really, what I am saying to you . . . is this is what I want for you. This is what I want for each one of you because you have earned it and you deserve it. Coaches in the back of the room and the players seated up front, you have earned this, and this is what I want for you.

"In 1990, when I was an assistant coach with the New York Giants, we had to go on the road. We had to beat San Francisco out there in the NFC Championship Game to play in the Super Bowl. We had to pack for two weeks because there was only one week between games. Desert Storm was going on, there was not even the assurance early on in the season that there would be a Super Bowl because, quite frankly, it was a dangerous time. We went to San Francisco and in a hellacious game against a great football team. We got a turnover late and took the ball down to kick the field goal and we won. We won. Now we go to Tampa and we land at four in the morning, we roll in there, it is a one-week game. We are out of bed at seven, we are in the game plan room. We are going to play the Buffalo Bills, who scored all kinds of points, broke all kinds of records: no-huddle, Jim Kelly, up and down the field, the whole deal. Well, they had beaten us. The Buffalo Bills beat us at the end of the season. We were 10–0 and went three and three the last six weeks of the season. Buffalo beat us in New York. Everybody figured, 'How are the Giants going to beat these guys?' The run and gun or whatever they called that offense at the time.

"We get in the game and I am in the press box and there is a helicopter gunship right here hovering to the right of where we sat. There are armed guards and when we came into the stadium we had to go through the metal detectors, the whole bit, the team, everybody. That was the climate of the game in 1990. It was a heck of a game back and forth—we held the ball for forty minutes on them, and it came down to one kick. The score was twenty to nineteen; they had a forty-seven-yard field goal attempt. We were all standing in the press box. The snap, the hold, the kick, the kick is wide right. We all in unison jumped up in the air because the feeling that comes over you is, 'We are the world champions!' I am not saying it is more important than family or the birth of your children or anything like that. I am just saying from a professional standpoint, what I want for all of you is that feeling. . . . All of a sudden it comes to you: you are the champions of the world. It sends goose bumps on top of my goose bumps now, and that was in 1990.

". . . I remember going to the back door and opening the door and letting my boys into the locker room and they are seeing this and they are running around. It is not just about you; your whole family feels it. Your whole family, whether it is your dad, your mom, your brothers, your sisters, your wife, everybody, they are all world champions. It is the greatest professional feeling in the world. The greatest satisfaction you ever have for one moment in time and we are sitting here Saturday night with one sixty-minute game to play for a chance to become the world champions. I know they are an excellent football team. Hell, they are eighteen and oh—naturally they are an excellent football team. But I know the heart of the people in this room, too, and I know the fight, and it is going to be a battle. I know it is going to be every play, every snap; you are going to go as hard as you can possibly go because you have your eye on that prize. Win one historic game. Why not us? We are sixty minutes away. I want that for every one of you, every guy in this room, because you have earned it."

When the meeting is over, I attend Mass, then grab a snack before retiring to my suite, where I sit down to review my notes, as I always do the night before games. Usually, I have a college football game on in the background; this night, it is replays of old Super Bowls. Judy, her sister Sandy, and our children are out at a Super Bowl function, so I am alone. And you may wonder how I slept the night before the biggest game of my life. I slept well, thank you. I still have my worries before shutting my eyes, such as how the players are going to react to so much time in the locker room before kickoff and at halftime. But in general, I feel confident in our preparation. I long ago expected to be coaching in the Super Bowl, so I can rest easy.

I am having the time of my life.

FOURTEEN

● ● ● ● ● ● ● ● ● ● ● ●

What lies behind us and what lies before us are
tiny matters compared to what lies within us.
— RALPH WALDO EMERSON

TYPICALLY ON GAME DAYS, I DON'T SEE MY FAMILY UNTIL THE
game is over, but this day is different in a lot of ways. First of all,
the kids and grandkids are staying on our floor at the Sheraton, and there
is a constant opening and closing of doors and visitors to our suite
throughout the stay. The kids seem to run in and out as if it were an open
gym. On Sunday morning, around eight o'clock, I sit at the desk in the
hotel room jotting down some notes. Before I know it, three of the five
grandkids are sitting around me, all dressed in Giants jerseys. Dylan gets
inside my arm and starts coloring right on my game notes, and Emma
soon follows his lead. Shea is crawling up and doodling, but he doesn't
last long. They stay close to thirty minutes, and their laughing parents
take plenty of pictures. Imagine that: here I am just hours before kickoff of the biggest game of my life, and I am in our hotel room messing
around with our grandkids!

I go for a run in the hotel gym around ten and head down to the pregame meal at eleven-thirty. I usually don't like to eat a lot of food before games—to be honest, I am not sure why.

The buses leave for the stadium after the pregame meal, and as usual, I sit in the first row of the first bus. What's going through my mind as we make our way to the stadium for the biggest game of our lives? Traffic. What kind of traffic will there be? Is there congestion near the stadium? How long will it take to walk from the buses to the locker room? There was a little football thought, four or five questions that arose from reviewing our game plan the previous night.

The pregame routine starts around 3:15 P.M. We still don't know about Plaxico. When we first arrived at the stadium, he had tried to run on the field but couldn't make cuts. After team trainers taped him up and treated him again, Plaxico sat and prayed in front of his locker. Now, typically, teams need to turn in an inactive roster 90 minutes before kickoff, but for the Super Bowl it is two hours. Well, Plaxico doesn't get cleared to play until two hours before kickoff and by the time that happens NFL officials are knocking on the locker room door.

One unfortunate by-product of Plaxico's being able to play is that Sinorice Moss, who practiced so well this week, will not be on the active roster, one of seven players along with the third quarterback. I pull Sinorice aside and tell him. I think he appreciates the personal gesture.

While the morning went fast, the pregame seems to last forever. On the field as the players warm up, I chat with referee Mike Carey, NFL Vice President of Officiating Mike Pereira, and the stand-by official, Walt Coleman. Mike inquires about my red cheeks in Green Bay.

"Did you get frostbite?" he asks.

"Mike, thanks for asking. Many people inquired, and it is nice to know this year people are concerned about my face," I say. "Last year it was my ass."

We go through our normal sequence until 3:53, then retreat to the locker room. At 4:07:15 exactly, we are on our way toward the field for introductions. As in all of our games, we decline to have individual players introduced, instead electing to run out as a team. But after the introductions, we still have another twenty-two minutes before kickoff. I have already instructed our players to go to the sideline during the pregame festivities, as I don't want them to expend nervous energy. A few jog on the field during lulls in the pregame, but most go toward the bench. As we wait on the sideline, an enormous American flag is unveiled on the field. The entire place is rich with colors, and the field and stands seem to shudder with anticipation.

When it is time for the national anthem to be performed by Jordin Sparks, I stand at attention and flash back almost fifteen years to the last time I coached in the Super Bowl, in 1991. The details of that day— "America the Beautiful," Whitney Houston, the national anthem, the Gulf War, the flyby—come rushing back in an instant. I have so much pride and love for America, a heart full of patriotism, that the anthem is always emotional for me. Maybe it is from growing up in Waterloo, New York, the birthplace of Memorial Day. I hold the game of football in such high regard, but first we have to take the time to pay our respects to our country and to those who defend it. I take a quick glance at Greg Gadson in his wheelchair on the sideline.

After the anthem, there is still another seven minutes before kickoff. At this point, the players warm up again and huddle around Michael Strahan for some pregame encouragement.

BEFORE THE CAPTAINS WALK OUT to midfield for the coin toss, they already know what we want in terms of possession and direction. A lot of thought goes into the choices made at the time of the coin toss. First, is there any kind of wind direction that should be considered? Which end zone do we want to be going toward at halftime? Which side is more convenient to the locker room? As for the coin flip itself, it is fifty-fifty, but don't think for a moment a football coach leaves it to chance. My old coaching colleague Fred Hoaglin used to chart and analyze players' success at guessing heads or tails to help determine which player should call it.

We win the toss and choose to receive the ball. In an average game, teams will get eleven offensive drives, and the more possessions you have, the higher your chance of scoring points. Besides, we don't want Tom Brady with the ball first.

Our first drive starts at our own 23, and from the get-go we look comfortable. Eli and a combination of Brandon Jacobs and Ahmad Bradshaw work the ball downfield, picking up four first downs and, more important, chewing up clock. Though Brandon is only gaining a few yards at a time, I tell the offensive coaches to be patient with the running game. Every time the Patriots have to tackle the big bruising back, it takes a toll, the effects of which will be seen later in the game. On 3rd and 11 from New England's 18, Eli works out of the shotgun with no tight end and hits Steve Smith on a short curl, picking up just 4 yards. We call on Lawrence Tynes for the field goal try from the left hash, his first attempt since the "kick heard round the world," and he drills it through the middle of the uprights. The good news from the opening possession is that we've moved the ball effectively, using up 9:59 of clock, making it the longest drive in Super Bowl history, and we've come away with three points. The bad news? We've come away with three points. We know that we have to get seven in the green zone to have a chance.

On the ensuing kickoff, our kick coverage is poor. Zak DeOssie leaves his lane, and Laurence Maroney takes the kick at his 1-yard line and makes it out to the 44, giving Brady great field position. At one point during the drive, we have the Pats facing a 3rd and 10 from our 17, a key moment early in the game. We get strong pressure on Brady, and his pass through traffic up the middle to Ben Watson goes incomplete. But wait— there's a flag. Antonio Pierce is called for pass interference, and now New England has a 1st and Goal from our 1-yard line. We make a stop on first down, but just three seconds into the second quarter, Maroney runs in and New England has the lead, 7–3. The penalty threatens to knock us down. How will we respond? We know from the regular-season game and from our first drive of the Super Bowl that we can move the ball on the Patriots, but can we respond to every score?

Patriot kicker Stephen Gostkowski pushes the kickoff out of bounds, giving us automatic possession on our own 40-yard line. On 3rd and 7 from the 43, Amani goes into motion from right to left. Brandon puts a huge block on the blitzing Brandon Meriweather, Amani beats Ellis Hobbs on the sideline route, and Eli delivers a perfect pass. Somehow, Amani manages to catch the ball 38 yards downfield *and* keep his feet in bounds while making the diving catch. He is one of the best ever at that tricky tandem. We are in a great position to take the lead back. After Brandon picks up 4 yards, giving us a 2nd and 6 from the 15, we are hit with a delay-of-game penalty, backing us up 5 yards. Whose fault is it?

Right now it doesn't matter. Right now we face a 2nd and 11 from just outside the 20. Out of the shotgun, Eli takes a three-step drop and finds David Tyree on a quick slant for a 6-yard pickup. On 3rd and 5 from the 14, we call a double level, or trailing pattern. One receiver starts outside and then turns inside, following another one across the field. The play usually results in a short pass, and Eli has to throw the ball through a gap in the defensive line. On this particular play, Steve Smith has trouble picking up the ball through all of those big bodies on the line and he tips it. Ellis Hobbs is in a perfect position to make the interception, and Ahmad Bradshaw pushes him out of bounds at the 33. It is our first offensive turnover of the play-offs. *Ninety-one percent of teams who win the turnover battle win the Super Bowl.*

But champions respond to swings of fortune with steadiness. Of course I am disappointed at the interception, but I am more concerned that it was our second trip to the green zone and again we did not come away with seven. But we don't get flustered. In two drives, the offense has proven that we can move the ball on this field against this defense. Now we just need to finish.

We stop the Patriots on their next two possessions, and they hold us to a three-and-out in between. On our third series of the second quarter, we again find ourselves nearing the green zone. We have 3rd and 4 from the 25 with 2:31 left in the half, which would mean a 43-yard field goal attempt, but it doesn't matter—Eli is sacked. Not only that, he fumbles the ball. Adalius Thomas got in the backfield quickly and hit Eli, knocking the ball out. The ball bounces forever as players scramble for it. It appears that Mike Vrabel is going to recover the ball, but Ahmad Bradshaw makes a seemingly brilliant decision to bat the ball with his hands. Steve

Smith beats Asante Samuel and Brandon Meriweather to the ball and smothers it. After much discussion, officials flag Ahmad for an illegal bat and it costs us 10 yards, but at least we maintain possession. Now we are at 3rd and 18 from the 39, and Eli's pass to Steve is almost picked off by Randall Gay. We are out of field goal range. We have no choice but to punt.

The Patriots begin to move the ball on us, but Justin Tuck beats Logan Mankins, hits Brady from behind, and forces the ball out; Osi Umenyiora recovers. With ten seconds left in the half, we try two passes from midfield, the last a Hail Mary flood tip, but Steve can't snare it. The half ends, 7–3.

We had two big goals coming in on offense: time of possession and scoring in the green zone. We accomplished one (19:27 to 10:30) but not the other. We have a lot of work to do in the second half if we're going to win this thing.

IN THE SUPER BOWL, HALFTIME is a whopping twenty-eight minutes. That is a lot of time. We have already planned it out to the second, and the official game clock hanging in the locker room reminds us of the time remaining. The first fifteen minutes, the players take care of their individual needs: they visit the training staff, eat a snack, drink fluids, fix any equipment issues. The coaches, meanwhile, are huddled into offense, defense, and special teams, discussing what has just happened and what might come next. For the offense, they have to answer questions like: What defenses are they throwing at us? In which situations are they blitzing? What did we do effectively in the first half? Those answers help us determine what formations and runs we will call in the second half. We also script the first few offensive plays. As for the defense, they analyze what the Patriots did that hurt us most and what formations and personnel they showed on those plays, so we can make adjustments.

The coaches then split into meetings with the players on opposite sides of the expansive locker room. I listen in first to the offense, then make my way over to lend an ear to Steve Spagnuolo.

Finally, the players huddle up around me.

"We are thirty minutes from being world champions," I remind them. "Thirty minutes. We need an all-out effort." After praising the team for ball possession, I *encourage* them to score touchdowns in the green zone and make a momentum–changing play on special teams. Just like against Tampa Bay, we need a stop to start the half to get the ball back, and then we need to go down and score.

We allow the Pats' offense two first downs and 35 yards but dig in to force them to punt on 4th and 2 from our 44. With just 2 yards to go for a first down and with the ball at midfield, we believe it is a prime opportunity for Bill Belichick to call for a fake punt. To counter that possibility, we call in the "gray team," which is not our usual punt return team. Rather, it is basically our defense with a punt returner added, and we call on them only in situations like this one. R. W. McQuarters can return the ball or step up into our defensive set if it is indeed a fake.

On all punts, it is the job of the middle linebacker to count the players to make sure we have eleven on the field. If we have more than eleven, it is his responsibility to run off to avoid a penalty. But somebody on our end believes it is normal punt return personnel on the field, not the gray team, and we get caught with twelve men. Chase Blackburn, the counter on the play, does his best to sprint off the field before the snap, but I see clearly, right in front of me, that he doesn't make it in time. New England punter Chris Hanson punts the ball to R.W., who runs out of bounds at the 14 yard line. There is no flag on the field.

A few weeks earlier, a similar situation occurred during a crucial game between the Washington Redskins and Minnesota Vikings. A Minnesota player had apparently not quite reached the sideline before the ball was snapped, so the Vikings had twelve men on the field. Redskins coach Joe Gibbs used a replay challenge, and after reviewing the play, the officials indeed ruled that Minnesota should be flagged. The coaches and officials in our game have that play on their minds, I am sure.

Mike Carey, the referee, jogs over to the Patriots' sideline to calm down an intense Bill Belichick. Mike is wired for NFL Films, and days later, while watching the highlights of the game, I hear Mike tell Bill at the time, "We [the officials] did not give them [the Giants] enough time to make substitutions." By rule, if the offense substitutes players, the defense must be given time to do the same. Belichick isn't taking the explanation well and challenges the call, and after reviewing the play, Carey flags us for twelve men on the field, a 5-yard penalty, which gives New England a first down at the 39.

It is a foolish penalty in our twentieth game of the year, and I am furious; the players can probably tell by my face. There's no way around it: the old Tom is making a return appearance. But at that moment, just when I am ready to explode, Michael Strahan, whose unit had just held them and who now has to go back on the field, comes up to me.

"Coach," he says, "we've been in tougher situations than this." And with that, he jogs onto the field.

EVERY PLAY MATTERS, BUT CHAMPIONS recognize those moments in a game that determine wins and losses. In our regular-season finale against the Patriots, we were leading 28–16 and 28–23 but did not seize the moment.

Now we allow Tom Brady to convert a 3rd and 13, but then our defense steps up. On the next third-down play from the 25, Michael comes up with a huge sack, pushing the Pats back to the 31. That makes for a 49-yard field goal, and Belichick hasn't asked his kicker to try one field goal from over 50 yards the entire season. They decide to go for it, and Brady's deep pass to Jabar Gaffney falls incomplete.

Amazingly, by the end of the third quarter, the score is still 7–3. Despite New England dominating the time of possession in the quarter, they didn't score.

Our first offensive play in the fourth quarter is from our own 20, and Eli runs play action, finding Kevin Boss in the middle of the field for a 45-yard gain to get us to the Patriots' 35-yard line. David Tyree, who has had such a traumatic season with the death of his mother, plays perhaps the best game of his life. After going into motion he fakes a block on the strong safety and breaks away for a 5-yard pass over the middle

to score our first touchdown of the game with just eleven minutes remaining. It is a well-executed play action pass that pulled the New England secondary to the line of scrimmage to defend the run.

Tom Brady goes to work with 7:54 remaining and leads his guys on
a twelve-play, 80-yard drive. As the Pats near our end zone, I am concerned about our time-outs. We have all three, plus the two-minute warning, but I want to save them for when we get the ball back, not when we
are on defense. Will the Patriots chew up too much clock and force me
to use our time-outs? Doesn't matter. Brady throws a TD pass to Randy
Moss, and New England is in front, 14–10.

The drive starts at our own 17-yard line. Eighty-three yards to pay
dirt, 2:39 on the clock. I get a brief look at Eli's eyes before he jogs onto
the field. This is his time.

"We are going to go down there and score," Eli tells the men in the
huddle.

On the sideline, Michael keeps yelling, "Seventeen to fourteen! Believe it, don't just say it!"

I know our team, so I know that we are good in the two-minute drill,
and we have proven that we can drive the ball on New England's great
defense. I have seen these guys at their best and at their worst, and I
know they can do this. I believe in this team.

From the shotgun, Eli completes an 11-yard pass to Amani to give
us another first down at the 28. His next two pass attempts to Plaxico are
incomplete. The two-minute warning gives us a breather. I huddle on
the sideline with Eli and offensive coordinator Kevin Gilbride, with
backup quarterbacks Anthony Wright and Jared Lorenzen looking on.
We call two successive plays. I remind Eli that we have all three time-
outs left.

Facing a 3rd and 10 from our 28, Eli hits Amani wide left and he
picks up 9 yards, but we are still short of the first-down marker. I have
already decided we are in four-down territory. We cannot punt the ball
back to the Patriots because I don't believe we will see the ball again.
The call on fourth down is for Brandon Jacobs to power the ball over

the line of scrimmage. He follows Madison Hedgecock's big body and leaps forward before he is stopped.

Does he make it?

Time freezes. The officials measure the distance. From where I am standing, I am confident he made it—but not by much.

He made it.

We get additional good news when the officials take an official time-out, since we don't have to use one of ours to change personnel.

After Eli scrambles for 5 yards and misses David Tyree deep on second down, it is 3rd and 5 from our own 44 with 1:15 remaining. Then the type of play that is reserved for only the greatest of all games occurs. Eli takes the snap and then promptly disappears in a mass of Patriots jerseys; I am sure that Jarvis Green and Richard Seymour have him wrapped up and he is going down. But then he reappears, regains his balance, holds the ball tight, and steps up into the pocket. I see his arm go back. I see the ball take flight. From the way it leaves his hand, the arc is too high— very dangerous, especially down the middle of the field. As David leaps for the ball, smothered by Patriots defenders, it appears that he won't be able to catch it, or at least won't be able to hold on after Rodney Harrison either hits him or rips the ball away. Somehow Harrison misses the ball; still, David barely gets *his* fingers on it. But now I am thinking he is going to break his back. He hits the ground as Harrison tries to disrupt the catch, desperately trying to knock the ball from David's hands. Old Tom is alive and well, but in a good way, and I scream into the headset, "Did he have possession? Did he have it?"

The coaches upstairs respond, "Yes!"

I ask them again and again, and they confirm that he caught it.

Yes, a football miracle has occurred. The catch was a remarkable play that will live forever in this organization's lore. But what is going to happen three snaps later is just as important.

After Eli's amazing escape and David's legendary catch, we call our second time-out with just under a minute to go, to give our big linemen a chance to get down to the 33-yard line and not waste too much time.

Coming out of the time-out, Eli is sacked by Adalius Thomas, and we are forced to use our last time-out with fifty seconds left. It is now 2nd and 11 from New England's 25. Under tremendous pressure, Eli throws a wobbly ball, which luckily goes through the hands of Brandon Meriweather and is not handled by David Tyree. 3rd and 11 from the 25.

We have confidence in this last minute of this final game because of one thing: preparation. We have prepared for every situation, and not just in the last two weeks. Go back to minicamp in the spring of 2007 when we were working on our two-minute drill. The hours and hours of routes that our receivers ran with Eli. The fact that our coaching staff reviewed every play of New England's 2007 games over and over again. When you are prepared, you are confident; when you are confident, you execute.

Coming into the game, there were three major things we had to do to win: put pressure on Tom Brady, control the time of possession, and score touchdowns in the green zone. Keep in mind that while we opened the game with a ten-minute drive that chewed up clock, we ended up with just a field goal. We have watched enough tape on the Patriots to know what they like to do when they have their backs against the wall. Typically, NFL teams do one of two things in the green zone: either they play a well-designed and difficult-to-penetrate zone coverage or they bring the house on the blitz. Most teams are good at both. The Patriots could rush two guys, or three or four or even five. Will the Pats blitz? On 3rd and 11, we guess they will be in zone coverage and not blitz.

We call 62 Café X Glance, with receivers running a curl route, a flag route, and a flat route. Teams usually don't pick up a lot of yardage with a flat route, but it is always a good option to have. Eli takes the snap in shotgun and quickly scans the field. The underneath coverage takes away the curl, and the flag route is covered by the deep third. Steve Smith seems to have a step in the flat but hasn't yet threatened the first-down marker. Eli spots Steve and delivers the ball into the wide flat, outside the angle of the defender, allowing Steve to square his shoulders and not only get the first down but also get out of bounds to stop the clock with thirty-nine seconds to go. Without that play, nothing before or after that moment means anything. Steve has battled his way back from injury and is making an impact in the biggest game of his life.

Now, with a 1st and 10 from the 13 with thirty-nine seconds left and no time-outs, we call 62 Café X Fade, a play that is very similar to the one before but contains a fade route. Out of the shotgun, Eli recognizes the blitz, and Brandon Jacobs and the O-line provide steady protection. Not only does Brandon block his assigned man, but also his big body takes up space. Plaxico starts his route as if he is running a slant, typical for this kind of call against a blitz. But instead of running a slant, he fakes the slant and executes a fade route in the corner of the end zone. Ellis Hobbs bites on the slant and has no chance at the ball, which is perfectly thrown by Eli. It is tough for me to see through all of the bodies whether Plaxico is in bounds, but it doesn't take long for me to realize we have scored.

We didn't know until Plaxico was on the field during the game if he could even play. But of course he did, and the result is an amazing moment. A young man who's battled every day of the season with ankle and now knee concerns and is doing all he can for his team.

The Patriots have one last chance to tie or win the game. Laurence Maroney returns the kickoff 17 yards before being tackled on an excellent play by Zak DeOssie and Chase Blackburn. With twenty-nine seconds left, New England has 1st and 10 from their 26. On first down, Brady's pass, intended for Jabar Gaffney, is incomplete. On second down, rookie Jay Alford comes up with a huge sack, dropping Brady for a 10-yard loss. It is our fifth sack of the day, to go along with nine hits on Brady, an impressive number considering New England had allowed only twenty-one sacks *all season*. On third down, Brady rolls right to buy extra time and launches the ball 70 yards downfield, where Corey Webster and Gibril Wilson converge on Moss and Corey manages to tip the ball away at the last second. On fourth down, the last deep gasp to Moss is no good. There is one second left.

At this point, most players, coaches, and fans believe the game is over, including Bill Belichick. He jogs across the field to shake my hand, but I am hesitant, as I know the NFL will not just tick off the last second. Madison Hedgecock dumps a bucket of Gatorade on my head, and even though we're in Arizona, it is a cool night and the liquid is freezing. I finally take a few steps onto the field and Bill pulls my ear close and congratulates me. Much was made after the game that Bill ran to the locker room before the clock hit 0:00, but I know him; he is gracious and sincere and there is no disrespect.

We still have one play to run, and we call 2 Tights 85, our victory formation. At the end of every Saturday practice, we always conclude with the Victory play. It is a psychological thing. Now we are running Victory for real, to seal the greatest win in Super Bowl history.

AFTER THE GAME, CHAOS REIGNS supreme. I raise one arm in the air, unleash a smile, and hug Osi. There is confetti in the air and at my feet. I turn and see the expressions on the faces of my family, expressions far different from those I noticed them wearing before the game and, for Tim, even more different from the one with which he confronted me a year before in my kitchen, when he and Katie and Judy stood strong for me. Dan Edwards, who was our public relations director in Jacksonville, is assigned to lead me to the podium, where Commissioner Roger Goodell waits with the Lombardi Trophy. The scene is confusing, and we go in just about every wrong direction. Finally we approach the platform stairs, and just as my foot is about to hit the first step, I hear a familiar voice calling my name. I turn around and give Judy a hug. Moments like this are made for family. I see Chris Snee holding Dylan with his arm around Katie. There is Tim hugging Emma with Andrea nearby, beaming. Brian and Susie wear big smiles, and Keli and Chris are hugging everyone.

The ownership of the Giants is onstage, Ann Mara, John Mara, Steve Tisch, and Joan Tisch, and I know Mr. Mara and Mr. Tisch are with us as well. Up on the stage, I praise the Patriots while relishing our great effort. By the time the presentations are over, Dylan and Emma are making snow angels in the confetti. This is what I meant when I told the team last night that their families are world champions, too. This is the time of *my* life.

I am quickly escorted to the main media tent. During the press conference, some of the Patriots' players stop by to extend a congratulatory hand, Tedy Bruschi and Rodney Harrison among them—that is class. I get a glance of Plaxico holding his son with one hand and his wife's hand with the other. Shortly thereafter he breaks down with emotion while talking to the press.

As it was right after the NFC Championship Game, the locker room is overflowing with media. There is no team meeting, no time to get the team together to revel in the end of our journey. By the time I get in there, Eli is sharing a private moment with Peyton, and I don't want to interrupt to give Eli a hug.

After the locker room, I am taken to the field to the set of the NFL Network for a brief interview. There are thousands of Giants fans still in the stadium, and I join in a few cheers. When I walk off the set, Judy is waiting along with Tim and Andrea and Emma, who is in her father's arms. Tim puts her on the ground, she runs as fast as her little legs can take her to me, and I scoop her up. She blinks a few times, looks me in the eye, and says, "Pop-Pop, did the Giants win?"

By the time we board the team bus to head back to the hotel, however, it all seems kind of normal. There is the subdued conversation as players and coaches sit in their usual seats, and I wonder for a moment if this is it. Is this how it feels? Has the moment already passed? But when we pull up to the Sheraton, there is nothing normal about it. All week we have been kept in seclusion from the public, but here we are, surrounded by fans and family members, who have jammed the hallways and lobby. We have to walk single file through the lobby just to get to the elevators. I am finally able to get up to our room, where our family is waiting for Judy and me. It is a special moment with our children, their spouses, and our grandkids, and we toast what we have accomplished.

We head downstairs for the official Giants party and then return to our suite with more family and friends to party.

Among those in our jam-packed suite: Keli, Tim, Brian, and Katie; their spouses, Chris, Andrea, Susie, and Chris; Judy's sister Sandy; my sister Carole and her husband, Bob, along with their sons, Kyle and Kevin, and Kevin's wife, Jolene; my sister Kathy and daughters Traci and Amy along with their boyfriends, Bobby and Pat; my sister Patty and her husband, Scott, and their children, Sean and Courtney, with Courtney's boyfriend, Justin; my sister Chris and her husband, Gabe, and their children, Caitlyn, Kevin, and Cara; Andrea's mother, Elsa Rubio, and Andrea's brother, Emir; Susie's parents, Mary Ann and Bill Collini, and Susie's sister, Amy Kelly and her son, Collin; my cousins, John Post, Jay Post and his sons Jay and Jimmy, Jerry Post and his wife Cappy and their son, Mark; and a contingent of close friends, including Ernie and Rita Bono, Nancy and Gary Chartrand, Ray and Carole Lanzi, Mike and Jane Lewis, and Fran and Lisa Floey, along with their children, Paige and Sean; also in the suite is Mike Murphy, the man who is always looking out for Judy and me.

Ernie approaches me and asks, "Do you know what you just did?"

My first thought is, *How can we use this momentum for the Jay Fund?*

By 3:30 A.M., it is time to go to bed—for me, at least. Most everyone else stays up, but I have to be up at six for a seven-thirty press conference.

Three hours later, I get dressed, and, when I open up the room door, there is Tim in the hallway wearing a jogging suit. He stayed up all night watching the game over and over, just to make sure it really happened. I give him a hug and head off to the press conference.

You know you have done something special when the president calls. The White House tries to reach me twice on Monday morning, but both times I am tied up with the media, along with Eli. On the way back to the hotel, we finally connect, and the president, an avid sportsman, congratulates me. Not only that, he knows about the heat that I and the team were under, and he jokes that "we know a little something about criticism here in the Oval Office."

THE SEASON IS OVER. THE journey is not.

We arrive back in New Jersey on Monday evening, and the players and coaches go home after a night of little or no sleep. We walk in our door around 11:00 P.M. or so, and Judy and I talk and listen to a few of our voice-mail messages.

The team reconvenes early Tuesday morning. After the players receive their exit physicals, we gather in the team meeting room, as we have done so many times over the past twelve months.

"Will the world champion New York Giants please stand up?" I ask, and they all rise to their feet with a holler. We kneel down for the Lord's Prayer, as we didn't have the chance to do after the game. I tell them how much I wished we could have all been together to celebrate. I show the players our team objectives, the same ones I revealed in late July in our first meeting of training camp. One by one, I check off those objectives. It has been an amazing journey.

We board a flotilla of buses—Judy and I are on the first bus and set out for the parade in New York City. We leave the Meadowlands and head through the Holland Tunnel into lower Manhattan. As soon as we exit the tunnel, there are thousands of people in the streets waiting to catch a glimpse. Ed Skiba, our assistant equipment manager, stands at the front of the bus holding up the Lombardi Trophy, and the fans go crazy. The closer we get to Broadway, the larger the crowd grows. People are everywhere—on the sidewalk, yelling out of windows, hanging on lampposts. It is overwhelming.

The buses take us to a holding area in Battery Park before we board the floats. Then-governor Eliot Spitzer introduces himself to me, and I have a brief conversation with Mayor Michael Bloomberg. A few minutes go by and then we climb onto the floats. On the one I am assigned to, I am joined by Eli, Michael, Chris Mara, Frank Mara, and Jerry Reese and his son, J.R., who enjoy standing up front showing off the Lombardi Trophy. In the back, I stand with Judy, Ann Mara, Joan Tisch, John Mara, and Steve Tisch. At one point, Michael comes and waves me to the front. Despite my reluctance, it is something I will never forget: the millions of fans and the ticker tape raining down. I think of President Harry S. Truman and General Douglas MacArthur parading down the Canyon of Heroes in a similar fashion after victory in World War II, and the great Yankee parades down this same street.

People are lined up as deep and as far as the eye can see. Even the side streets are filled with thousands, clad in red, white, and blue Giants jerseys. I wonder, *Are they here because our victory was so unexpected?*

It is a little chilly, and I am dressed in an overcoat and a black turtleneck, a wardrobe New Jersey Senate president Dick Codey will joke makes me look like a priest. But a real member of the clergy is indeed present. As the procession makes its way past Trinity Episcopal Church, I spot its pastor, Jim Cooper, a friend, standing on a ladder, dressed in full vestments with a Super Bowl championship hat, wafting incense smoke among the people. It was a sight to behold.

In a brief ceremony in front of City Hall, as raindrops fall, we receive the warm congratulations of dignitaries. Michael pleases the crowd with his vertical stomp. Then it is back on the buses and back to New Jersey for a rally at Giants Stadium. Senator Codey is humorous and energetic and says everything there is to be said to the thirty-five thousand or so fans in the stadium. David Tyree sends them into a frenzy when he grabs a football and holds it to his head, reenacting his now-famous catch, which is not even forty-eight hours old.

Standing on the stage at the center of such wonderful enthusiasm, I think about how far we have come. Here we are, more than a hundred coaches, players, and staff, who came together for one purpose. We believed. We believed in ourselves when others didn't. We did what no one thought we could do. We did it for our team, for our families, for Mr. Mara and Mr. Tisch, for the New York Giants, for the NFL, for American soldiers, and for anyone who has ever been told, "You can't." But most fundamentally, *we did it.* We reached our destination. And what an incredible journey it has been.

EPILOGUE

● ● ● ● ● ● ● ● ● ● ●

AS YOU MIGHT IMAGINE, IN THE DAYS, WEEKS, AND MONTHS FOL-
lowing the Super Bowl, I received thousands of messages through
the mail and via e-mail, text, and phone. Many were from people I had
never met—just regular guys and gals who wrote thoughtful notes about
what we had accomplished. Some were from Giants fans who were just
giddy. Some were from the people in and out of my profession who have
been a part of my lifetime journey. There was a litany of congratulatory
notes from coaches with whom I had worked or competed against over
the years: Bill Parcells, Randy Edsall, Mike Maser, Al Groh, John Fox,
Bobby Ross, Mack Brown, Jerry Glanville, Lou Holtz, Bruce Coslet,
Tony Dungy, Lovie Smith, Andy Reid, Dick Jauron, Eric Mangini, Dom
Capers, Mike McCarthy, and dozens more. Then there were the personal
letters from Wayne Weaver, Navy athletic director Chet Gladchuk, and
Father Donald Monan, three former bosses. Surprising and very mean-

ingful were notes from more than twenty former players of mine at Rochester Institute of Technology. There was a kind note from the widow of the late George Young and from Tony Boselli. There were messages from judges and nuns, from coaches in hockey, including the New York Rangers' Tom Renney, and in baseball, including Joe Torre, and one from golf legend Arnold Palmer. There were even a handful from members of the media, including John Madden, who had left me the emotional voice mail after the regular-season New England game. It really was overwhelming.

One of the more unusual letters I received was one from Fox News host Bill O'Reilly, a Giants fan. He sent me a script of what he had said on air about me and the Giants' remarkable run. In his "Talking Points," O'Reilly said that we had toughed it out, despite the mock and scorn, and that is the key to success. That sums up our season pretty well.

In late March, one of our Super Bowl heroes, David Tyree, stopped in my office, something he rarely did. In an honest and emotional few minutes, David thanked me for my coaching adjustment in 2007 and for being more open and caring. At the ripe old age of sixty-one, I had made the necessary adjustments, and David just wanted to say thank you. Of course, I should have been thanking him for believing in the team, for his courage, for sharing his thoughts with me—and for an incredible catch.

If you have learned one thing about me from reading these pages, it's probably that winning a Super Bowl will not change who I am or how I coach. Just because we had an amazing run means nothing for 2008. So it was right back to work for me.

In 1994, when I was the head coach in Jacksonville, a year in which we still didn't have a team, I was invited by President Bill Clinton to the White House for a state dinner honoring the prime minister of Ireland, with many prominent Irish Americans on the guest list. I was honored to be invited, and I know Judy would have liked to have gone, but there was work to do. I couldn't afford to give up a day in building the franchise. That's just me, and you probably think I am crazy. Flash forward to April 2008, after we were on top of the world as Super Bowl champions. I was fortunate to receive an invitation to attend a small Mass with

Pope Benedict XVI in New York City. I am a devout Catholic, and this was the honor of honors. But the Pope's trip coincided with our NFL draft meetings, so I turned down the chance. Duty first has always been my doctrine.

What was so great about our championship run was the amount of joy it brought to so many people. I treasure the accomplishment for the assistant coaches and their families, who have sacrificed so much. Every member of the Giants organization in public relations, marketing, medicine, finance, equipment, and video played a role in the season, and every one of them should share in the joy. Pat Hanlon is such a tremendous reason for our success and my ability to change. And the players, of course. The fact that Jeff Feagles has been in the NFL for twenty years and almost walked away after 2005 made the season even more special for him. Jeff's is just one story of many.

So how did we do it? How did we go from being the brunt of harsh words and jokes to being on top of the football world?

- Our players maintained a great attitude. There was no finger-pointing and no blaming others; there was only support, especially when times were tough.
- Our players took responsibility seriously and held themselves and their teammates accountable for their actions. Along this line, I believe the Leadership Council allowed for better communication between me and them.
- We brought in talented new staff members, including Steve Spagnuolo, Chris Palmer, Thomas McGaughey and Sean Ryan, and we elevated people such as Kevin Gilbride and Tom Quinn.
- Our 2007 draft class performed way beyond expectations. Guys such as Aaron Ross, Michael Johnson, Steve Smith, Kevin Boss, Zak DeOssie, Jay Alford, and Ahmad Bradshaw all contributed in big ways.
- We saw significant on-field performances on offense, defense, and special teams, too many to identify here. We were at our best when our best was needed, as John Wooden would point out.

- Lastly, yes, you could probably add my changes to the list: my willingness to open up a bit, to allow myself and those around me to enjoy the game of football. I didn't change my values; I just added some compassion to the passion. I believe that by opening up and letting the players see me as I really am, I helped construct a better sense of team unity. And for all of that, I give credit to Judy, who finds ways to teach me everything I need to know.

After the season, the players went right back to work. In each of the past seven years, at least one of the teams that participated in a Super Bowl did not make the play-offs the following season. Perhaps it is a result of complacency, of too many people fawning, or of too many of the distractions that come with a championship. Whatever it is, we have no interest in having that happen to us. The coaches were still hard at work, preparing for the April draft, evaluating our players and looking into free agents. I was able to do some work with the Jay Fund and spend time with my grandkids. Sundays during the off-season are my time to do whatever I want, and often that means visiting the little ones. They make me see life through the eyes of children.

There are certain things that only age can provide—besides wrinkles and retirement homes—and one is perspective. As we grow older, we begin to cherish the important things in life: an embrace from a spouse, a phone call from a child, an afternoon with a grandchild. Professionally speaking, we usually come to an understanding that getting to the top is hard; it is something that takes years to truly understand, and that is why if you ever get there, you'd better cherish the moment. I've been coaching for forty years and have coached in two Super Bowls, just one as a head coach. The journey is as important as the end result. So I have taken a moment to look around, because moments are gone in an instant.

THE GROUNDS OF WALTER REED Army Medical Hospital in Washington, D.C., are meticulously kept. The 113-acre property is one of America's leading medical facilities and home to the Wounded Warrior program for soldiers injured while in uniform. It is the home for so many months of Greg Gadson, and it is the temporary home for thousands of soldiers adjusting to life's new challenges. When we received word in February that President George W. Bush wanted to honor us at a ceremony at the White House, we took advantage of the trip to spend time with some of our military heroes.

On the second floor of the Military Advanced Training Center lies the heart of the recovery and rehabilitation program for soldiers who have lost arms or legs or some combination of both. It is here that they strain to entice small movements in limbs and learn how to walk again, acclimating themselves to their new prosthetic limbs. At first glance, the large rehab center looks like a typical gym, with mats, weight sets, cardio machines, and an indoor track. But look closely and you'll notice the silver track railings on the ceiling mirroring the track on the floor, railings that help harness soldiers as they learn how to walk and run again.

I'm not sure what to expect when I first encounter the soldiers. We have been briefed to feel comfortable asking about their injuries and their tours of duty, but to hear the details from these brave soldiers is difficult.

The first young man I meet is wearing a Brett Favre Green Bay Packers jersey and a Green Bay hat. He smiles as I approach. Michael Cain is twenty-seven and from Berlin, Wisconsin. This is his second stint at Walter Reed after being injured in 2003. While on a resupply mission in Tikrit, Iraq, his vehicle struck an antitank land mine. The blast tore apart his leg. Here he is, four years later, still rehabbing. When he is finished with his rehab, he wants to get a job with the Veterans Administration to help other soldiers.

As I work my way around the room to other soldiers, I hear Greg Gadson's voice. Dressed for his White House appearance, Greg is walking with his crutches on his prosthetic legs. We have not seen each other since the Super Bowl in Phoenix, and he looks well. We share a few laughs, and Greg asks when we are moving on to next year. He has the right attitude. But I already knew that.

A few minutes later, I meet Mark Little from Virginia, a soldier who served in the National Guard and Army. Ninety-two days into his tour in Iraq, a bomb cost him his legs—on the same road south of Baghdad where Greg lost his legs, at the same exact spot, exactly six months to the day later. The road had been swept by American forces for explosives just six and a half minutes before the blast injured Mark. I could imagine the truth of all that crushing a man's spirit, but here is Mark, upbeat, wearing a smile the whole time.

We meet so many other proud warriors, from all walks of life and from all parts of America. What they have in common is sacrifice, courage, and knowledge of the difficulties that lie ahead. A few minutes into a conversation with one young solider who is sitting in a wheelchair and missing a leg, he asks me what I do for the Giants. I tell him I am the head coach. He congratulates me on the Super Bowl and thanks us for visiting Walter Reed.

"No," I say, "you're the hero. We should be thanking you."

It is an emotional hour or so for me, as I am sure it is for Judy and the players. I am struck by how positive the soldiers' attitudes are, despite the tremendous adversity they face. I am amazed at just how young so many of these men and women are, and the extent of their multiple injuries is almost incomprehensible. Some have suffered broken ribs and legs, some burns and head injuries. But the one thing that really stands out to me is just how grateful they are to us for taking the time to visit.

As we ride on the buses over to the White House, Judy and I talk about what we have just experienced. We're thankful the Super Bowl win allows us the opportunity to impact a few lives, if only for a handful of minutes.

I have never been to the White House, and as an aficionado of history, I am looking forward to walking in the shadows of greats. We are able to tour the main floor and the ground floor, walking into the State Room, the East Room, the Blue Room, and so many other places I have only seen in the movies. Right before the ceremony on the South Lawn commences, I have the opportunity, along with Eli, Amani, Jerry Reese,

Greg Gadson, Steve Tisch and John Mara and their mothers, to meet the president and vice president in the Rose Garden. President Bush is gracious and knowledgeable about our win.

After introducing many of the dignitaries and welcoming the Giants family at the start of the ceremony, President Bush introduces Judy and me and then quips, "He got the extension, that's a good thing. Makes it a little easier to be standing up here."

A few minutes later, he notes, "And it was interesting, in the last game of the season [by which he means the late December game against the Patriots], a lot of folks thought the coach would just kind of lay down and let New England cruise to a perfect season. I remember a lot of people speculating about that last game of the season. And yet you didn't, Coach. Your team didn't win on the scoreboard, but you won the hearts of a lot of Americans for contesting the game."

When it is my turn to speak, I look out to the audience of a thousand, including soldiers from Walter Reed who hail from New York and New Jersey.

"The New York Giants of 2007 were called the 'Road Warriors.' Well, we pale in comparison to the real warriors, the warriors we visited today at Walter Reed. The thing that impressed me—all of us—so much was their attitude, their positive attitude, the look in their eye, their patriotism, their knowledge of what they were fighting for. And as I always say, we receive great inspiration from our soldiers, and it's an honor to be with them, and it's an honor to have Greg Gadson with us in our drive to the Super Bowl Championship XLII."

As Eli presents the president with a football signed by all the members of the team, I ask a favor of the president. "When you place this championship ball in your trophy case and you pass by the ball, we would ask hopefully that you would reflect on the accomplishments of this great group of young men," I say of the New York Giants. "A group of men who believed in themselves, who refused to be beaten, and brought really greater honor and glory to the great game of professional football."

New York Giants vs New England Patriots
Sunday, February 03, 2008 at University of Phoenix Stadium

PATRIOTS

No	Name	Pos
3	Gostkowski,Stephen	K
6	Hanson,Chris	P
7	Gutierrez,Matt	QB
10	Gaffney,Jabar	WR
12	Brady,Tom	QB
15	Washington,Kelley	WR
16	Cassel,Matt	QB
17	Jackson,Chad	WR
18	Stallworth,Donte'	WR
21	Gay,Randall	CB
22	Samuel,Asante	CB
23	Andrews,Willie	DB
26	Wilson,Eugene	DB
27	Hobbs,Ellis	CB
28	Spann,Antwain	CB
31	Meriweather,Brandon	DB
33	Faulk,Kevin	RB
36	Sanders,James	S
37	Harrison,Rodney	SS
38	Eckel,Kyle	FB
39	Maroney,Laurence	RB
41	Ventrone,Raymond	DB
44	Evans,Heath	RB
50	Vrabel,Mike	LB
52	Alexander,Eric	LB
53	Izzo,Larry	LB
54	Bruschi,Tedy	LB
55	Seau,Junior	LB
58	Woods,Pierre	LB
61	Neal,Steve	G
65	Britt,Wesley	T
66	Paxton,Lonie	LS
67	Koppen,Dan	C
68	O'Callaghan,Ryan	T
70	Mankins,Logan	G
71	Hochstein,Russ	G/C
72	Light,Matt	T
74	Yates,Billy	G
75	Wilfork,Vince	DL
77	Kaczur,Nick	T
80	Brown,Troy	WR
81	Moss,Randy	WR
82	Spach,Stephen	TE
83	Welker,Wes	WR
84	Watson,Benjamin	TE
88	Brady,Kyle	TE
90	Smith,Le Kevin	DL
92	Thomas,Santonio	DL
93	Seymour,Richard	DL
94	Warren,Ty	DL
95	Moore,Rashad	DL
96	Thomas,Adalius	LB
97	Green,Jarvis	DL

PATRIOTS OFFENSE

WR	83	W.Welker	18	D.Stallworth	80	T.Brown
					17	C.Jackson
LT	72	M.Light	65	W.Britt		
LG	70	L.Mankins	71	R.Hochstein	74	B.Yates
C	67	D.Koppen	71	R.Hochstein		
RG	61	S.Neal	71	R.Hochstein	74	B.Yates
RT	77	N.Kaczur	68	R.O'Callaghan		
TE	84	B.Watson	88	K.Brady	82	S.Spach
WR	81	R.Moss	10	J.Gaffney	15	K.Washington
QB	12	T.Brady	16	M.Cassel	7	M.Gutierrez (3rd)
RB	39	L.Maroney	33	K.Faulk		
FB	44	H.Evans	38	K.Eckel		

GIANTS DEFENSE

LE	92	M.Strahan	71	D.Tollefson		
DT	96	B.Cofield	99	R.Davis	75	M.Wright
DT	98	F.Robbins	93	J.Alford		
RE	72	O.Umenyiora	91	J.Tuck		
SLB	53	R.Torbor	51	Z.DeOssie	52	T.Daniels
MLB	58	A.Pierce	57	C.Blackburn		
WLB	55	K.Mitchell	59	G.Wilkinson		
LCB	31	A.Ross	25	R.McQuarters	35	K.Dockery
RCB	29	S.Madison	23	C.Webster	33	G.Pope
SS	37	Ja.Butler	43	M.Johnson		
FS	28	G.Wilson	43	M.Johnson		

PATRIOTS SPECIALISTS

K	3	S.Gostkowski	6	C.Hanson
P	6	C.Hanson	3	S.Gostkowski
H	6	C.Hanson	16	M.Cassel
PR	83	W.Welker	33	K.Faulk
KR	27	E.Hobbs	23	W.Andrews
LS	66	L.Paxton	71	R.Hochstein

TODAY"S OFFICIALS: Referee-Carey, Mike (94); Umpire-Michalek, Tony (115); Head Linesman-Slaughter, Gary (30); Line Judge-Johnson, Carl (101); Field Judge-Cheek, Boris (41); Side Judge-Rose, Larry (128); Back Judge-Helverson, Scott (93); Replay assistant-Baker, Ken; Video Operator-Grant, Jim

PATRIOTS DEFENSE

Pos	No	Name	No	Name	No	Name
LE	94	T.Warren	90	L.Smith		
NT	75	V.Wilfork	95	R.Moore		
RE	93	R.Seymour	97	J.Green	92	S.Thomas
OLB	50	M.Vrabel	58	P.Woods		
ILB	55	J.Seau	52	E.Alexander		
ILB	54	T.Bruschi	53	L.Izzo		
OLB	96	A.Thomas	58	P.Woods		
LCB	22	A.Samuel	21	R.Gay		
RCB	27	E.Hobbs	31	B.Meriweather	28	A.Spann
SS	37	R.Harrison	23	W.Andrews	41	R.Ventrone
FS	36	J.Sanders	26	E.Wilson		

GIANTS OFFENSE

Pos	No	Name	No	Name	No	Name
WR	17	P.Burress	85	D.Tyree	87	D.Hixon
LT	66	D.Diehl	79	G.Whimper		
LG	69	R.Seubert	77	K.Boothe		
C	60	S.O'Hara	65	G.Ruegamer		
RG	76	C.Snee	77	K.Boothe		
RT	67	K.McKenzie	61	A.Koets		
TE	89	K.Boss	88	M.Matthews	86	J.Collins
WR	81	A.Toomer	12	S.Smith	83	S.Moss
QB	10	E.Manning	2	A.Wright	13	J.Lorenzen
FB	39	M.Hedgecock				
RB	27	B.Jacobs	44	A.Bradshaw	22	R.Droughns
					26	D.Ware

GIANTS SPECIALISTS

Pos	No	Name	No	Name	No	Name
K	9	L.Tynes				
P	18	J.Feagles				
H	18	J.Feagles				
KC	93	J.Alford				
PC	51	Z.DeOssie	65	G.Ruegamer		
PR	25	R.McQuarters	31	A.Ross	83	S.Moss
KR	87	D.Hixon	44	A.Bradshaw	22	R.Droughns

GIANTS

No	Name	Pos
2	Wright,Anthony	QB
9	Tynes,Lawrence	K
10	Manning,Eli	QB
12	Smith,Steve	WR
13	Lorenzen,Jared	QB
17	Burress,Plaxico	WR
18	Feagles,Jeff	P
22	Droughns,Reuben	RB
23	Webster,Corey	CB
25	McQuarters,R.W.	CB
26	Ware,Danny	RB
27	Jacobs,Brandon	RB
28	Wilson,Gibril	S
29	Madison,Sam	CB
31	Ross,Aaron	CB
33	Pope,Geoffrey	CB
35	Dockery,Kevin	CB
37	Butler,James	S
39	Hedgecock,Madison	FB
43	Johnson,Michael	S
44	Bradshaw,Ahmad	RB
51	DeOssie,Zak	LB
52	Daniels,Torrance	LB
53	Torbor,Reggie	LB
55	Mitchell,Kawika	LB
57	Blackburn,Chase	LB
58	Pierce,Antonio	LB
59	Wilkinson,Gerris	LB
60	O'Hara,Shaun	C
61	Koets,Adam	T
65	Ruegamer,Grey	G
66	Diehl,David	T
67	McKenzie,Kareem	T
69	Seubert,Rich	G
71	Tollefson,Dave	DE
72	Umenyiora,Osi	DE
75	Wright,Manuel	DT
76	Snee,Chris	G
77	Boothe,Kevin	G
79	Whimper,Guy	T
81	Toomer,Amani	WR
83	Moss,Sinorice	WR
85	Tyree,David	WR
86	Collins,Jerome	TE
87	Hixon,Domenik	WR
88	Matthews,Michael	TE
89	Boss,Kevin	TE
91	Tuck,Justin	DE
92	Strahan,Michael	DE
93	Alford,Jay	DT
96	Cofield,Barry	DT
98	Robbins,Fred	DT
99	Davis,Russell	DT

New York Giants vs New England Patriots
Sunday, February 03, 2008 at University of Phoenix Stadium

NEW ENGLAND PATRIOTS

No	Name	Pos		No	Name	Pos	Ht	Wt	Age	Ex	School
52	Alexander,Eric	LB		3	Stephen Gostkowski	K	6'01"	210	24	2	Memphis
23	Andrews,Willie	DB		6	Chris Hanson	P	6'02"	202	32	7	Marshall
88	Brady,Kyle	TE		7	Matt Gutierrez	QB	6'04"	231	24	R	Idaho State
12	Brady,Tom	QB		10	Jabar Gaffney	WR	6'01"	205	28	6	Florida
65	Britt,Wesley	T		12	Tom Brady	QB	6'04"	225	31	7	Michigan
80	Brown,Troy	WR		15	Kelley Washington	WR	6'03"	218	29	5	Tennessee
54	Bruschi,Tedy	LB		16	Matt Cassel	QB	6'04"	225	26	2	Southern California
16	Cassel,Matt	QB		17	Chad Jackson	WR	6'01"	215	23	2	Florida
38	Eckel,Kyle	FB		18	Donte' Stallworth	WR	6'00"	196	28	6	Tennessee
44	Evans,Heath	RB		21	Randall Gay	CB	5'11"	190	26	4	Louisiana State
33	Faulk,Kevin	RB		22	Asante Samuel	CB	5'10"	185	27	5	Central Florida
10	Gaffney,Jabar	WR		23	Willie Andrews	DB	5'10"	195	25	2	Baylor
21	Gay,Randall	CB		26	Eugene Wilson	DB	5'10"	195	28	5	Illinois
3	Gostkowski,Stephen	K		27	Ellis Hobbs	CB	5'09"	190	25	3	Iowa State
97	Green,Jarvis	DL		28	Antwain Spann	CB	6'00"	190	25	2	Louisiana-Lafayette
7	Gutierrez,Matt	QB		31	Brandon Meriweather	DB	6'00"	200	24	R	Miami
6	Hanson,Chris	P		33	Kevin Faulk	RB	5'08"	202	32	9	Louisiana State
37	Harrison,Rodney	SS		36	James Sanders	S	5'10"	210	25	3	Fresno State
27	Hobbs,Ellis	CB		37	Rodney Harrison	SS	6'01"	220	36	14	Western Illinois
71	Hochstein,Russ	G/C		38	Kyle Eckel	FB	5'11"	245	27	1	Navy
53	Izzo,Larry	LB		39	Laurence Maroney	RB	5'11"	220	23	2	Minnesota
17	Jackson,Chad	WR		41	Raymond Ventrone	DB	5'10"	200	26	1	Villanova
77	Kaczur,Nick	T		44	Heath Evans	RB	6'00"	250	30	7	Auburn
67	Koppen,Dan	C		50	Mike Vrabel	LB	6'04"	261	33	11	Ohio State
72	Light,Matt	T		52	Eric Alexander	LB	6'02"	240	26	3	Louisiana State
70	Mankins,Logan	G		53	Larry Izzo	LB	5'10"	228	34	11	Rice
39	Maroney,Laurence	RB		54	Tedy Bruschi	LB	6'01"	247	35	12	Arizona
31	Meriweather,Brandon	DB		55	Junior Seau	LB	6'03"	248	39	18	Southern California
95	Moore,Rashad	DL		58	Pierre Woods	LB	6'05"	250	26	2	Michigan
81	Moss,Randy	WR		61	Steve Neal	G	6'04"	305	32	5	Cal St.-Bakersfield
61	Neal,Steve	G		65	Wesley Britt	T	6'08"	320	27	2	Alabama
68	O'Callaghan,Ryan	T		66	Lonie Paxton	LS	6'02"	260	30	8	Sacramento State
66	Paxton,Lonie	LS		67	Dan Koppen	C	6'02"	296	29	5	Boston College
22	Samuel,Asante	CB		68	Ryan O'Callaghan	T	6'07"	330	25	2	California
36	Sanders,James	S		70	Logan Mankins	G	6'04"	310	26	3	Fresno State
55	Seau,Junior	LB		71	Russ Hochstein	G/C	6'04"	305	31	6	Nebraska
93	Seymour,Richard	DL		72	Matt Light	T	6'04"	305	30	7	Purdue
90	Smith,Le Kevin	DL		74	Billy Yates	G	6'02"	305	28	4	Texas A&M
82	Spach,Stephen	TE		75	Vince Wilfork	DL	6'02"	325	27	4	Miami
28	Spann,Antwain	CB		77	Nick Kaczur	T	6'04"	315	29	3	Toledo
18	Stallworth,Donte'	WR		80	Troy Brown	WR	5'10"	196	37	15	Marshall
96	Thomas,Adalius	LB		81	Randy Moss	WR	6'04"	210	31	10	Marshall
92	Thomas,Santonio	DL		82	Stephen Spach	TE	6'04"	250	26	2	Fresno State
41	Ventrone,Raymond	DB		83	Wes Welker	WR	5'09"	185	27	4	Texas Tech
50	Vrabel,Mike	LB		84	Benjamin Watson	TE	6'03"	255	28	3	Georgia
94	Warren,Ty	DL		88	Kyle Brady	TE	6'06"	280	36	13	Penn State
15	Washington,Kelley	WR		90	Le Kevin Smith	DL	6'01"	308	26	2	Nebraska
84	Watson,Benjamin	TE		92	Santonio Thomas	DL	6'04"	305	27	1	Miami
83	Welker,Wes	WR		93	Richard Seymour	DL	6'06"	310	29	7	Georgia
75	Wilfork,Vince	DL		94	Ty Warren	DL	6'05"	300	27	5	Texas A&M
26	Wilson,Eugene	DB		95	Rashad Moore	DL	6'03"	325	29	4	Tennessee
58	Woods,Pierre	LB		96	Adalius Thomas	LB	6'02"	270	31	8	Southern Mississippi
74	Yates,Billy	G		97	Jarvis Green	DL	6'03"	285	29	6	Louisiana State

Head Coach: Bill Belichick
Assistant Coaches: Josh Boyer (Quality Control), Nick Caserio (Wide recievers), Joel Collier (Assistant Secondary), Brian Daboll (Wide Receivers), Don Davis (Assistant Strength and Conditioning), Don Davis (Assistant Strength and Conditioning), Ivan Fears (Running Backs), Pepper Johnson (Defensive Line), Pete Mangurian (Tight Ends), Josh McDaniels (Offensive Coordinator), Berj Najarian (Director of Football/Head Coach Administration), Harold Nash (Assistant Strength and Conditioning), Matt Patricia (Assistant Offensive Line), Dean Pees (Defensive Coordinator), Dante Scarnecchia (Assistant Head Coach/Offensive Line), Brad Seely (Special Teams), Mike Woicik (Strength and Conditioning

NEW YORK GIANTS

No	Name	Pos	Ht	Wt	Age	Ex	School
2	Anthony Wright	QB	6'01"	211	32	7	South Carolina
9	Lawrence Tynes	K	6'01"	202	30	4	Troy
10	Eli Manning	QB	6'04"	225	27	4	Mississippi
12	Steve Smith	WR	6'00"	195	23	R	Southern California
13	Jared Lorenzen	QB	6'04"	285	27	2	Kentucky
17	Plaxico Burress	WR	6'05"	232	31	8	Michigan State
18	Jeff Feagles	P	6'01"	215	42	20	Miami
22	Reuben Droughns	RB	5'11"	220	30	7	Oregon
23	Corey Webster	CB	6'00"	202	26	3	Louisiana State
25	R.W. McQuarters	CB	5'10"	194	32	10	Oklahoma State
26	Danny Ware	RB	6'1"	222	23	R	Georgia
27	Brandon Jacobs	RB	6'04"	264	26	3	Southern Illinois
28	Gibril Wilson	S	6'00"	209	27	4	Tennessee
29	Sam Madison	CB	5'11"	180	34	11	Louisville
31	Aaron Ross	CB	6'01"	192	26	R	Texas
33	Geoffrey Pope	CB	6'0"	185	24	R	Howard
35	Kevin Dockery	CB	5'08"	188	24	2	Mississippi State
37	James Butler	S	6'03"	215	26	3	Georgia Tech
39	Madison Hedgecock	FB	6'03"	266	27	3	North Carolina
43	Michael Johnson	S	6'02"	205	24	R	Arizona
44	Ahmad Bradshaw	RB	5'11"	192	22	R	Marshall
51	Zak DeOssie	LB	6'04"	240	24	R	Brown
52	Torrance Daniels	LB	6'03"	248		2	Harding
53	Reggie Torbor	LB	6'02"	250	27	4	Auburn
55	Kawika Mitchell	LB	6'01"	253	29	5	South Florida
57	Chase Blackburn	LB	6'03"	247	25	3	Akron
58	Antonio Pierce	LB	6'01"	238	30	7	Arizona
59	Gerris Wilkinson	LB	6'03"	231	25	2	Georgia Tech
60	Shaun O'Hara	C	6'03"	303	31	8	Rutgers
61	Adam Koets	T	6'06"	300	24	R	Oregon State
65	Grey Ruegamer	G	6'04"	299	32	8	Arizona State
66	David Diehl	T	6'05"	319	28	5	Illinois
67	Kareem McKenzie	T	6'06"	327	29	7	Penn State
69	Rich Seubert	G	6'03"	310	29	6	Western Illinois
71	Dave Tollefson	DE	6'04"	265	27	1	N.W. Missouri
72	Osi Umenyiora	DE	6'03"	261	27	5	Troy
75	Manuel Wright	DT	6'06"	329	24	2	Southern California
76	Chris Snee	G	6'03"	317	26	4	Boston College
77	Kevin Boothe	G	6'05"	315	25	2	Cornell
79	Guy Whimper	T	6'04"	304	25	2	East Carolina
81	Amani Toomer	WR	6'03"	203	34	12	Michigan
83	Sinorice Moss	WR	5'08"	185	25	2	Miami
85	David Tyree	WR	6'00"	206	28	5	Syracuse
86	Jerome Collins	TE	6'04"	270	26	2	Notre Dame
87	Domenik Hixon	WR	6'02"	190	24	1	Akron
88	Michael Matthews	TE	6'04"	270	25	R	Georgia Tech
89	Kevin Boss	TE	6'07"	255	24	R	Western Oregon
91	Justin Tuck	DE	6'05"	274	25	3	Notre Dame
92	Michael Strahan	DE	6'05"	255	37	15	Texas Southern
93	Jay Alford	DT	6'03"	304	25	R	Penn State
96	Barry Cofield	DT	6'04"	306	24	2	Northwestern
98	Fred Robbins	DT	6'04"	317	31	8	Wake Forest
99	Russell Davis	DT	6'04"	315	33	9	North Carolina

No	Name	Pos
93	Alford, Jay	DT
57	Blackburn, Chase	LB
77	Boothe, Kevin	G
89	Boss, Kevin	TE
44	Bradshaw, Ahmad	RB
17	Burress, Plaxico	WR
37	Butler, James	S
96	Cofield, Barry	DT
86	Collins, Jerome	TE
52	Daniels, Torrance	LB
99	Davis, Russell	DT
51	DeOssie, Zak	LB
66	Diehl, David	T
35	Dockery, Kevin	CB
22	Droughns, Reuben	RB
18	Feagles, Jeff	P
39	Hedgecock, Madison	FB
87	Hixon, Domenik	WR
27	Jacobs, Brandon	RB
43	Johnson, Michael	S
61	Koets, Adam	T
13	Lorenzen, Jared	QB
29	Madison, Sam	CB
10	Manning, Eli	QB
88	Matthews, Michael	TE
67	McKenzie, Kareem	T
25	McQuarters, R.W.	CB
55	Mitchell, Kawika	LB
83	Moss, Sinorice	WR
60	O'Hara, Shaun	C
58	Pierce, Antonio	LB
33	Pope, Geoffrey	CB
98	Robbins, Fred	DT
31	Ross, Aaron	CB
65	Ruegamer, Grey	G
69	Seubert, Rich	G
12	Smith, Steve	WR
76	Snee, Chris	G
92	Strahan, Michael	DE
71	Tollefson, Dave	DE
81	Toomer, Amani	WR
53	Torbor, Reggie	LB
91	Tuck, Justin	DE
9	Tynes, Lawrence	K
85	Tyree, David	WR
72	Umenyiora, Osi	DE
26	Ware, Danny	RB
23	Webster, Corey	CB
79	Whimper, Guy	T
59	Wilkinson, Gerris	LB
28	Wilson, Gibril	S
2	Wright, Anthony	QB
75	Wright, Manuel	DT

Head Coach: Tom Coughlin
Assistant Coaches: Andre Curtis (Quality Control - Defense), Dave DeGuglielmo (Assistant Offensive Line), Pat Flaherty (Offensive Line), Kevin Gilbride (Offensive Coordinator), Peter Giunta (Secondary/Corners), Jerald Ingram (Running Backs), Thomas McGauhey (Assistant Special Teams), David Merritt (Secondary/Safeties), Chris Palmer (Quarterbacks), Jerry Palmieri (Strength and Conditioning), Markus Paul (Assistant Strength and Conditioning), Mike Pope (Tight Ends), Tom Quinn (Special Teams Coordinator), Sean Ryan (Quality Control - Offense), Bill Sheridan (Linebackers), Steve Spagnuolo (Defensive Coordinator), Mike Sullivan (Wide Receivers), Mike Waufle (Defensive Line

ABOUT THE AUTHORS

TOM COUGHLIN is head coach of the New York Giants. He was also head coach of the expansion Jacksonville Jaguars for nine seasons, where he led the team to two appearances in the AFC Championship Game and was named NFL Coach of the Year in 1996; head football coach at Boston College; and an assistant coach for the Green Bay Packers, Philadelphia Eagles, and New York Giants. Coughlin and his wife, Judy, have been married for forty-one years and have four children and five grandchildren.

BRIAN CURTIS is the author of *Every Week a Season* and *The Men of March*, as well as co-author (with Jerry Rice) of the *New York Times* bestseller *Go Long!* and (with Nick Saban) of *How Good Do You Want to Be?* A former reporter for Fox Sports Net and a former host and analyst on CBS College Sports, he lives in New York with his wife, Tamara, and two daughters.

ABOUT THE TYPE

This book was set in Times Roman, designed by Stanley Morrison specifically for *The Times* of London. The typeface was introduced in the newspaper in 1932. Times Roman had its greatest success in the United States as a book and commercial typeface, rather than one used in newspapers.